600 Easy and Delicious Recipes for Breville Convection Oven to Air Fry, Bake, Broil, Roast and Dehydrate Favorite Meals for 1000 Days

By Adam Martin

# Table of Content

# Chapter 4 Poultry ................................................ 31

## Chapter 5 Beef ......................................................................... 52

# Chapter 7 Fish and Seafood.......................................... 83

## Chapter 8 Vegetable ......................................................... 99

## Chapter 9 Bread, Sandwiches and Pizza .................................. 115

## Chapter 10 Snacks and Appetizers ............................................ 125

# Chapter 11 Desserts ...................................... 139

# Chapter 12 Sauces, Dipping, and Spice Mixes .......................... 152

# Introduction

Dear readers

I'm glad you can see my first cookbook, which I've been writing for 6 months since I started use this Breville Smart Oven Air Fryer pro. In this cookbook, I wrote down some of my experience and collected the most common recipes which you can cook with the Breville, and if you buy the Smart Oven Air Fryer Pro, I hope this cookbook will help you make delicious food in your own kitchen. Now Let me briefly tell you the story of my relationship with Breville.

Shopping for kitchen appliances can be a real piece of work and I had already resigned myself to the tedious routine before choosing to purchase the Smart Oven Air Fryer Pro. It turned out to be the best choice I have made recently because of its 13 preset functions, and I can imagine that you understand how easy it is for anyone.

It has a lot to do with the smart technology of the oven which more or less brings my kitchen dreams to life. It merges the roles of different kitchen appliances into one, making it easier to execute multiple cooking techniques.

In this cookbook, we'll examine some unique innovations of the Smart Oven Air Fryer Pro, such as the Element IQ and super convection to deliver exquisitely finished meals at any time.

We all love our fries fine and crispy; the first bite you take while the flavor settles on my taste buds is an experience to live for. I want to share my experience with you now. This is why this cookbook is specially made for you to make the best use of your Smart Oven Air Fryer pro. In this review, I will mention some tips that I found helpful when starting with my new Breville Smart Oven Air Fryer Pro. You will also learn different cooking techniques, basic usage instructions, and precautions to take when operating the oven.

The most important thing is that I collected about 600 air fryer recipes, most of which were cooked and tested by myself. My family and friends highly praised me for the deliciousness I made.

I hope this book will give you a good start and that you get a good memory of Breville Smart Oven Air Fryer Pro in the future. Now let's get you started on how to cook delicious meals with yours.

# Chapter 1 All about the Breville Smart Oven Air Fryer Pro

The Breville Smart Oven Air Fryer Pro is one of the most popular electric ovens on the market today and you can easily guess why. The all-in-one appliance allows you to cook everything from French fries and breaded chicken to cheese fries and deep-fried treats using high-heat air. And guess what? The best part is that you don't even need the slightest drop of oil!

The Breville Smart Oven Air Fryer Pro has benefit me so much and I will go ahead to share some basic tips and tricks I have found useful. I will also share some precautions you have to observe. It will be out of place for you to purchase the Breville Smart Oven Air Fryer Pro without knowing how to use it for maximal benefits, especially after reading through the reviews and making an informed choice. This book is designed to help get you familiar with the oven so that your meals come out in the most mouth-watering flavor.

As stated earlier, the Breville Smart Oven Air Fryer Pro comes with the well-known and highly sophisticated Element IQ technology. This makes the oven ideal for you, especially if you want a large countertop to prepare fries for large gatherings. You know, those crispy French fries get you happily crunching with no drip of oil to soil your fingers and forearms. I will be highlighting the different controls present on this interesting device, all of which have contributed to making Breville the toast of many users worldwide.

Following my purchase of the product, I discovered the unit comes with a choice of two programmable digital temperature controls and a really smart navigation system. This system uses a color-coded ring to display the interior temperature of the food. You will also find a protected LED screen that displays different settings such as how much cooking time you have left, the temperature of your food, convection settings, and so many others.

The design of the oven is clearly for multiple purposes, and I discovered up to 10 specialized cooking techniques. Trust me when I say that the level of sophistication and versatility I got to experience. Using the Breville Smart Oven Air Fryer Pro has made it my favorite latest addition to my kitchen.

# Features of the Breville Smart Oven Air Fryer Pro

The Breville Smart Oven Air Fryer Pro comes with a lot of unique features that allow easy use which makes me enjoy cooking more since purchasing the appliance. It's not surprising that Breville has become a beloved product among other cooks, kitchen workers, and homeowners alike.

- **Smart Technology:** Breville Smart Oven Air Fryer Pro uses the Element IQ Technology to cook foods faster and better by intelligently directing the power to where it is most needed inside the oven. It has an in-built algorithm to control the six quartz heat-generating elements for cooking and uses heat sensors and temperature control elements to detect and cancel out cold parts.

  I use the available preset recommended settings for cooking; however, you can choose to override these settings manually. Your personalized settings will be stored in the oven's memory, even if it is unplugged from the power source.

- **Specialized Air Fry Setting:** With this setting, I effectively cook crispy air-fried foods such as chicken wings, French fries, and many more. The Breville Smart Oven Air Fryer Pro uses a blend of higher temperature and super convection. With the presence of this function, the oven makes stand-alone air Fryers completely obsolete.

- **Dual Speed Convection:** This technology speeds up cooking time by sinking colder air and raising warmer air for a more rapid heating process. I found out that my cooking time has decreased by more than 30%, thanks to the dual-speed convection. It has saved me a great deal of time for my other activities. It's good for many cooking techniques such as air frying, dehydrating, proofing and roasting.

- **LCD Display:** The LCD screen display on the Breville Smart Oven Air Fryer Pro makes it easier to engage with the device's many functions, adjust a wide range of settings, and cook food with more freedom and control. It helps me know when different cooking techniques are completed, shows countdown timers, and ultimately acts as my command center for all my cooking activities.

- **Oven Light:** The smart lighting system within the oven automatically turns on when you open the oven door and when a cooking cycle is completed. I use the light at any period during a cooking cycle to see what is inside the oven.

- **Larger Capacity:** The Breville Smart Oven Air Fryer Pro is large enough to perfectly fit a 14-pound turkey, a 5-quart Dutch oven, most 9-inch pans, and 12-cup muffin trays. It measures one cubic foot in dimensions, a whooping size for an electric oven! I use it for more wholesome cooking and spend less time with my cooking techniques. This also means that once you have a Breville Smart Oven Air Fryer Pro, you may not need to purchase another oven.

- **Accessories and Warranty:** The Smart Oven Air Fryer Pro comes with extra accessories such as bamboo cutting boards, pizza stones, and pizza crisper pans. I also discovered there are more air fry baskets, enamel roasting pans, wire racks as well as broiling racks.

  Even better, the oven comes with a 2-year limited product warranty that is valid from your purchase date. If you detect any issue with your purchase, you can get it changed at any approved store as long as you follow the warranty instructions.

- **Versatility:** If you are looking for an all-in-one cooking station, you found one in Breville Smart Oven Air Fryer Pro. The behemoth has 13 functions put into one big machine, with the ultimate goal of giving you the best cooking experience every time. You can cook for prolonged periods at any desired temperature and time settings, giving you the luxury to relax while preparing your favorite dish.

## Functions of the Breville Smart Air Fryer Oven Pro

The functions are even more fun to explore as you will find out the following ones:

∞ **Toast Function:** With this, you can adjust the level of darkness you want to achieve with selected food items and the number of slices you want to toast. The cooking time is automatically calculated, depending on the temperature, number of slices, and other variables. You can also manually change the cooking duration by adjusting the TIME dial during a toasting cycle which I mostly use for browning and crisping the outside of breads, English muffins, and waffles.

∞ **Bagel Function:** This is one of the preset cooking techniques that require no preheat cycle. I enjoyed using this for my bagel. To use, I cut my bagel, placed it face up in the oven, and set the oven to the Bagel function. I find this setting incredibly useful because it helps to crisp the insides of my bagels while toasting the outsides.

∞ **Broil Function:** This function is good for foods such as thin slices of meat, sandwiches, poultry products, fish,

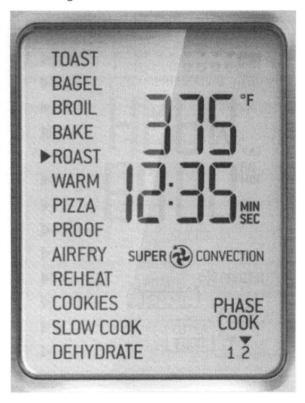

and vegetables. I also use it for sausages, desserts, casseroles, and gratins. This function automatically ensures that air and heat are evenly distributed around whatever food you are cooking.

∞ **Bake Function:** Unlike the one-sided Crumpet function, the Bake function uses all six quartz heating elements intelligently and I found it useful for cakes, brownies, lasagna, and muffins. After preheating, you can place your food in the oven for optimal baking.

∞ **Roast Function:** With the roast function, I have a mini-barbeque experience, all within the comfort of my kitchen. Asides from temperature and time settings, roasting also uses convection settings of the Fryer. You can adjust these settings during a roasting cycle.

∞ **Pizza Function:** This function is specifically designed to bring the best out of every pizza you eat by melting and browning the cheese and toppings on the pizza while also crisping the crusts. It also requires a preheating cycle and uses convection, temperature, and time settings. When using a pizza pan or stone, you must place it in the oven before preheating so that you can get the best results.

∞ **Proof Function:** This cooking technique uses convection to equally distribute low temperatures around the oven. This allows for proofing foods such as doughs, breads, rolls, and pizza. For doughs, I use an oven-proof container, place it at the center of the oven and cover it. With the Smart Oven's automatic cooking function, I can leave my food for as long as 2 hours, resting assured of an optimal output.

∞ **Air Fry Function:** This function is the golden horse of the Breville Smart Oven Air Fryer. It employs virtually every technology available in the oven to produce well-cooked, crispy, and browned foods. I use this function for different kinds of foods, from chicken wings to pizza. The Air Fry function combines the heating power of the quartz elements with the smart heat control and airflow systems [super convection] of the oven to produce satisfying results.

∞ **Cookies Function:** Aside from the Bake function, the Cookies function is another cooking technique that can be used to bake certain food items. I found it particularly useful for cookies and small cupcakes. To achieve optimal baking, it requires a preheat cycle and uses convection settings to ensure the food is evenly heated.

∞ **Dehydrate Function:** The availability of this function on the Breville Smart Oven Air Fryer has turned out to be a massive plus for many owners. With this function, the oven combines efficient airflow and low consistent heat to achieve a faster and more uniform drying of food items. What I find particularly useful is that I can choose how long to leave my food for, without fear of overheating or burning the food.

∞ **Slow Cook Function:** The Slow Cook Function is most useful for cooking food over long periods at rather low temperatures. I find this useful especially when I want to have a nap or do some other time-consuming and attention-demanding activities while cooking. All you need is to observe the preheating cycle, choose an appropriate temperature, time, and convection setting, and you can switch your attention to your next task.

∞ **Reheat Function:** Preparing for guests can be very tedious especially when you have to get different dishes ready. It gets worse when it all gets cold so fast and leaves you exhausted. Not to worry anymore, as the reheat function is great for leftover foods or foods that get cold shortly after serving.

∞ **Warm Function:** After a long day at work, a warm meal is one of the best things I could ever ask for and the oven's Warm function gives me just this. Research has shown that most foods require temperatures of at least 70°C to prevent the growth of harmful bacteria. What more could we ask for than a single appliance that can serve to warm our meals also? I recommend you use the Warm function for leftover meals and those which have cooled after serving.

# The Control Panel

To give you the most engaging cooking experience, the Breville Smart Oven Air Fryer Pro is equipped with a powerful control center, pivoted around the LCD and different knobs. The control panel is located on the right edge of the oven and it houses a handful of useful buttons and dials.

- **Interactive LCD:** Over the years, as the world keeps evolving, I have come to accept that I have to be more dynamic with my kitchen choices, and I believe the same goes for you. One key factor in my choice of the Breville Smart Oven Air Fryer Pro is its Led Crystal Display. It adds to the allure of the machine, and with the aid of brilliant algorithms, the LCD serves as an in-built command and reporting center for all functionalities of the Smart Oven Air Fryer Pro. It gives a view into the depth of sophistication of the oven, allowing you to monitor and control even the tiniest bit of detail while cooking your meals.

- **Temperature Knob:** You can use the temperature control knob to select how much heat you wish to expose your food items to. The temperature knob is also used to select toast darkness levels, depending on what cooking technique you wish to use.

- **Temperature Conversion Button:** You can also switch from the Celsius to Fahrenheit unit just by pushing a button. You can also use this button to adjust the volume of sound produced by your oven.

- **Start/Stop Button:** After you've selected your desired cooking settings, the Start button is what you will use to commence the cooking cycle. When you feel the cooking is done, you can also use it to manually end the cooking cycle.

- **Time Knob:** For most cooking techniques, the time knob helps you select the cooking duration. When using the Toast functions, you can also use the time dial for selections.

- **Oven Light Button:** The oven lights automatically turn on when you open the oven door. However, with this button, you can manually turn the oven lights on or off at any time during a cooking cycle.

- **Convection Button:** This helps you select the super convection settings suitable for the meal you wish to cook.

# Benefits of Using the Breville Smart Oven Air Fryer Pro

Needless to say, I have enjoyed countless benefits since I began using the Breville Smart Oven Air Fryer Pro. If you have one, by now you will be able to bear credence to this claim. The ingenious manner in which a single appliance incorporates so many functions into one remains a technological marvel. Besides helping me get the optimal levels of productivity every day, here are a few reasons why I find the Breville Smart Oven Air Fryer Pro very alluring.

- It has a lot of space and is particularly wonderful for large cooking dinners, such as family get-togethers and hosting friends. I have also been able to make use of all the functions of the oven air fryer and get amazing results with every recipe I have so far tried on it.

- The quality of the racks and baskets made of stainless steel is indeed impressive, especially with proper maintenance.

- My cooking time has been reduced by about 30%, just as claimed in the product package. This is majorly because of the super convection setting that helps bring extra crispness to French fries and other family meals which require dehydration.

- The Toast and Bagel functions allow me to make my bread the exact way I want it. You get to choose how browned you want your bread to be and have it finished to exactness.

- The Smart Oven Air Fryer Pro has different pans including a pizza pan, roasting pan as well as wire basket that has the perfect fit into my oven. This saves your finances from the additional demands of buying these specialized cooking containers.

- Breville Smart Oven Air Fryer Pro comes in different colors for you to choose from and helps you bring radiance to your kitchen through its numerous glowing options.

# How to Use the Breville Smart Air Fryer Oven?

Your air fryer oven really couldn't be easier to use. The following are some steps to help you get going!

- Step 1: Start by checking all the components of the Breville Smart Air Fryer Oven and see if they are in good shape, especially the power cord, because any fault in the power cord can be hazardous.

- Step 2: Remove the air fryer oven from the box. Place it on a level surface near a grounded power outlet. Plug the air fryer oven.

- Step 3: Remove the trays from the oven. (Before using the oven, make sure to clean the trays with soap and water thoroughly.) Right after unboxing the device, it is essential to clean the appliance inside out using a clean piece of cloth and wash all the removable accessories of the oven before the use.

- Step 4: Set the oven to the PIZZA function and use the TIME button to select 18 minutes.

- Step 5: Press the START button and allow finishing the cooking cycle. Once the cooking cycle has finished, your Breville Smart Oven is ready to use.

# Basic Tips and Precautions

The Breville Smart Oven Air Fryer Pro is a perfect multitasking machine for everyday kitchen use. In one appliance, you have an oven, a toaster, as well as a technology-driven air fryer. It was fantastic when I tried baking a few cupcakes and muffins. I also did toast a few slices of bread, which I did not regret. My large 8-inch cakes and chocolate chip cookies came out nice, a quite interesting achievement given it was the first time I did with my new oven air fryer pro. Now as it is, I have mostly let go of using the traditional oven for my cooking activities. You will also find it is quite easy and fun to use the air fryer oven, especially after finding the right recipe.

Here are some tips about things that came in handy for me after using the Breville Smart Oven Air Fryer Pro for a few months:

1. Always place a lid over the cookware when you are using the slow cook function.

2. Cut large chunks of chicken into manageable bits when cooking. I find this particularly useful because it allows the food to be uniformly radiated and evenly cooked.

3. Do not fill any cookware to the brim. It is better if you keep the contents to just half the capacity, to avoid spills.

4. Ensure your choice of cookware is lightweight and oven-proof.

5. Discard all the excess oil when you are grilling, cooking fatty foods, or air frying.

6. Do not use the appliance when your power outlet is unstable and do not use an adapter.

While using the Breville Smart Oven Air Fryer Pro could be engrossing, there are a couple of things to be aware of while handling the appliance. After running myself into a few troubles, I came up with a list of useful precautions to take with the oven.

∞ It is important to note that if your recipe features foods that drip grease or oil, you should make sure to use the grilling rack inside the roasting pan, instead of the air frying basket.

∞ Do not forget to unplug the oven from the power outlet before beginning to clean it out.

∞ Be careful with handling the oven air fryer especially around children. The metallic parts could be especially hot, enough to inflict burning injuries. When I use it, I typically leave the oven to cool for at least half an hour before disassembling the parts for cleaning. Asides from saving you or any wandering kid from pain, it also helps to preserve the stainless steel racks and the air fry baskets.

∞ To clean, I use a soft sponge, dampened moderately to gently rub along the length of the heating element. I believe this is a great habit you should copy. It is much wiser to ignore the standard oven cleaner because it makes the metal surface of the interior deteriorate faster. Ideally, non-abrasive sponges together with non-corrosive cleaning liquid soaps are what you should use on your oven. By doing this, you are improving the lifespan of your oven while making it sparkling clean at the same time.

∞ It is also important that you insert the crumb tray into the oven, and place the broiling rack appropriately into the roasting pan. It is safer if you leave it to rest on the wire rack at the middle height position.

∞ Make sure your Breville Smart Oven Air Fryer Pro is dry at all times, more particularly when you are not using it. In addition, I have learned to always keep the oven door closed, to maintain the integrity of the interior heating system.

∞ For all it's worth, always keep your Smart Oven Air Fryer Pro in an upright position. I have also learned to not keep anything on the top of the oven. Doing that can prevent serious accidents such as electrical problems, especially when liquids from whatever you placed on the oven finds their way into the electrical circuitry.

# Chapter 2 Basics in 30 Minutes

## Spinach-Bacon Rollups

**Prep time: 5 minutes | Cook time: 8 minutes | Serves 4**

| | |
|---|---|
| 4 (6- or 7-inch) flour tortillas | 1 cup baby spinach leaves |
| 4 slices Swiss cheese | 4 slices turkey bacon |

1. Preheat air fryer oven to 390ºF (200ºC).
2. On each tortilla, place one slice of cheese and ¼ cup of spinach.
3. Roll up tortillas and wrap each with a strip of bacon. Secure each end with a toothpick.
4. Place the rollups on air fryer cooking tray, leaving a little space in between them.
5. Select Bake, and set time to 4 minutes. Turn and rearrange the rollups (for more even cooking) and bake for 4 to 5 minutes longer, until bacon is crisp.

## Hard-Boiled Eggs

**Prep time: 5 minutes | Cook time: 10 minutes | Serves 6**

| | |
|---|---|
| 6 eggs | 1/2 cup ice water |

1. Place the eggs in the air fryer cooking tray. (You can put the eggs in an oven-safe bowl if you are worried about them rolling around and breaking.)
2. Select Air Fry. Set the temperature to 250ºF (120ºC). Set the timer and air fry for 10 minutes
3. Meanwhile, fill a medium mixing bowl with 1/2 cup ice water.
4. Use tongs to remove the eggs from the air fryer cooking tray, and transfer them to the ice water bath.
5. Let the eggs sit for 5 minutes in the ice water.
6. Peel and eat on the spot or refrigerate for up to 1 week.

## French Toast Sticks

**Prep time: 10 minutes | Cook time: 13 minutes | Makes 12 sticks**

| | |
|---|---|
| 4 slices Texas toast (or any thick bread, such as challah) | 1 teaspoon ground cinnamon |
| 1 tablespoon butter | ¼ cup milk |
| 1 egg | 1 teaspoon vanilla extract |
| 1 teaspoon stevia | Cooking oil |

1. Cut each slice of toast into 3 pieces (for 12 sticks total).
2. Place the butter in a small, microwave-safe bowl. Microwave for 15 seconds, or until the butter has melted.
3. Remove the bowl from the microwave. Add the egg, stevia, cinnamon, milk, and vanilla extract. Whisk until fully combined.
4. Spray the air fryer cooking tray with cooking oil.
5. Dredge each of the toast sticks in the egg mixture.
6. Place the French toast sticks in the oven. It is okay to stack them. Spray the French toast sticks with cooking oil. Select Bake. Set time to 8 minutes.
7. Open the oven and flip each of the French toast sticks. Bake for an additional 4 minutes, or until the French toast sticks are crisp.
8. Cool before serving.

## Golden Onion Rings

**Prep time: 5 minutes | Cook time: 12 minutes | Serves 4**

| | |
|---|---|
| 1 large onion | tablespoons |
| ½ cup flour, plus 2 tablespoons | 1 cup crushed panko breadcrumbs |
| ½ teaspoon salt | Oil for misting or cooking spray |
| ½ cup beer, plus 2 | |

1. Peel onion, slice, and separate into rings.
2. In a large bowl, mix together the flour and salt. Add beer and stir until it stops foaming and makes a thick batter.
3. Place onion rings in batter and stir to coat.
4. Place breadcrumbs in a sealable plastic bag or container with lid.
5. Work with a few at a time, remove onion rings from batter, shake off excess, and drop into breadcrumbs. Shake to coat, then lay out onion rings on cookie sheet or wax paper.
6. When finished, spray onion rings with oil or cooking spray and pile into air fryer cooking tray.
7. Select Roast. Set temperature to 390ºF (200ºC), and set time to 5 minutes. Shake cooking tray and mist with oil. Cook 5 minutes and mist again. Cook an additional 2 to 4 minutes, until golden brown and crispy.

## Corn on the Cob

**Prep time: 5 minutes | Cook time: 12 minutes | Serves 4**

2 large ears fresh corn    Salt (optional)
Olive oil for misting

1. Shuck corn, remove silks, and wash.
2. Cut or break each ear in half crosswise.
3. Spray corn with olive oil.
4. Select Roast. Set temperature to 390ºF (200ºC), and set time to 12 to 15 minutes or until browned as much as you like.
5. Serve plain or with coarsely ground salt.

## Nacho Chicken Fries

**Prep time: 10 minutes | Cook time: 12 minutes | Serves 4 to 6**

1 pound (454 g) chicken tenders
Salt, to taste
¼ cup flour
2 eggs
¾ cup panko breadcrumbs
¾ cup crushed organic nacho cheese tortilla chips

Oil for misting or cooking spray
For the Seasoning Mix:
1 tablespoon chili powder
1 teaspoon ground cumin
½ teaspoon garlic powder
½ teaspoon onion powder

1. Stir together all seasonings in a small cup and set aside.
2. Cut chicken tenders in half crosswise, then cut into strips no wider than about ½ inch.
3. Preheat air fryer oven to 390ºF (200ºC).
4. Salt chicken to taste. Place strips in large bowl and sprinkle with 1 tablespoon of the seasoning mix. Stir well to distribute seasonings.
5. Add flour to chicken and stir well to coat all sides.
6. Beat eggs together in a shallow dish.
7. In a second shallow dish, combine the panko, crushed chips, and the remaining 2 teaspoons of seasoning mix.
8. Dip chicken strips in eggs, then roll in crumbs. Mist with oil or cooking spray.
9. Chicken strips will cook best if done in two batches. They can be crowded and overlapping a little but not stacked in double or triple layers.
10. Air fry for 4 minutes. Shake cooking tray, mist with oil, and air fry 2 to 3 more minutes, until chicken juices run clear and outside is crispy.
11. Repeat step 10 to cook the remaining chicken fries.

## French Toast

**Prep time: 10 minutes | Cook time: 6 minutes | Serves 2**

4 slices bread of your choosing
2 tablespoons soft butter
2 eggs, lightly beaten
Pinch of salt

Pinch of cinnamon
Pinch of ground nutmeg
Pinch of ground cloves
Nonstick cooking spray
Sugar, for serving

1. In a shallow bowl, mix together the salt, spices and eggs.
2. Butter each side of the slices of bread and slice into strips. You may also use cookie cutters for this step.
3. Set your oven to 350ºF (175ºC) and allow to warm up briefly.
4. Dredge each strip of bread in the egg and transfer to the fryer. Select Bake. Set time to 2 minutes, ensuring the toast turns golden brown.
5. At this point, spritz the tops of the bread strips with cooking spray, flip, and bake for another 4 minutes on the other side. Top with a light dusting of sugar before serving.

## Fried Potatoes with Onion and Pepper

**Prep time: 10 minutes | Cook time: 23 minutes | Serves 4**

3 large russet potatoes
1 tablespoon canola oil
1 tablespoon extra-virgin olive oil
1 teaspoon paprika
Salt, to taste

Pepper, to taste
1 cup chopped onion
1 cup chopped red bell pepper
1 cup chopped green bell pepper

1. Cut the potatoes into ½-inch cubes. Place the potatoes in a large bowl of cold water and allow them to soak for at least 30 minutes, preferably an hour.
2. Drain the potatoes and dry thoroughly with paper towels. Return them to the empty bowl.
3. Add the canola and olive oils, paprika, and salt and pepper to taste. Toss to fully coat the potatoes.
4. Transfer the potatoes to the air fryer oven. Select Air Fry, and set time to 20 minutes, shaking the air fryer cooking tray every 5 minutes (a total of 4 times).
5. Add the onion and red and green bell peppers to the air fryer cooking tray. Select Air Fry, and set time to an additional 3 to 4 minutes, or until the potatoes are cooked through and the peppers are soft.
6. Cool before serving.

## Air-Fried Shrimp

**Prep time: 5 minutes | Cook time: 6 minutes | Serves 4**

1½ pounds (680 g) raw shrimp, peeled and deveined
1 tablespoon olive oil
1 teaspoon garlic, minced
1 teaspoon cayenne pepper
½ teaspoon lemon pepper
Sea salt, to taste

1. Toss all ingredients in a lightly greased Air Fryer cooking tray.
2. Select Air Fry. Set temperature to 400ºF (205ºC), and set time to 6 minutes, tossing the cooking tray halfway through the cooking time.
3. Bon appétit!

## Garlic Chicken Wings

**Prep time: 15 minutes | Cook time: 13 minutes | Serves 4**

2 pounds (907 g) chicken wings
Oil for misting
Cooking spray
For the Marinade:
1 cup buttermilk
2 cloves garlic, mashed flat
1 teaspoon
Worcestershire sauce
1 bay leaf
For the Coating:
1½ cups grated Parmesan cheese
¾ cup breadcrumbs
1½ tablespoons garlic powder
½ teaspoon salt

1. Mix all marinade ingredients together.
2. Remove wing tips (the third joint) and discard or freeze for stock. Cut the remaining wings at the joint and toss them into the marinade, stirring to coat well. Refrigerate for at least an hour but no more than 8 hours.
3. When ready to cook, combine all coating ingredients in a shallow dish.
4. Remove wings from marinade, shake off excess, and roll in coating mixture. Press coating into wings so that it sticks well. Spray wings with oil.
5. Spray air fryer cooking tray with cooking spray. Place wings in cooking tray in single layer, close but not touching.
6. Select Roast. Set temperature to 360ºF (180ºC), and set time to 13 to 15 minutes or until wings are done and juices run clear.
7. Repeat previous step to cook remaining wings.

## Air-Fried Bacon

**Prep time: 5 minutes | Cook time: 5 minutes | Serves 5**

10 slices bacon

1. Cut the bacon slices in half, so they will fit in the air fryer oven.
2. Place the half-slices in the air fryer cooking tray in a single layer. (You may need to cook the bacon in more than one batch.)
3. Select Air Fry. Set the temperature to 400ºF (205ºC). Set the timer and air fry for 5 minutes.
4. Open the oven and check the bacon. (The power of the fan may cause the bacon to fly around during the cooking process. If so, use a fork or tongs to rearrange the slices.)
5. Reset the timer and air fry for 5 minutes or more.
6. When the time has elapsed, check the bacon again. If you like your bacon crispier, air fry it for another 1 to 2 minutes.

## Simple Chicken Breasts

**Prep time: 5 minutes | Cook time: 14 minutes | Serves 4**

½ teaspoon garlic powder
1 teaspoon salt
½ teaspoon freshly ground black pepper
1 teaspoon dried parsley
2 tablespoons olive oil, divided
4 boneless, skinless chicken breasts

1. In a small mixing bowl, mix together the garlic powder, salt, pepper, and parsley.
2. Using 1 tablespoon of olive oil and half of the seasoning mix, rub each chicken breast with oil and seasonings.
3. Place the chicken breast in the air fryer cooking tray.
4. Select Roast. Set temperature to 370ºF (190ºC). Set the timer and cook for 7 minutes.
5. Using tongs, flip the chicken and brush the remaining olive oil and spices onto the chicken.
6. Reset the timer and grill for 7 minutes or more.
7. Check that the chicken has reached an internal temperature of 165ºF (75ºC). Add cooking time if needed.
8. Once the chicken is fully cooked, transfer it to a platter and serve.

# Lemony Chicken Thighs

**Prep time: 10 minutes | Cook time: 20 minutes | Serves 4**

4 to 6 chicken thighs
1 teaspoon salt
1 teaspoon freshly ground black pepper
2 tablespoons olive oil

2 tablespoons Italian seasoning
2 tablespoons freshly squeezed lemon juice
1 lemon, sliced

1. Place the chicken thighs in a medium mixing bowl and season them with the salt and pepper.
2. Add the olive oil, Italian seasoning, and lemon juice and toss until the chicken thighs are thoroughly coated with oil.
3. Add the sliced lemons.
4. Place the chicken thighs into the air fryer cooking tray in a single layer.
5. Set the temperature to 350ºF (175ºC). Select Roast. Set temperature to 10 minutes.
6. Using tongs, flip the chicken.
7. Reset the timer and cook for 10 minutes or more.
8. Check that the chicken has reached an internal temperature of 165ºF (75ºC). Add cooking time if needed.
9. Once the chicken is fully cooked, plate, serve, and enjoy!

French Toast Sticks, page 10

Golden Onion Rings, page 10

Air-Fried Shrimp, page 12

Air-Fried Bacon, page 12

# Chapter 3 Breakfast

## Ham and Cheese Sandwiches

**Prep time: 5 minutes | Cook time: 8 minutes | Serves 2**

| | |
|---|---|
| 1 teaspoon butter | ham |
| 4 slices bread | 4 slices Cheddar cheese |
| 4 slices smoked country | 4 thick slices tomato |

1. Spread ½ teaspoon of butter onto one side of 2 slices of bread. Each sandwich will have 1 slice of bread with butter and 1 slice without it.
2. Assemble each sandwich by layering 2 slices of ham, 2 slices of cheese, and 2 slices of tomato on the unbuttered pieces of bread. Top with the other bread slices, buttered side up.
3. Place the sandwiches in the oven buttered-side down. Select Bake, and set time to 4 minutes.
4. Open the oven. Flip the grilled cheese sandwiches. Bake for an additional 4 minutes.
5. Cool before serving. Cut each sandwich in half and enjoy.

## Breakfast Cheesy Scramble Casserole

**Prep time: 10 minutes | Cook time: 13 minutes | Serves 4**

| | |
|---|---|
| 6 slices bacon, crumbled | pepper |
| 6 eggs | ½ cup chopped green bell pepper |
| Salt, to taste | |
| Pepper, to taste | ½ cup chopped onion |
| Cooking oil | ¾ cup shredded Cheddar cheese |
| ½ cup chopped red bell | |

1. In a skillet over medium-high heat, select Air Fry, and set time to 5 to 7 minutes, flipping to evenly crisp. Drain on paper towels, crumble, and set aside.
2. In a medium bowl, whisk the eggs. Add salt and pepper to taste.
3. Spray a barrel pan with cooking oil. Make sure to cover the bottom and sides of the pan.
4. Add the beaten eggs, crumbled bacon, red bell pepper, green bell pepper, and onion to the cooking tray. Place the cooking tray in the oven. Air fry for 6 minutes.
5. Open the oven and sprinkle the cheese over the casserole. Broil for an additional 2 minutes.
6. Cool before serving.

## Salmon and Brown Rice Frittata

**Prep time: 10 minutes | Cook time: 15 minutes | Serves 4**

| | |
|---|---|
| Olive oil, for greasing the pan | salmon |
| | ½ cup fresh baby spinach |
| 1 egg | ¼ cup chopped red bell pepper |
| 4 egg whites | |
| ½ teaspoon dried thyme | 1 tablespoon grated Parmesan cheese |
| ½ cup cooked brown rice | |
| ½ cup cooked, flaked | |

1. Rub a 6-by-2-inch pan with a bit of olive oil and set aside.
2. In a small bowl, beat the egg, egg whites, and thyme until well mixed.
3. In the prepared pan, stir together the brown rice, salmon, spinach, and red bell pepper.
4. Pour the egg mixture over the rice mixture and sprinkle with the Parmesan cheese.
5. Select Bake. Set time to about 15 minutes, or until the frittata is puffed and golden brown. Serve.

## Asparagus, Carrot, and Bell Pepper Strata

**Prep time: 10 minutes | Cook time: 15 minutes | Serves 4**

| | |
|---|---|
| 8 large asparagus spears, trimmed and cut into 2-inch pieces | whole-wheat bread, cut into ½-inch cubes |
| | 3 egg whites |
| ⅓ cup shredded carrot | 1 egg |
| ½ cup chopped red bell pepper | 3 tablespoons 1 percent milk |
| 2 slices low-sodium | ½ teaspoon dried thyme |

1. In a 6-by-2-inch pan, combine the asparagus, carrot, red bell pepper, and 1 tablespoon of water. Bake in the air fryer oven for 3 to 5 minutes, or until crisp-tender. Drain well.
2. Add the bread cubes to the vegetables and gently toss.
3. In a medium bowl, whisk the egg whites, egg, milk, and thyme until frothy.
4. Pour the egg mixture into the pan. Select Bake. Set time to 11 to 15 minutes, or until the strata is slightly puffy and set and the top starts to brown. Serve.

## Ricotta Butternut Squash Frittata

**Prep time: 10 minutes | Cook time: 13 minutes | Serves 2**

1 cup cubed (½-inch) butternut squash
2 tablespoons olive oil
Kosher salt and freshly ground black pepper, to taste
4 fresh sage leaves,
thinly sliced
6 large eggs, lightly beaten
½ cup ricotta cheese
Cayenne pepper, for garnish

1. In a bowl, toss the squash with the olive oil and season with salt and black pepper until evenly coated. Sprinkle the sage on the bottom of a 7-inch round cake pan insert, metal cake pan, or foil pan and place the squash on top. Place the pan in the air fryer oven and select Bake. Set temperature to 400ºF (205ºC), and set time to 10 minutes. Stir to incorporate the sage, then cook until the squash is tender and lightly caramelized at the edges, about 3 minutes.
2. Pour the eggs over the squash, dollop the ricotta all over, and sprinkle with cayenne. Bake at 300ºF (150ºC) until the eggs are set and the frittata is golden brown on top, about 20 minutes. Remove the pan from the oven and cut the frittata into wedges to serve.

## Chocolate Almond Crescent Rolls

**Prep time: 5 minutes | Cook time: 8 minutes | Serves 4 to 6**

1 (8-ounce / 227-g) tube of crescent roll dough
⅔ cup semi-sweet or bittersweet chocolate chunks
1 egg white, lightly beaten
¼ cup sliced almonds
Powder sugar, for dusting
Butter or oil

1. Preheat the air fryer oven to 350ºF (175ºC).
2. Unwrap the crescent roll dough and separate it into triangles with the points facing away from you. Place a row of chocolate chunks along the bottom edge of the dough. (If you are using chips, make it a double row.) Roll the dough up around the chocolate and then place another row of chunks on the dough. Roll again and finish with one or two chocolate chunks. Be sure to leave the end free of chocolate so that it can adhere to the rest of the roll.
3. Brush the tops of the crescent rolls with the lightly beaten egg white and sprinkle the almonds on top, pressing them into the crescent dough so they adhere.
4. Brush the bottom of the air fryer cooking tray with butter or oil and transfer the crescent rolls to the air fryer cooking tray. Select Air Fry. Set temperature to 350ºF (175ºC), and set time to 8 minutes. Remove and let the crescent rolls cool before dusting with powdered sugar and serve.

## Creamy Cinnamon-Glazed Butter-Pecan Roll

**Prep time: 15 minutes | Cook time: 25 minutes | Serves 2**

8 ounces (227 g) pizza dough
All-purpose flour, for dusting
2 tablespoons unsalted butter, melted
¼ cup packed dark brown sugar
¼ cup chopped pecans
¼ teaspoon kosher salt
1 tablespoon maple syrup, or dark agave syrup
½ cup powdered sugar
1 ounce (28 g) cream cheese, at room temperature
1 tablespoon milk
⅛ teaspoon ground cinnamon

1. Using a rolling pin, roll the pizza dough out on a lightly floured work surface into a rough 12 x 8-inch rectangle. Brush the dough all over with the melted butter, then sprinkle evenly with the brown sugar, pecans, and salt, then drizzle with the syrup. Using a pizza cutter or knife, cut the rectangle lengthwise into 8 equal strips. Roll up one strip like a snail shell, and then continue rolling each spiral up in the next strip until you have one giant spiral.
2. Cut a piece of parchment paper or foil to the size of the bottom of your air fryer cooking tray and line the bottom with it. Carefully lay the spiral in the oven and cover with a round of foil cut to fit the size of the spiral. Select Bake. Set temperature to 325ºF (165ºC), and set time to 15 minutes. Remove the foil round from the top and bake the roll until golden brown and cooked through in the middle, about 10 minutes or more.
3. Meanwhile, in a bowl, whisk together the powdered sugar, cream cheese, milk, and cinnamon until smooth.
4. Once the roll is cooked, let it cool in the cooking tray for 10 minutes, then carefully lift it out of the oven, using the parchment paper bottom as an aid. Transfer the roll to a plate and pour the icing over the roll to cover it completely. Let the roll and icing cool together for at least 10 minutes to set before cutting into wedges to serve.

## Egg English Muffins

**Prep time: 5 minutes | Cook time: 8 minutes | Serves 4**

4 eggs
Salt and pepper, to taste
Olive oil
4 English muffins, split
1 cup shredded Colby Jack cheese
4 slices ham or Canadian bacon

1. Preheat air fryer oven to 390ºF (200ºC).
2. Beat together eggs and add salt and pepper to taste. Spray air fryer cooking tray lightly with oil and add eggs. Bake for 2 minutes, stir, and continue cooking for 3 or 4 minutes, stirring every minute, until eggs are scrambled to your preference. Remove the cooking tray from oven.
3. Place bottom halves of English muffins in air fryer cooking tray. Take half of the shredded cheese and divide it among the muffins. Top each with a slice of ham and one-quarter of the eggs. Sprinkle the remaining cheese on top of the eggs. Use a fork to press the cheese into the egg a little so it doesn't slip off before it melts.
4. Select Toast, cook at 360ºF (180ºC) for 1 minute. Add English muffin tops and toast for 2 to 4 minutes to heat through and toast the muffins.

## Bread Boat Eggs

**Prep time: 10 minutes | Cook time: 13 minutes | Serves 4**

4 pistolette rolls
1 teaspoon butter
¼ cup diced fresh mushrooms
½ teaspoon dried onion flakes
4 eggs
½ teaspoon salt
¼ teaspoon dried dill weed
¼ teaspoon dried parsley
1 tablespoon milk

1. Cut a rectangle in the top of each roll and scoop out center, leaving ½-inch shell on the sides and bottom.
2. Place butter, mushrooms, and dried onion in air fryer cooking tray and bake for 1 minute. Stir and cook 3 more minutes.
3. In a medium bowl, beat together the eggs, salt, dill, parsley, and milk. Pour mixture into the cooking tray with mushrooms.
4. Select Bake. Set temperature to 390ºF (200ºC), and set time to 2 minutes. Stir. Continue cooking for 3 or 4 minutes, stirring every minute, until eggs are scrambled to your liking.
5. Remove the cooking tray from oven and fill rolls with scrambled egg mixture.
6. Place filled rolls in air fryer cooking tray and select Bake. Set temperature to 390ºF (200ºC), and set time to 2 to 3 minutes or until rolls are lightly browned.

## Eggs with Bacon and Tomato Sauce

**Prep time: 10 minutes | Cook time: 27 minutes | Serves 1**

1 teaspoon olive oil
2 tablespoons finely chopped onion
1 teaspoon chopped fresh oregano
pinch crushed red pepper flakes
1 (14-ounce / 397-g) can crushed or diced tomatoes
1 teaspoon salt, divided
1 teaspoon freshly ground black pepper, divided
2 slices of bacon, chopped
2 large eggs
¼ cup grated Cheddar cheese
Fresh parsley, chopped

1. Start by making the tomato sauce. Preheat a medium saucepan over medium heat on the stovetop. Add the olive oil and sauté the onion, oregano and pepper flakes for 5 minutes. Add the tomatoes and bring to a simmer. Season with salt and freshly ground black pepper and simmer for 10 minutes.
2. Meanwhile, preheat the oven to 400ºF (205ºC) and pour a little water into the bottom of the air fryer drawer. (This will help prevent the grease that drips into the bottom drawer from burning and smoking.) Place the bacon in the air fryer cooking tray and air fry at 400ºF (205ºC), and set time to 5 minutes, shaking the cooking tray every once in a while.
3. When the bacon is almost crispy, remove it to a paper-towel-lined plate and rinse out the air fryer drawer, draining away the bacon grease.
4. Transfer the tomato sauce to a shallow 7-inch pie dish. Crack the eggs on top of the sauce and scatter the cooked bacon back on top. Season with the rest salt and freshly ground black pepper and transfer the pie dish into the air fryer cooking tray. You can use an aluminum foil sling to help with this by taking a long piece of aluminum foil, folding it in half lengthwise twice until it is roughly 26-inches by 3-inches. Place this under the pie dish and hold the ends of the foil to move the pie dish in and out of the air fryer cooking tray. Tuck the ends of the foil beside the pie dish while it cooks in the oven.
5. Select Air Fry. Set temperature to 400ºF (205ºC), and set time to 5 minutes, or until the eggs are almost cooked to your liking. Sprinkle cheese on top and air-fry for an additional 2 minutes. When the cheese has melted, remove the pie dish from the oven, sprinkle with a little chopped parsley and let the eggs cool for a few minutes – just enough time to toast some buttered bread in your air fryer oven!

## Cheddar and Vegetable Egg Cups

**Prep time: 10 minutes | Cook time: 19 minutes | Serves 2**

Vegetable oil, for greasing
2 large eggs
½ cup mixed diced vegetables, such as onions, bell peppers, mushrooms, tomatoes
½ cup shredded sharp Cheddar cheese
2 tablespoons half-and-half
1 tablespoon chopped fresh cilantro (or other fresh herbs of your choice)
Kosher salt and black pepper, to taste

1. Grease two 6-ounce ramekins with vegetable oil.
2. In a medium bowl, whisk together the eggs, vegetables, ¼ cup of the cheese, the half-and-half, cilantro, and salt and pepper to taste. Divide the mixture between the prepared ramekins.
3. Place the ramekins in the air fryer cooking tray. Select Bake. Set temperature to 300ºF (150ºC), and set time to 15 minutes.
4. Top the cups with the remaining ¼ cup cheese. Select Broil. Set temperature to 400ºF (205ºC) and broil for 4 minutes, until the cheese on top is melted and lightly browned.
5. Serve immediately, or store in an airtight container in the refrigerator up to a week.

## Pancake Muffins

**Prep time: 15 minutes | Cook time: 28 minutes | Serves 4**

1 cup flour
2 tablespoons sugar (optional)
½ teaspoon baking soda
1 teaspoon baking powder
¼ teaspoon salt
1 egg, beaten
1 cup buttermilk
2 tablespoons melted butter
1 teaspoon pure vanilla extract
24 foil muffin cups
Cooking spray
For the Suggested Fillings:
1 teaspoon of jelly or fruit preserves
1 tablespoon or less fresh blueberries

1. In a large bowl, stir together flour, optional sugar, baking soda, baking powder, and salt.
2. In a small bowl, combine egg, buttermilk, butter, and vanilla. Mix well.
3. Pour egg mixture into dry ingredients and stir to mix well.
4. Double up the muffin cups and remove the paper liners from the top cups. Spray the foil cups lightly with cooking spray.
5. Place 6 sets of muffin cups in air fryer cooking tray. Pour just enough batter into each cup to cover the bottom. Sprinkle with desired filling. Pour in more batter to cover the filling and fill the cups about ¾ full.
6. Select Bake. Set temperature to 330ºF (165ºC), and set time to 7 to 8 minutes.
7. Repeat steps 5 and 6 for the remaining 6 pancake muffins.

## Apple Cider Doughnut Holes

**Prep time: 15 minutes | Cook time: 6 minutes | Makes 10 mini doughnuts**

For the Doughnut Holes:
1½ cups all-purpose flour
2 tablespoons granulated sugar
2 teaspoons baking powder
1 teaspoon baking soda
½ teaspoon kosher salt
Pinch of freshly grated nutmeg
¼ cup plus 2 tablespoons buttermilk, chilled
2 tablespoons apple cider (hard or nonalcoholic),
chilled
1 large egg, lightly beaten
Vegetable oil, for brushing
For the Glaze:
½ cup powdered sugar
2 tablespoons unsweetened applesauce
¼ teaspoon vanilla extract
Pinch of kosher salt

Make the Doughnut Holes
1. In a bowl, whisk together the flour, granulated sugar, baking powder, baking soda, salt, and nutmeg until smooth. Add the buttermilk, cider, and egg and stir with a small rubber spatula or spoon until the dough just comes together.
2. Using a 1-ounce ice cream scoop or 2 tablespoons, scoop and drop 10 balls of dough into the air fryer cooking tray, spaced evenly apart, and brush the tops lightly with oil. Select Bake. Set temperature to 350ºF (175ºC) until the doughnut holes are golden brown and fluffy, about 6 minutes. Transfer the doughnut holes to a wire rack to cool completely.

Make the Glaze
3. In a small bowl, stir together the powdered sugar, applesauce, vanilla, and salt until smooth.
4. Dip the tops of the doughnuts holes in the glaze, then let them stand until the glaze sets before serving. If you're impatient and want warm doughnuts, have the glaze ready to go while the doughnuts are being cooked. Use the glaze as a dipping sauce for the warm doughnuts fresh out of the air fryer oven.

## Crispy Tofu

**Prep time: 15 minutes | Cook time: 14 minutes | Serves 4**

| | |
|---|---|
| 1 (8-ounce / 227-g) package firm or extra-firm tofu | yeast |
| | 1 teaspoon dried rosemary |
| 4 teaspoons tamari or shoyu | 1 teaspoon dried dill |
| 1 teaspoon onion granules | 2 teaspoons arrowroot (or cornstarch) |
| ½ teaspoon garlic granules | 2 teaspoons neutral-flavored oil (such as sunflower, safflower, or melted refined coconut) |
| ½ teaspoon turmeric powder | |
| ¼ teaspoon freshly ground black pepper | Cooking oil spray (sunflower, safflower, or refined coconut) |
| 2 tablespoons nutritional | |

1. Cut the tofu into slices and press out the excess water.
2. Cut the slices into ½-inch cubes and place in a bowl. Sprinkle with the tamari and toss gently to coat. Set aside for a few minutes.
3. Toss the tofu again, then add the onion, garlic, turmeric, and pepper. Gently toss to thoroughly coat.
4. Add the nutritional yeast, rosemary, dill, and arrowroot. Toss gently to coat.
5. Finally, drizzle with the oil and toss one last time. Spray the air fryer cooking tray with the oil. Place the tofu in the air fryer cooking tray and, select Bake, and set time to 7 minutes. Remove, shake gently (so that the tofu cooks evenly), and bake for another 7 minutes, or until the tofu is crisp and browned.

## Toast and Turkey Sausage Roll-Ups

**Prep time: 10 minutes | Cook time: 22 minutes | Serves 3**

| | |
|---|---|
| 6 links turkey sausage | ½ tsp. vanilla extract |
| 6 slices of white bread, crusts removed | 1 tbsp. butter, melted |
| 2 eggs | powdered sugar (optional) |
| ½ cup milk | Maple syrup, for serving |
| ½ tsp. ground cinnamon | |

1. Preheat the air fryer oven to 380ºF (195ºC) and pour a little water into the bottom of the air fryer drawer. (This will help prevent the grease that drips into the bottom drawer from burning and smoking.)
2. Air Fry the sausage links at 380ºF (195ºC), and set time to 8 minutes, turning them a couple of times

during the cooking process. (If you have pre-cooked sausage links, omit this step.)
3. Roll each sausage link in a piece of bread, pressing the finished seam tightly to seal shut.
4. Combine the eggs, milk, cinnamon, and vanilla in a shallow dish. Dip the sausage rolls in the egg mixture and let them soak in the egg for 30 seconds. Spray or brush the bottom of the air fryer cooking tray with oil and transfer the sausage rolls to the air fryer cooking tray, seam side down.
5. Air Fry the rolls at 370ºF (190ºC), and set time to 9 minutes. Brush melted butter over the bread, flip the rolls over and air fry for an additional 5 minutes. Remove the French toast roll-ups from the cooking tray and dust with powdered sugar, if using. Serve with maple syrup and enjoy.

## Brown Sugar-Pumpkin Donut Holes

**Prep time: 10 minutes | Cook time: 5 minutes | Makes 12 donut holes**

| | |
|---|---|
| 1 cup whole-wheat pastry flour, plus more as needed | added pumpkin purée |
| | 3 tablespoons 2 percent milk, plus more as needed |
| 3 tablespoons packed brown sugar | 2 tablespoons unsalted butter, melted |
| ½ teaspoon ground cinnamon | 1 egg white |
| 1 teaspoon low-sodium baking powder | Powdered sugar (optional) |
| ⅓ cup canned no-salt- | |

1. In a medium bowl, mix the pastry flour, brown sugar, cinnamon, and baking powder.
2. In a small bowl, beat the pumpkin, milk, butter, and egg white until combined. Add the pumpkin mixture to the dry ingredients and mix until combined. You may need to add more flour or milk to form a soft dough.
3. Divide the dough into 12 pieces. With floured hands, form each piece into a ball.
4. Cut a piece of parchment paper or aluminum foil to fit inside the air fryer cooking tray but about 1 inch smaller in diameter. Poke holes in the paper or foil and place it in the cooking tray.
5. Put 6 donut holes into the cooking tray, leaving some space around each. Select Bake. Set time to 5 to 7 minutes, until the donut holes reach an internal temperature of 200ºF (95ºC) and are firm and light golden brown.
6. Cool for 5 minutes. Remove from the cooking tray and roll in powdered sugar, if desired. Repeat with the remaining donut holes and serve.

## Scotch Eggs

**Prep time: 10 minutes | Cook time: 15 minutes | Serves 4**

1 pound (454 g) bulk pork sausage
2 tablespoons finely chopped fresh parsley
1 tablespoon finely chopped fresh chives
⅛ teaspoon freshly grated nutmeg
⅛ teaspoon kosher salt
⅛ teaspoon black pepper
4 hard-cooked large eggs, peeled
1 cup shredded Parmesan cheese
Vegetable oil spray
Coarse mustard, for serving

1.  In a large bowl, gently mix the sausage, parsley, chives, nutmeg, salt, and pepper until well combined. Shape the mixture into four equal-size patties.
2.  Place one egg on each sausage patty and shape the sausage around the egg, covering it completely. Dredge each sausage-covered egg in the shredded cheese to cover completely, pressing lightly to adhere. (Make sure the cheese well adheres to the meat so shreds of cheese don't end up flying around in the oven.)
3.  Arrange the Scotch eggs in the air fryer cooking tray. Spray lightly with vegetable oil spray. Select Air Fry. Set temperature to 400ºF (205ºC), and set time to 15 minutes. Halfway through the cooking time, turn eggs and spray again.
4.  Serve with mustard.

## Apples Stuffed with Granola

**Prep time: 5 minutes | Cook time: 20 minutes | Serves 4**

4 apples
1 cup granola
2 tablespoons light brown sugar
¾ teaspoon cinnamon
2 tablespoons unsalted
butter, melted
1 cup water or apple juice
crème fraîche or yogurt (optional)

1.  Working one apple at a time, cut a circle around the apple stem and scoop out the core, taking care not to cut all the way through to the bottom. (This should leave an empty cavity in the middle of the apple for the granola.) Repeat with the remaining apples.
2.  In a small bowl, combine the granola, brown sugar, and cinnamon. Pour the melted butter over the ingredients and stir with a fork. Divide the granola mixture among the apples, packing it tightly into the empty cavity.
3.  Place the apples in the cooking tray insert for the oven. Pour the water or juice around the apples. Select Bake. Set temperature to 350ºF (175ºC), and set time to 20 minutes until the apples are soft all the way through. (If the granola begins to scorch before the apples are fully cooked, cover the top of the apples with a small piece of aluminum foil.)
4.  Serve warm with crème fraîche or yogurt, if desired.

## Quick Shakshuka

**Prep time: 15 minutes | Cook time: 30 minutes | Serves 2**

For the Tomato Sauce:
3 tablespoons extra-virgin olive oil
1 small yellow onion, diced
1 jalapeño pepper, seeded and minced
1 red bell pepper, diced
¼ teaspoon salt
2 cloves garlic, minced
1 teaspoon cumin
1 teaspoon sweet paprika
Pinch cayenne pepper
1 tablespoon tomato
paste
1 can (28-ounce / 794-g) whole plum tomatoes with juice
2 teaspoons granulated sugar
For the Shakshuka:
4 eggs
1 tablespoon heavy cream
1 tablespoon chopped cilantro
Kosher salt and pepper, to taste

1.  Heat the olive oil in a large, deep skillet over medium heat. Add the onion and peppers, season with salt, and sauté until softened, about 10 minutes. Add the garlic and spices and sauté a few additional minutes until fragrant. Add the tomato paste and stir to combine. Add the plum tomatoes along with their juice—breaking up the tomatoes with a spoon—and the sugar. Turn the heat to high and bring the mixture to a boil. Turn the heat down and simmer until the tomatoes are thickened, about 10 minutes. Turn off the heat. (May be done in advance. Refrigerate the sauce if not used right away.)
2.  Crack the eggs into a 7-inch round cake pan insert for the air fryer oven. Remove 1 cup of the tomato sauce from the skillet and spoon it over the egg whites only, leaving the yolks exposed. Drizzle the cream over the yolks.
3.  Place the cake pan in the oven and select Bake. Set temperature to 300ºF (200ºC), and set time to 10 to 12 minutes, until the egg whites are set and the yolks still runny. Remove the pan from the air fryer and garnish with chopped cilantro. Season with salt and pepper.
4.  Serve immediately with crusty bread to mop up the sauce.

## Red Rolls

**Prep time: 10 minutes | Cook time: 15 minutes | Serves 6**

7 cups minced meat
1 small onion, diced
1 packet spring roll sheets
2 ounces (57 g) Asian noodles

3 cloves garlic, crushed
1 cup mixed vegetables
1 tablespoon sesame oil
2 tablespoons water
1 teaspoon soy sauce

1. Cook the noodles in hot water until they turn soft. Drain and cut to your desired length.
2. Grease the wok with sesame oil. Put it over a medium-high heat and fry the minced meat, mixed vegetables, garlic, and onion, stirring regularly to ensure the minced meat cooks through. The cooking time will vary depending on the pan you are using – 3 to 5 minutes if using a wok, and 7 to 10 if using a standard frying pan.
3. Drizzle in the soy sauce and add to the noodles, tossing well to allow the juices to spread and absorb evenly.
4. Spoon the stir-fry diagonally across a spring roll sheet and fold back the top point over the filling. Fold over the sides. Before folding back the bottom point, brush it with cold water, which will act as an adhesive.
5. Repeat until all the filling and sheets are used.
6. Preheat your oven at 360ºF (180ºC).
7. If desired, drizzle a small amount of oil over the top of the spring rolls to enhance the taste and ensure crispiness.
8. Select Bake. Set time to 8 minutes, in multiple batches if necessary. Serve and enjoy.

## Carrot and Raisin Muffins

**Prep time: 10 minutes | Cook time: 12 minutes | Makes 8 muffins**

1½ cups whole-wheat pastry flour
1 teaspoon low-sodium baking powder
⅓ cup brown sugar
½ teaspoon ground cinnamon
1 egg

2 egg whites
⅔ cup almond milk
3 tablespoons safflower oil
½ cup finely shredded carrots
⅓ cup golden raisins, chopped

1. In a medium bowl, combine the flour, baking powder, brown sugar, and cinnamon, and mix well.
2. In a small bowl, combine the egg, egg whites, almond milk, and oil and beat until combined. Stir the egg mixture into the dry ingredients just until combined. Don't overbeat; some lumps should be in the batter—that's just fine.
3. Stir the shredded carrot and chopped raisins gently into the batter.
4. Double up 16 foil muffin cups to make 8 cups. Put 4 of the cups into the oven and fill ¾ full with the batter.
5. Select Bake. Set time to 12 minutes or until the tops of the muffins spring back when lightly touched with your finger.
6. Repeat with remaining muffin cups and the remaining batter. Cool the muffins on a wire rack for 10 minutes before serving.

## Cherry Breakfast Tarts

**Prep time: 10 minutes | Cook time: 20 minutes | Serves 6**

For the Tarts:
2 refrigerated piecrusts
⅓ cup cherry preserves
1 teaspoon cornstarch
Cooking oil
For the Frosting:

½ cup vanilla yogurt
1 ounce (28 g) cream cheese
1 teaspoon stevia
Rainbow sprinkles, for garnish

Make the Tarts
1. Place the piecrusts on a flat surface. Using a knife or pizza cutter, cut each piecrust into 3 rectangles, for 6 total. (I discard the unused dough left from slicing the edges.)
2. In a small bowl, combine the preserves and cornstarch. Mix well.
3. Scoop 1 tablespoon of the preserves mixture onto the top half of each piece of piecrust.
4. Fold the bottom of each piece up to close the tart. Using the back of a fork, press along the edges of each tart to seal.
5. Spray the breakfast tarts with cooking oil and place them in the oven. I do not recommend stacking the breakfast tarts. They will stick together if stacked. You may need to prepare them in two batches. Select Bake, and set time to 10 minutes.
6. Allow the breakfast tarts to cool fully before removing from the oven.
7. If necessary, repeat steps 5 and 6 for the remaining breakfast tarts.
Make the Frosting
8. In a small bowl, combine the yogurt, cream cheese, and stevia. Mix well.
9. Spread the breakfast tarts with frosting and top with sprinkles, and serve.

Cinnamon Rolls, page 29

Sweet Oat Bran Muffins, page 27

Banana Chia Seed Pudding, page 28

Asparagus Spears and Goat Cheese Frittata, page 26

## Classic Quesadillas

**Prep time: 10 minutes | Cook time: 18 minutes | Serves 4**

4 eggs
2 tablespoons skim milk
Salt and pepper, to taste
Oil for misting or cooking spray
4 flour tortillas

4 tablespoons salsa
2 ounces (57 g) Cheddar cheese, grated
½ small avocado, peeled and thinly sliced

1. Preheat air fryer to 270ºF (130ºC).
2. Beat together eggs, milk, salt, and pepper.
3. Spray a 6 x 6-inch air fryer cooking tray lightly with cooking spray and add egg mixture.
4. Bake 8 to 9 minutes, stirring every 1 to 2 minutes, until the eggs are scrambled to your liking. Remove and set aside.
5. Spray one side of each tortilla with oil or cooking spray. Flip over.
6. Divide eggs, salsa, cheese, and avocado among the tortillas, covering only half of each tortilla.
7. Fold each tortilla in half and press down lightly.
8. Place 2 tortillas in air fryer cooking tray and select Bake. Set temperature to 390ºF (200ºC), and set time to 3 minutes or until cheese melts and outside feels slightly crispy. Repeat with remaining two tortillas.
9. Cut each cooked tortilla into halves or thirds.

## Fruity Beignets

**Prep time: 10 minutes | Cook time: 8 minutes | Makes 16 beignets**

1 teaspoon active quick-rising dry yeast
⅓ cup buttermilk
3 tablespoons packed brown sugar
1 egg
1½ cups whole-wheat pastry flour

3 tablespoons chopped dried cherries
3 tablespoons chopped golden raisins
2 tablespoons unsalted butter, melted
Powdered sugar, for dusting (optional)

1. In a medium bowl, mix the yeast with 3 tablespoons of water. Let it stand for 5 minutes, or until it bubbles.
2. Stir in the buttermilk, brown sugar, and egg until well mixed.
3. Stir in the pastry flour until combined.
4. With your hands, work the cherries and raisins into the dough. Let the mixture stand for 15 minutes.
5. Pat the dough into an 8-by-8-inch square and cut into 16 pieces. Gently shape each piece into a ball.

6. Drizzle the balls with the melted butter. Place them in a single layer in the air fryer cooking tray so they don't touch. You may have to bake these in batches. Select Bake. Set time to 5 to 8 minutes, or until puffy and golden brown.
7. Dust with powdered sugar before serving, if desired.

## Delicious Donut Holes

**Prep time: 15 minutes | Cook time: 8 minutes | Makes 12 donut holes**

1 tablespoon ground flaxseed
1½ tablespoons water
¼ cup non-dairy milk, unsweetened
2 tablespoons neutral-flavored oil (sunflower, safflower, or refined coconut)
1½ teaspoons vanilla
1½ cups whole-wheat pastry flour or all-purpose

gluten-free flour
¾ cup coconut sugar, divided
2½ teaspoons cinnamon, divided
½ teaspoon nutmeg
¼ teaspoon sea salt
¾ teaspoon baking powder
Cooking oil spray (refined coconut, sunflower, or safflower)

1. In a medium bowl, stir the flaxseed with the water and set aside for 5 minutes, or until gooey and thick.
2. Add the milk, oil, and vanilla. Stir well and set this wet mixture aside.
3. In a small bowl, combine the flour, ½ cup coconut sugar, ½ teaspoon cinnamon, nutmeg, salt, and baking powder. Stir very well. Add this mixture to the wet mixture and stir together—it will be stiff, so you'll need to knead it lightly, just until all of the ingredients are thoroughly combined.
4. Spray the air fryer cooking tray with oil. Pull off bits of the dough and roll into balls (about 1 inch in size each). Place in the cooking tray, leaving room in between as they'll increase in size a smidge. (You'll need to work in batches, as you probably won't be able to cook all 12 at a time.) Spray the tops with oil and select Air Fry, and set time to 6 minutes.
5. Remove the pan, spray the donut holes with oil again, flip them over, and spray them with oil again. Air fry them for 2 minutes, or until golden-brown.
6. During these last 2 minutes of frying, place the remaining 4 tablespoons coconut sugar and 2 teaspoons cinnamon in a bowl, and stir to combine.
7. When the donut holes are done frying, remove them one at a time and coat them as follows: Spray with oil again and toss with the cinnamon sugar mixture. Spray one last time, and coat with the cinnamon sugar one last time. Enjoy fresh and warm if possible, as they're the best that way.

## Apple Sauce-Walnut Muffins

**Prep time: 15 minutes | Cook time: 20 minutes | Makes 8 muffins**

1 cup flour
⅓ cup sugar
1 teaspoon baking powder
¼ teaspoon baking soda
¼ teaspoon salt
1 teaspoon cinnamon
¼ teaspoon ginger
¼ teaspoon nutmeg
1 egg
2 tablespoons pancake syrup, plus 2 teaspoons

2 tablespoons melted butter, plus 2 teaspoons
¾ cup unsweetened applesauce
½ teaspoon vanilla extract
¼ cup chopped walnuts
¼ cup diced apple
8 foil muffin cups, liners removed and sprayed with cooking spray

1. Preheat air fryer to 330ºF (165ºC).
2. In a large bowl, stir together flour, sugar, baking powder, baking soda, salt, cinnamon, ginger, and nutmeg.
3. In a small bowl, beat egg until frothy. Add syrup, butter, applesauce, and vanilla and mix well.
4. Pour egg mixture into dry ingredients and stir until just moistened.
5. Gently stir in nuts and diced apple.
6. Divide batter among the 8 muffin cups.
7. Place 4 muffin cups in air fryer cooking tray and select Bake. Set temperature to 330ºF (165ºC), and set time to 9 to 11 minutes.
8. Repeat with the remaining 4 muffins or until toothpick inserted in center comes out clean.

## Fried PB&J

**Prep time: 10 minutes | Cook time: 7 minutes | Serves 4**

½ cup cornflakes, crushed
¼ cup shredded coconut
8 slices oat nut bread or any whole-grain, oversize bread
6 tablespoons peanut butter

2 medium bananas, cut into ½-inch-thick slices
6 tablespoons pineapple preserves
1 egg, beaten
Oil for misting or cooking spray

1. Preheat air fryer to 360ºF (180ºC).
2. In a shallow dish, mix together the cornflake crumbs and coconut.
3. For each sandwich, spread one bread slice with 1½ tablespoons of peanut butter. Top with banana slices. Spread another bread slice with 1½ tablespoons of preserves. Combine to make a sandwich.
4. Using a pastry brush, brush top of sandwich lightly with beaten egg. Sprinkle with about 1½ tablespoons of crumb coating, pressing it in to make it stick. Spray with oil.
5. Turn sandwich over and repeat to coat and spray the other side.
6. Cooking 2 at a time, place sandwiches in air fryer cooking tray and select Air Fry, and set time to 6 to 7 minutes or until the coating is golden brown and crispy. If sandwich doesn't brown enough, spray with a little more oil and air fry at 390ºF (200ºC), and set time for another minute.
7. Cut cooked sandwiches in half and serve warm.

## Pork Sausage Quiche Cups

**Prep time: 5 minutes | Cook time: 22 minutes | Makes 10 quiche cups**

¼ pound all-natural ground pork sausage
3 eggs
¾ cup milk

20 foil muffin cups
Cooking spray
4 ounces (113 g) sharp Cheddar cheese, grated

1. Divide sausage into 3 portions and shape each into a thin patty.
2. Place patties in air fryer cooking tray and select Bake. Set temperature to 390ºF (200ºC), and set time to 6 minutes.
3. While sausage is cooking, prepare the egg mixture. A large measuring cup or bowl with a pouring lip works best. Combine the eggs and milk and whisk until well blended. Set aside.
4. When sausage has cooked fully, remove patties from cooking tray, drain well, and use a fork to crumble the meat into small pieces.
5. Double the foil cups into 10 sets. Remove paper liners from the top muffin cups and spray the foil cups lightly with cooking spray.
6. Divide crumbled sausage among the 10 muffin cup sets.
7. Top each with grated cheese, divided evenly among the cups.
8. Place 5 cups in air fryer cooking tray.
9. Pour egg mixture into each cup, filling until each cup is at least ⅔ full.
10. Select Bake, and set time to 8 minutes and test for doneness. A knife inserted into the center shouldn't have any raw egg on it when removed.
11. If needed, bake 1 to 2 more minutes, until the egg completely sets.
12. Repeat steps 8 through 11 for the remaining quiches.

## Eggs in a Basket

**Prep time: 5 minutes | Cook time: 6 minutes | Serves 1**

| | |
|---|---|
| 1 thick slice country, sourdough, or Italian bread | unsalted butter, melted |
| | 1 egg |
| 2 tablespoons (28 g) | Kosher salt and pepper, to taste |

1. Brush the bottom of the air fryer cooking tray insert and both sides of the bread with melted butter. Using a small round cookie or biscuit cutter, cut a hole out of the middle of the bread and set it aside.
2. Place the slice of bread in the air fryer cooking tray insert. Crack the egg into the hole in the bread, taking care not to break the yolk. Season with salt and pepper. Place the cut-out bread hole next to the slice of bread. Place the cooking tray insert into the oven.
3. Select Bake. Set temperature to 300ºF (150ºC), and set time to 6 to 8 minutes until the egg white is set but the yolk is still runny. Using a silicone spatula, remove the bread slice to a plate. Serve with the cut-out bread circle on the side or place it on top of the egg.

## Barbecue Chicken Flatbreads

**Prep time: 10 minutes | Cook time: 10 minutes | Serves 2 to 4**

| | |
|---|---|
| 2 cups chopped cooked chicken | Gouda cheese |
| ¾ cup prepared barbecue sauce | ¾ cup shredded Mozzarella cheese |
| 2 prepared naan flatbreads | ½ small red onion, halved and thinly sliced |
| ½ cup shredded smoked | 2 tablespoons chopped fresh cilantro |

1. In a medium bowl, toss together the chicken and ¼ cup of the barbecue sauce.
2. Spread half the remaining barbecue sauce on one of the flatbreads. Top with half the chicken and half each of the Gouda and Mozzarella cheeses. Sprinkle with half the red onion. Gently press the cheese and onions onto the chicken with your fingers.
3. Carefully place one flatbread in the air fryer cooking tray. Select Bake. Set temperature to 400ºF (205ºC), and set time to 10 minutes, until the bread is browned around the edges and the cheese is bubbling and golden brown. If not, bake for another 2 minutes. Transfer the flatbread to a plate and repeat to cook the second flatbread.
4. Sprinkle with the chopped cilantro before serving.

## Cheddar-Ham Muffins

**Prep time: 10 minutes | Cook time: 12 minutes | Makes 8 muffins**

| | |
|---|---|
| ¾ cup yellow cornmeal | ½ cup milk |
| ¼ cup flour | ½ cup shredded sharp Cheddar cheese |
| 1½ teaspoons baking powder | ½ cup diced ham |
| ¼ teaspoon salt | 8 foil muffin cups, liners removed and sprayed |
| 1 egg, beaten | with cooking spray |
| 2 tablespoons canola oil | |

1. Preheat air fryer oven to 390ºF (200ºC).
2. In a medium bowl, stir together the cornmeal, flour, baking powder, and salt.
3. Add egg, oil, and milk to dry ingredients and mix well.
4. Stir in shredded cheese and diced ham.
5. Divide batter among the muffin cups.
6. Place 4 filled muffin cups in air fryer cooking tray and select Bake, and set time to 5 minutes.
7. Reduce temperature to 330ºF (165ºC) and bake for 1 to 2 minutes or until toothpick inserted in center of muffin comes out clean.
8. Repeat steps 6 and 7 to cook the remaining muffins.

## French Toast Sticks with Maple Syrup

**Prep time: 10 minutes | Cook time: 15 minutes | Serves 4**

| | |
|---|---|
| 2 eggs | each slice cut into 4 strips |
| ½ cup milk | Oil for misting or cooking spray |
| ⅛ teaspoon salt | |
| ½ teaspoon pure vanilla extract | Maple syrup or honey, for serving |
| ¾ cup crushed cornflakes | |
| 6 slices sandwich bread, | |

1. In a small bowl, beat together eggs, milk, salt, and vanilla.
2. Place crushed cornflakes on a plate or in a shallow dish.
3. Dip bread strips in egg mixture, shake off excess, and roll in cornflake crumbs.
4. Spray both sides of bread strips with oil.
5. Place bread strips in air fryer cooking tray in single layer.
6. Select Bake. Set temperature to 390ºF (200ºC), and set time to 5 to 7 minutes or until they're dark golden brown.
7. Repeat steps 5 and 6 to cook the remaining French toast sticks.
8. Serve with maple syrup or honey for dipping.

# Cran-Bran Muffins

**Prep time: 10 minutes | Cook time: 30 minutes | Makes 8 muffins**

1½ cups bran cereal flakes
1 cup plus 2 tablespoons whole-wheat pastry flour
3 tablespoons packed brown sugar
1 teaspoon low-sodium

baking powder
1 cup 2 percent milk
3 tablespoons safflower oil or peanut oil
1 egg
½ cup dried cranberries

1. In a medium bowl, mix the cereal, pastry flour, brown sugar, and baking powder.
2. In a small bowl, whisk the milk, oil, and egg until combined.
3. Stir the egg mixture into the dry ingredients until just combined.
4. Stir in the cranberries.
5. Double up 16 foil muffin cups to make 8 cups. Put 4 cups into the air fryer oven and fill each three-fourths full with batter. Select Bake. Set time to about 15 minutes, or until the muffin tops spring back when lightly touched with your finger.
6. Repeat with the remaining muffin cups and batter.
7. Cool on a wire rack for 10 minutes before serving.

# Asparagus Spears and Goat Cheese Frittata

**Prep time: 10 minutes | Cook time: 25 minutes | Serves 2 to 4**

1 cup asparagus spears, cut into 1-inch pieces
1 teaspoon vegetable oil
6 eggs
1 tablespoon milk
2 ounces (57 g) goat

cheese
1 tablespoon minced chives (optional)
Kosher salt and pepper, to taste

1. Toss the asparagus pieces with the vegetable oil in a small bowl. Place the asparagus in a 7-inch round air fryer cake pan insert and place the pan in the oven. Select Bake. Set temperature to 400ºF (205ºC), and set time to 5 minutes until the asparagus is softened and slightly wrinkled. Remove the pan.
2. Whisk together the eggs and milk and pour the mixture over the asparagus in the pan. Crumble the goat cheese over the top of the eggs and add the chives, if using. Season with a pinch of salt and pepper. Return the pan to the oven and broil at 320ºF (160ºC), and set time to 20 minutes, until the eggs are set and cooked through. Serve immediately.

# Scotch Eggs with Sausage

**Prep time: 10 minutes | Cook time: 20 minutes | Serves 4**

2 tablespoons flour, plus extra for coating
1 pound (454 g) ground breakfast sausage
4 hard-boiled eggs, peeled

1 raw egg
1 tablespoon water
Oil for misting or cooking spray
¾ cup Crumb Coating
¾ cup flour

1. Combine flour with ground sausage and mix thoroughly.
2. Divide into 4 equal portions and mold each around a hard-boiled egg so the sausage completely covers the egg.
3. In a small bowl, beat together the raw egg and water.
4. Dip sausage-covered eggs in the remaining flour, then the egg mixture, then roll in the crumb coating.
5. Select Bake. Set temperature to 360ºF (180ºC), and set time to 10 minutes. Spray eggs, turn, and spray another side.
6. Continue cooking for another 10 to 15 minutes or until sausage is well done.

# American Chickpeas Donuts

**Prep time: 10 minutes | Cook time: 10 minutes | Serves 6**

1 cup flour
¼ cup sugar, plus ½ teaspoon
1 teaspoon baking powder
½ teaspoon salt
½ teaspoon cinnamon,

divided
1 tablespoon coconut oil, melted
2 tablespoons aquafaba or liquid from canned chickpeas
¼ cup milk

1. Put the sugar, flour and baking powder in a bowl and combine. Mix in the salt and cinnamon.
2. In a separate bowl, combine the aquafaba, milk and coconut oil.
3. Slowly pour the dry ingredients into the wet ingredients and combine well to create a sticky dough.
4. Refrigerate for at least an hour.
5. Preheat your Air Fryer oven at 370ºF (190ºC).
6. Using your hands, shape the dough into several small balls and place each one inside the fryer. Select Bake. Set time to 10 minutes, refraining from shaking the cooking tray as they cook.
7. Lightly dust the balls with sugar and cinnamon and serve with a hot cup of coffee.

## Paprika Hash Browns

**Prep time: 5 minutes | Cook time: 20 minutes | Serves 4**

4 russet potatoes
1 teaspoon paprika
Salt, to taste

Pepper, to taste
Cooking oil

1. Peel the potatoes using a vegetable peeler. Using a cheese grater, shred the potatoes. If your grater has different-size holes, use the area of the tool with the largest holes.
2. Place the shredded potatoes in a large bowl of cold water. Let them sit for 5 minutes. Cold water helps remove excess starch from the potatoes. Stir to help dissolve the starch.
3. Drain the potatoes and dry with paper towels or napkins. Make sure the potatoes are completely dry.
4. Season the potatoes with the paprika and salt and pepper to taste.
5. Spray the potatoes with cooking oil and transfer them to the oven. Select Air Fry, and set time to 20 minutes, shaking the cooking tray every 5 minutes (a total of 4 times).
6. Cool before serving.

## Blueberry Muffins

**Prep time: 10 minutes | Cook time: 28 minutes | Makes 8 muffins**

1⅓ cups flour
½ cup sugar
2 teaspoons baking powder
¼ teaspoon salt
⅓ cup canola oil

1 egg
½ cup milk
⅔ cup blueberries, fresh or frozen and thawed
8 foil muffin cups including paper liners

1. Preheat air fryer oven to 330ºF (165ºC).
2. In a medium bowl, stir together flour, sugar, baking powder, and salt.
3. In a separate bowl, combine oil, egg, and milk and mix well.
4. Add egg mixture to dry ingredients and stir until just moistened.
5. Gently stir in blueberries.
6. Spoon batter evenly into muffin cups.
7. Place 4 muffin cups in air fryer cooking tray and select Bake. Set temperature to 330ºF (165ºC), and set time to 12 to 14 minutes or until tops spring back when touched lightly.
8. Repeat the previous step to cook the remaining muffins.

## Egg Porridge

**Prep time: 5 minutes | Cook time: 10 minutes | Serves 1**

2 organic free-range eggs
⅓ cup organic heavy cream without food additives
2 packages of your

preferred sweetener
2 tablespoons grass-fed butter
Ground organic cinnamon, to taste

1. In a bowl add the eggs, cream and sweetener, and mix together.
2. Melt the butter in a saucepan over a medium heat. Lower the heat once the butter is melted.
3. Combine together with the egg and cream mixture.
4. Select Bake, set the temperature to 350ºF (175ºC), and set the time to 10 minutes. While Cooking, mix until it thickens and curdles.
5. Pour the porridge into a bowl. Sprinkle cinnamon on top and serve immediately.

## Sweet Oat Bran Muffins

**Prep time: 10 minutes | Cook time: 20 minutes | Makes 8 muffins**

⅔ cup oat bran
½ cup flour
¼ cup brown sugar
1 teaspoon baking powder
½ teaspoon baking soda
⅛ teaspoon salt
½ cup buttermilk

1 egg
2 tablespoons canola oil
½ cup chopped dates, raisins, or dried cranberries
24 paper muffin cups
Cooking spray

1. Preheat air fryer oven to 330ºF (165ºC).
2. In a large bowl, combine the oat bran, flour, brown sugar, baking powder, baking soda, and salt.
3. In a small bowl, beat together the buttermilk, egg, and oil.
4. Pour buttermilk mixture into bowl with dry ingredients and stir just until moistened. Do not beat.
5. Gently stir in dried fruit.
6. Use triple baking cups to help muffins hold shape during baking. Spray them with cooking spray, place 4 sets of cups on air fryer cooking tray at a time, and fill each one ¾ full of batter.
7. Select Bake, and set time to 10 minutes, until the top springs back when lightly touched and toothpick inserted in center comes out clean.
8. Repeat for the remaining muffins.

## Banana Chia Seed Pudding

**Prep time: 5 minutes | Cook time: 0 minutes | Serves 1**

1 can full-fat coconut milk
1 medium- or small-sized banana, ripe

½ teaspoon cinnamon
1 teaspoon vanilla extract
¼ cup chia seeds

1. In a bowl, mash the banana until soft.
2. Add the remaining ingredients and mix until incorporated.
3. Cover and place in your refrigerator overnight.
4. Serve!

## Sweet Potato-Cinnamon Toast

**Prep time: 5 minutes | Cook time: 8 minutes | Makes 6 to 8 slices**

1 small sweet potato, cut into ⅜-inch slices
Oil, for misting

Ground cinnamon, to taste

1. Preheat air fryer oven to 390ºF (200ºC).
2. Spray both sides of sweet potato slices with oil. Sprinkle both sides with cinnamon to taste.
3. Place potato slices in air fryer cooking tray in a single layer.
4. Select Bake, and set time to 4 minutes, turn, and bake for 4 more minutes or until potato slices are barely fork-tender.

## Canadian Bacon and Cheese English Muffins

**Prep time: 5 minutes | Cook time: 8 minutes | Serves 4**

4 English muffins
8 slices Canadian bacon

4 slices cheese
Cooking oil

1. Split each English muffin. Assemble the breakfast sandwiches by layering 2 slices of Canadian bacon and 1 slice of cheese onto each English muffin bottom. Top with the other half of the English muffin.
2. Place the sandwiches in the air fryer oven. Spray the top of each with cooking oil. Select Bake, and set time to 4 minutes.
3. Open the oven and flip the sandwiches. Bake for an additional 4 minutes.
4. Cool before serving.

## Veggie Omelet

**Prep time: 5 minutes | Cook time: 10 minutes | Serves 2**

extra-virgin olive oil
3 eggs
Pinch of cayenne or

black pepper
½ cup finely chopped vegetables

1. In a pan on high heat, stir-fry the vegetables in extra-virgin olive oil until lightly crispy.
2. Select Bake, set the temperature to 350ºF (175ºC), and set the time to 10 minutes. Bake the eggs with one tablespoon of water and a pinch of pepper.
3. When almost cooked, top with the vegetables and flip to cook briefly.
4. Serve.

## Strawberry-Rhubarb Parfait with Coconut Flakes

**Prep time: 5 minutes | Cook time: 0 minutes | Serves 1**

1 package crème fraiche or plain full-fat yogurt
2 tablespoons toasted flakes
2 tablespoons toasted

coconut flakes
6 tablespoons homemade strawberry and rhubarb jam

1. Add the jam into a dessert bowl.
2. Add the crème fraîche and garnish with the toasted and coconut flakes.
3. Serve!

## Smoked Salmon and Pork Sausage Omelet

**Prep time: 5 minutes | Cook time: 10 minutes | Serves 2**

3 eggs
1 smoked salmon
3 links pork sausage

¼ cup onions
¼ cup provolone cheese

1. Whisk the eggs and pour them into the cooking tray.
2. Select Bake, set the temperature to 350ºF (175ºC), and set the time to 10 minutes.
3. Add the onions, salmon and cheese before turning the omelet over.
4. Sprinkle the omelet with cheese and serve with the sausages on the side.
5. Serve!

# Cinnamon Rolls

**Prep time: 5 minutes | Cook time: 12 minutes | Makes 8 cinnamon rolls**

1 can of cinnamon rolls     Cooking spray

1. Spray the air fryer cooking tray with olive oil.
2. Separate the canned cinnamon rolls and place them in the air fryer cooking tray.
3. Select Bake. Set the temperature to 340ºF (170ºC). Set the timer and bake for 6 minutes.
4. Using tongs, flip the cinnamon rolls. Reset the timer and bake for another 6 minutes.
5. When the rolls are done cooking, use tongs to remove them from the oven. Transfer them to a platter and spread them with the icing that comes in the package.

# Eggs Florentine

**Prep time: 5 minutes | Cook time: 15 minutes | Serves 2**

| | |
|---|---|
| 1 cup washed, fresh spinach leaves | taste |
| 2 tablespoons freshly grated Parmesan cheese | 1 tablespoon white vinegar |
| Sea salt and pepper, to | 2 eggs |

1. Select Air Fry. Air Fry the spinach in the oven until wilted.
2. Sprinkle with Parmesan cheese and seasoning.
3. Slice into bite-size pieces and place on a plate.
4. Simmer a pan of water and add the vinegar. Stir quickly with a spoon.
5. Break an egg into the center. Turn off the heat and cover until set.
6. Repeat with the second egg.
7. Place the eggs on top of the spinach and serve.

# Cheddar Bacon Muffins

**Prep time: 5 minutes | Cook time: 20 minutes | Serves 1**

| | |
|---|---|
| 1 medium egg | 1 ounce (28 g) Cheddar cheese |
| ¼ cup heavy cream | Salt and black pepper, to taste |
| 1 slice cooked bacon (cured, pan-fried, cooked) | |

1. Preheat your fryer to 350ºF (175ºC).
2. In a bowl, mix the egg with the cream, salt and pepper.
3. Spread into muffin tin and fill the cup half full.
4. Place 1 slice of bacon into the muffin hole and half ounce of cheese on top of the muffin.
5. Select Bake. Set time to around 15 to 20 minutes or until slightly browned.
6. Add another ½ ounce of cheese onto the muffin and broil until the cheese is slightly browned. Serve!

# Coconut-Cream Cheese Pancakes

**Prep time: 5 minutes | Cook time: 5 minutes | Serves 1**

| | |
|---|---|
| 2 ounces (57 g) cream cheese | flour |
| 2 eggs | ½ to 1 packet of sugar |
| ½ teaspoon cinnamon | butter and sugar for garnish |
| 1 tablespoon coconut | |

1. Mix together all the ingredients until smooth.
2. Heat up a non-stick pan or skillet with butter or coconut oil on medium-high.
3. Put the mix in the oven. Select Bake. Bake it on one side and then flip to cook the other side!
4. Top with some butter and sugar.

# Sausage and Cream Cheese Biscuits

**Prep time: 5 minutes | Cook time: 15 minutes | Serves 5**

| | |
|---|---|
| 12 ounces (340 g) chicken breakfast sausage | 1 (6-ounce/ 170-g) can biscuit dough |
| | ⅛ cup cream cheese |

1. Form the sausage into 5 small patties.
2. Place the sausage patties in the air fryer oven. Select Air Fry for 5 minutes.
3. Open the oven. Flip the patties. Air fry for an additional 5 minutes.
4. Remove the cooked sausages from the oven.
5. Separate the biscuit dough into 5 biscuits.
6. Place the biscuits in the air fryer. Select Air Fry, and set time to 3 minutes.
7. Open the air fryer. Flip the biscuits. Air fry for an additional 2 minutes.
8. Remove the cooked biscuits from the oven.
9. Split each biscuit in half. Spread 1 teaspoon of cream cheese onto the bottom of each biscuit. Top with a sausage patty and the other half of the biscuit, and serve.

# Chapter 4 Poultry

## Turkey Wings

**Prep time: 5 minutes | Cook time: 26 minutes | Serves 4**

2 pounds (907 g) turkey wings
3 tablespoons olive oil or
sesame oil
3 to 4 tablespoons chicken rub (any type)

1. Put the turkey wings in a large mixing bowl.
2. Pour the olive oil into the bowl and add the rub.
3. Using your hands, rub the oil mixture over the turkey wings.
4. Place the turkey wings in the air fryer cooking tray.
5. Set the temperature to 380ºF (195ºC). Select Air Fry for 13 minutes.
6. Using tongs, flip the wings.
7. Reset the timer and roast for 13 minutes or more.
8. Remove the turkey wings from the oven, plate, and serve.

## Buttermilk-Fried Drumsticks

**Prep time: 10 minutes | Cook time: 20 minutes | Serves 2**

1 egg
½ cup buttermilk
¾ cup self-rising flour
¾ cup seasoned panko breadcrumbs
1 teaspoon salt
¼ teaspoon ground
black pepper (to mix into coating)
4 chicken drumsticks, skin on
Oil for misting or cooking spray

1. Beat together egg and buttermilk in shallow dish.
2. In a second shallow dish, combine the flour, panko crumbs, salt, and pepper.
3. Sprinkle chicken legs with additional salt and pepper to taste.
4. Dip legs in buttermilk mixture, then roll in panko mixture, pressing in crumbs to make coating stick. Mist with oil or cooking spray.
5. Spray air fryer cooking tray with cooking spray.
6. Roast drumsticks at 360ºF (180ºC), and set time to 10 minutes. Turn pieces over and roast for an additional 10 minutes.
7. Turn pieces to check for browning. If you have any white spots that haven't begun to brown, spritz them with oil or cooking spray. Continue cooking for 5

minutes or until crust is golden brown and juices run clear. Larger, meatier drumsticks will take longer to cook than small ones.

## Spiced Chicken Chimichangas

**Prep time: 15 minutes | Cook time: 10 minutes | Serves 4**

2 cups cooked chicken, shredded
2 tablespoons chopped green chiles
½ teaspoon oregano
½ teaspoon cumin
½ teaspoon onion powder
¼ teaspoon garlic powder
Salt and pepper, to taste
8 (6- or 7-inch diameter) flour tortillas
Oil for misting or cooking spray
For the Chimichanga Sauce:
2 tablespoons butter
2 tablespoons flour
1 cup chicken broth
¼ cup light sour cream
¼ teaspoon salt
2 ounces (57 g) Pepper Jack or Monterey Jack cheese, shredded

1. Make the sauce by melting butter in a saucepan over medium-low heat. Stir in flour until smooth and slightly bubbly. Gradually add broth, stirring constantly until smooth. Cook and stir for 1 minute, until the mixture slightly thickens. Remove from heat and stir in sour cream and salt. Set aside.
2. In a medium bowl, mix together the chicken, chiles, oregano, cumin, onion powder, garlic, salt, and pepper. Stir in 3 to 4 tablespoons of the sauce, using just enough to make the filling moist but not soupy.
3. Divide filling among the 8 tortillas. Place filling down the center of tortilla, stopping about 1 inch from edges. Fold one side of tortilla over filling, fold the two sides in, and then roll up. Mist all sides with oil or cooking spray.
4. Place chimichangas in air fryer cooking tray seam side down. To fit more into the cooking tray, you can stand them on their sides with the seams against the sides of the cooking tray.
5. Select Roast. Set temperature to 360ºF (180ºC), and set time to 8 to 10 minutes or until heated through and crispy brown outside.
6. Add the shredded cheese to the remaining sauce. Stir over low heat, warming just until the cheese melts. Don't boil or sour cream may curdle.
7. Drizzle the sauce over the chimichangas.

## Chicken Cordon Bleu

**Prep time: 10 minutes | Cook time: 16 minutes | Serves 4**

| | |
|---|---|
| 4 small boneless, skinless chicken breasts | slices deli Swiss cheese |
| Salt and pepper, to taste | 2 tablespoons olive oil |
| 4 slices deli ham | 2 teaspoons marjoram |
| 4 (3- to 4-inch square) | ¼ teaspoon paprika |

1. Split each chicken breast horizontally almost in two, leaving one edge intact.
2. Lay breasts open flat and sprinkle with salt and pepper to taste.
3. Place a ham slice on top of each chicken breast.
4. Cut cheese slices in half and place one half atop each breast. Set aside the remaining halves of cheese slices.
5. Roll up chicken breasts to enclose cheese and ham and secure with toothpicks.
6. Mix together the olive oil, marjoram, and paprika. Rub all over outsides of chicken breasts.
7. Place chicken in air fryer cooking tray and select Roast. Set temperature to 360ºF (180ºC), and set time to 15 to 20 minutes, until well done and juices run clear.
8. Remove all toothpicks. To avoid burns, place chicken breasts on a plate to remove toothpicks, then immediately return them to the air fryer cooking tray.
9. Place a half cheese slice on top of each chicken breast and cook for a minute or so just to melt cheese.

## Chicken Hand Pies

**Prep time: 10 minutes | Cook time: 15 minutes | Makes 8 pies**

| | |
|---|---|
| ¾ cup chicken broth | 1 tablespoon milk |
| ¾ cup frozen mixed peas and carrots | Salt and pepper, to taste |
| 1 cup cooked chicken, chopped | 1 can organic flaky biscuits |
| 1 tablespoon cornstarch | Oil for misting or cooking spray |

1. In a medium saucepan, bring chicken broth to a boil. Stir in the frozen peas and carrots and cook for 5 minutes over medium heat. Stir in chicken.
2. Mix the cornstarch into the milk until it dissolves. Stir it into the simmering chicken broth mixture and cook just until thickened.
3. Remove from heat, add salt and pepper to taste, and let it cool slightly.

4. Lay biscuits out on wax paper. Peel each biscuit apart in the middle to make 2 rounds so you have 16 rounds total. Using your hands or a rolling pin, flatten each biscuit round slightly to make it larger and thinner.
5. Divide chicken filling among 8 of the biscuit rounds. Place the remaining biscuit rounds on top and press edges all around. Use the tines of a fork to crimp biscuit edges and make sure they are sealed well.
6. Spray both sides lightly with oil or cooking spray.
7. Roast in a single layer, 4 at a time, at 330ºF (165ºC), and set time to 10 minutes or until biscuit dough is cooked through and golden brown.

## Parmesan Breaded Chicken with Spaghetti

**Prep time: 10 minutes | Cook time: 10 minutes | Serves 4**

| | |
|---|---|
| 4 chicken tenders | cheese, plus more for serving |
| Italian seasoning, to taste | |
| Salt, to taste | Oil for misting or cooking spray |
| ¼ cup cornstarch | |
| ½ cup Italian salad dressing | 8 ounces (227 g) spaghetti, cooked |
| ¼ cup panko breadcrumbs | 1 (24-ounce / 680.4-g) jar marinara sauce |
| ¼ cup grated Parmesan | |

1. Pound chicken tenders with meat mallet or rolling pin until about ¼-inch thick.
2. Sprinkle both sides with Italian seasoning and salt to taste.
3. Place cornstarch and salad dressing in 2 separate shallow dishes.
4. In a third shallow dish, mix together the panko crumbs and Parmesan cheese.
5. Dip flattened chicken in cornstarch, then salad dressing. Dip in the panko mixture, pressing into the chicken so the coating sticks well.
6. Spray both sides with oil or cooking spray. Place in air fryer cooking tray in a single layer.
7. Select Air Fry. Set temperature to 390ºF (200ºC), and set time for 5 minutes. Spray with oil again, turning chicken to coat both sides.
8. Air fry for an additional 4 to 6 minutes or until chicken juices run clear and outside is browned.
9. While chicken is cooking, heat marinara sauce and stir into cooked spaghetti.
10. To serve, divide spaghetti with sauce among 4 dinner plates, and top each with a fried chicken tender. Pass additional Parmesan at the table for those who want extra cheese.

## Peach-Chicken Breast with Cherries

**Prep time: 10 minutes | Cook time: 14 minutes | Serves 4**

⅓ cup peach preserves
1 teaspoon ground rosemary
½ teaspoon black pepper
½ teaspoon salt
½ teaspoon marjoram
1 teaspoon light olive oil
1 pound (454 g) boneless chicken breasts, cut in

1½-inch chunks
Oil for misting or cooking spray
10 ounces (283 g) package frozen unsweetened dark cherries, thawed and drained

1. In a medium bowl, mix together peach preserves, rosemary, pepper, salt, marjoram, and olive oil.
2. Stir in chicken chunks and toss to coat well with the preserve mixture.
3. Spray air fryer cooking tray with oil or cooking spray and lay chicken chunks in cooking tray.
4. Select Roast. Set temperature to 390ºF (200ºC), and set time to 7 minutes. Stir. Cook for 6 to 8 more minutes or until chicken juices run clear.
5. When chicken has cooked through, scatter the cherries over and cook for additional minute to heat cherries.

## Panko-Crusted Chicken Nuggets

**Prep time: 10 minutes | Cook time: 26 minutes | Makes 20 to 24 nuggets**

1 pound (454 g) boneless, skinless chicken thighs, cut into 1-inch chunks
¾ teaspoon salt
½ teaspoon black pepper
½ teaspoon garlic powder
½ teaspoon onion

powder
½ cup flour
2 eggs, beaten
½ cup panko breadcrumbs
3 tablespoons plain breadcrumbs
Oil for misting or cooking spray

1. In the bowl of a food processor, combine chicken, ½ teaspoon salt, pepper, garlic powder, and onion powder. Process in short pulses until chicken is very finely chopped and well blended.
2. Place flour in one shallow dish and beaten eggs in another. In a third dish or plastic bag, mix together the panko crumbs, plain breadcrumbs, and ¼ teaspoon salt.
3. Shape chicken mixture into small nuggets. Dip nuggets in flour, then eggs, then panko crumb mixture.

4. Spray nuggets on both sides with oil or cooking spray and place in air fryer cooking tray in a single layer, close but not overlapping.
5. Select Air Fry. Set temperature to 360ºF (180ºC), and set time to 10 minutes. Spray with oil and cook 3 to 4 minutes, until chicken is done and coating is golden brown.
6. Repeat step 5 to cook the remaining nuggets.

## Buffalo Egg Rolls with Blue Cheese

**Prep time: 15 minutes | Cook time: 18 minutes | Makes 8 egg rolls**

1 teaspoon water
1 tablespoon cornstarch
1 egg
2½ cups cooked chicken, diced or shredded
⅓ cup chopped green onion
⅓ cup diced celery
⅓ cup buffalo wing sauce
8 egg roll wraps
Oil for misting or cooking spray

For the Blue Cheese Dip:
3 ounces (85 g) cream cheese, softened
⅓ cup blue cheese, crumbled
1 teaspoon Worcestershire sauce
¼ teaspoon garlic powder
¼ cup buttermilk (or sour cream)

1. Mix water and cornstarch in a small bowl until dissolved. Add egg, beat well, and set aside.
2. In a medium-size bowl, mix together chicken, green onion, celery, and buffalo wing sauce.
3. Divide chicken mixture evenly among 8 egg roll wraps, spooning ½ inch from one edge.
4. Moisten all edges of each wrap with beaten egg wash.
5. Fold the short ends over filling, then roll up tightly and press to seal edges.
6. Brush outside of wraps with egg wash, then spritz with oil or cooking spray.
7. Place 4 egg rolls in air fryer cooking tray.
8. Select Roast. Set temperature to 390ºF (200ºC), and set time to 9 minutes or until outside is brown and crispy.
9. While the rolls are cooking, prepare the Blue Cheese Dip. With a fork, mash together cream cheese and blue cheese.
10. Stir in remaining ingredients.
11. Dip should be just thick enough to slightly cling to egg rolls. If too thick, stir in buttermilk or milk 1 tablespoon at a time until it reach the desired consistency.
12. Cook remaining 4 egg rolls as in steps 7 and 8.
13. Serve while hot with blue cheese dip, more buffalo wing sauce, or both.

## Poblano Bake

**Prep time: 10 minutes | Cook time: 12 minutes | Serves 4**

2 large poblano peppers (approx. 5½ inches long excluding stem)
¾ pound (340.2 g) ground turkey, raw
¾ cup cooked brown rice
1 teaspoon chile powder
½ teaspoon ground

cumin
½ teaspoon garlic powder
4 ounces (113 g) sharp Cheddar cheese, grated
1 (8-ounce / 227-g) jar salsa, warmed

1. Slice each pepper in half lengthwise so that you have four wide, flat pepper halves.
2. Remove seeds and membrane and discard. Rinse inside and out.
3. In a large bowl, combine turkey, rice, chile powder, cumin, and garlic powder. Mix well.
4. Divide turkey filling into 4 portions and stuff one into each of the 4 pepper halves. Press lightly to pack down.
5. Place 2 pepper halves in air fryer cooking tray and select Roast. Set temperature to 390ºF (200ºC), and set time to 10 minutes or until turkey is well done.
6. Top each pepper half with ¼ of the grated cheese. Cook 1 more minute or just until cheese melts.
7. Repeat steps 5 and 6 to cook remaining pepper halves.
8. To serve, place each pepper half on a plate and top with ¼ cup warm salsa.

## Taquitos

**Prep time: 15 minutes | Cook time: 10 minutes | Makes 12 taquitos**

1 teaspoon butter
2 tablespoons chopped green onions
1 cup cooked chicken, shredded
2 tablespoons chopped green chiles
2 ounces (57 g) Pepper Jack cheese, shredded
4 tablespoons salsa

½ teaspoon lime juice
¼ teaspoon cumin
½ teaspoon chile powder
⅛ teaspoon garlic powder
12 corn tortillas
Oil for misting or cooking spray
guacamole, sour cream or salsa for serve

1. Melt butter in a saucepan over medium heat. Add green onions and sauté a minute or two, until tender.
2. Remove from heat and stir in the chicken, green chiles, cheese, salsa, lime juice, and seasonings.
3. Preheat air fryer oven to 390ºF (200ºC).

4. To soften refrigerated tortillas, wrap in damp paper towels and microwave for 30 to 60 seconds, until slightly warmed.
5. Remove one tortilla at a time, keeping others covered with the damp paper towels. Place a heaping tablespoon of filling into tortilla, roll up and secure with toothpick. Spray all sides with oil or cooking spray.
6. Place taquitos in air fryer cooking tray, either in a single layer or stacked. To stack, leave plenty of space between taquitos and alternate the direction of the layers, 4 on the bottom lengthwise, then 4 more on top crosswise.
7. Air fry for 4 to 6 minutes or until brown and crispy.
8. Repeat steps 6 and 7 to cook the remaining taquitos.
9. Serve hot with guacamole, sour cream or salsa!

## Peanut Butter-Barbecue Chicken

**Prep time: 10 minutes | Cook time: 20 minutes | Serves 4**

1 pound (454 g) boneless, skinless chicken thighs
Salt and pepper, to taste
1 large orange
½ cup barbecue sauce

2 tablespoons smooth peanut butter
2 tablespoons chopped peanuts for garnish (optional)
Cooking spray

1. Season chicken with salt and pepper to taste. Place in a shallow dish or plastic bag.
2. Grate orange peel, squeeze orange and reserve 1 tablespoon of juice for the sauce.
3. Pour remaining juice over chicken and marinate for 30 minutes.
4. Mix together the reserved 1 tablespoon of orange juice, barbeque sauce, peanut butter, and 1 teaspoon grated orange peel.
5. Place ¼ cup of sauce mixture in a small bowl for basting. Set remaining sauce aside to serve with cooked chicken.
6. Preheat the oven to 360ºF (180ºC). Spray cooking tray with nonstick cooking spray.
7. Remove chicken from marinade, letting excess drip off. Place in air fryer cooking tray and cook for 5 minutes. Turn chicken over and cook for 5 minutes longer.
8. Brush both sides of chicken lightly with sauce.
9. Roast chicken 5 minutes, then turn thighs one more time, again brushing both sides lightly with sauce. Roast for 5 more minutes or until chicken is done and juices run clear.
10. Serve chicken with remaining sauce on the side and garnish with chopped peanuts if you like.

# Butter Chicken Breast

**Prep time: 5 minutes | Cook time: 14 minutes | Serves 2**

2 (8-ounce / 227-g) boneless, skinless chicken breasts
1 sleeve Ritz crackers

4 tablespoons cold unsalted butter, cut into 1-tablespoon slices
cooking spray

1. Spray the air fryer cooking tray with olive oil, or spray an air fryer–size baking sheet with olive oil or cooking spray.
2. Dip the chicken breasts in water.
3. Put the crackers in a resealable plastic bag. Using a mallet or your hands, crush the crackers.
4. Place the chicken breasts inside the bag one at a time and coat them with the cracker crumbs.
5. Place the chicken in the greased air fryer cooking tray, or on the greased baking sheet set into the air fryer cooking tray.
6. Put 1 to 2 dabs of butter onto each piece of chicken.
7. Select Roast 370ºF (190ºC). Set the timer and cook for 7 minutes.
8. Using tongs, flip the chicken. Spray the chicken generously with olive oil to avoid uncooked breading.
9. Reset the timer and bake for 7 minutes more.
10. Check that the chicken has reached an internal temperature of 165ºF (75ºC). Add cooking time if needed.
11. Using tongs, remove the chicken from the oven and serve.

# Fiesta Chicken Plate

**Prep time: 15 minutes | Cook time: 15 minutes | Serves 4**

1 pound (454 g) boneless, skinless chicken breasts (2 large breasts)
2 tablespoons lime juice
1 teaspoon cumin
½ teaspoon salt
½ cup grated Pepper Jack cheese
1 (16-ounce / 454-g) can refried beans

½ cup salsa
2 cups shredded lettuce
1 medium tomato, chopped
2 avocados, peeled and sliced
1 small onion, sliced into thin rings
Sour cream
Tortilla chips (optional)

1. Split each chicken breast in half lengthwise.
2. Mix lime juice, cumin, and salt together and brush on all surfaces of chicken breasts.
3. Place in air fryer cooking tray and select Roast. Set temperature to 390ºF (200ºC), and set time to 12 to

15 minutes, until well done.
4. Divide the cheese evenly over chicken breasts and cook for an additional minute to melt cheese.
5. While chicken is cooking, heat refried beans on stovetop or in microwave.
6. When ready to serve, divide beans among 4 plates. Place chicken breasts on top of beans and spoon salsa over. Arrange the lettuce, tomatoes, and avocados artfully on each plate and scatter with the onion rings.
7. Pass sour cream at the table and serve with tortilla chips if desired.

# Southern Fried Chicken

**Prep time: 10 minutes | Cook time: 26 minutes | Serves 4**

½ cup buttermilk
2 teaspoons salt, plus 1 tablespoon
1 teaspoon freshly ground black pepper
1 pound (454 g) chicken thighs and drumsticks
1 cup all-purpose flour

2 teaspoons onion powder
2 teaspoons garlic powder
½ teaspoon sweet paprika
Southern Fried Chicken

1. In a large mixing bowl, whisk together the buttermilk, 2 teaspoons of salt, and pepper.
2. Add the chicken pieces to the bowl, and let the chicken marinate for at least an hour, covered, in the refrigerator.
3. About 5 minutes before the chicken is done marinating, prepare the dredging mixture. In a large mixing bowl, combine the flour, 1 tablespoon of salt, onion powder, garlic powder, and paprika.
4. Spray the air fryer cooking tray with olive oil.
5. Remove the chicken from the buttermilk mixture and dredge it in the flour mixture. Shake off any excess flour.
6. Place the chicken pieces into the greased air fryer cooking tray in a single layer, leaving space between each piece. (You may have to fry the chicken in more than one batch.) Spray the chicken generously with olive oil.
7. Select Air Fry. Set temperature to 390ºF (200ºC). Set the timer and cook for 13 minutes.
8. Using tongs, flip the chicken. Spray generously with olive oil.
9. Reset the timer and fry for 13 minutes or more.
10. Check that the chicken has reached an internal temperature of 165ºF (75ºC). Add cooking time if needed.
11. Once the chicken is fully cooked, plate, serve, and enjoy!

## Turkey Breast

**Prep time: 10 minutes | Cook time: 50 minutes | Serves 4**

| | |
|---|---|
| 2 tablespoons unsalted butter | 1 teaspoon dried thyme |
| 1 teaspoon salt | 1 teaspoon dried oregano |
| ½ teaspoon freshly ground black pepper | 1 (3½-pound / 1.6-kg) boneless turkey breast |
| | 1 tablespoon olive oil |

1. Melt the butter in a small microwave-safe bowl on low for about 45 seconds.
2. Add the salt, pepper, thyme, and oregano to the melted butter. Let the butter cool until you can handle it without burning yourself.
3. Rub the butter mixture all over the turkey breast, then rub on the olive oil, over the butter.
4. Place the turkey breast in the air fryer cooking tray, skin-side down.
5. Select Roast. Set temperature to 350ºF (175ºC). Set the timer and cook for 20 minutes.
6. Using tongs, flip the turkey.
7. Reset the timer and roast the turkey breast for another 30 minutes. Check that it has reached an internal temperature of 165ºF (75ºC). Add cooking time if needed.
8. Using tongs, remove the turkey from the oven and let it rest for about 10 minutes before carving.

## Spicy Roast Chicken Thighs

**Prep time: 10 minutes | Cook time: 10 minutes | Serves 4**

| | |
|---|---|
| 1 teaspoon ground turmeric | vinegar |
| ½ teaspoon cayenne pepper | 2 tablespoons olive oil |
| ½ teaspoon ground cinnamon | 1 pound (454 g) boneless, skinless chicken thighs, cut crosswise into thirds |
| ¼ teaspoon ground cloves | Zoodles, steamed rice, naan bread, or a mixed salad, for serving |
| ¼ teaspoon kosher salt | |
| 1 tablespoon cider | |

1. In a small bowl, combine the turmeric, cayenne, cinnamon, cloves, salt, vinegar, and oil. Stir to form a thick paste.
2. Place the chicken in a resealable plastic bag and add the marinade. Seal the bag and massage until the chicken is well coated. Marinate at room temperature for 30 minutes or in the refrigerator for up to 24 hours.

3. Place the chicken in the air fryer cooking tray. Select Roast. Set temperature to 350ºF (175ºC), and set time to 10 minutes, turning the chicken halfway through the cooking time. Use a meat thermometer to ensure that the chicken has reached an internal temperature of 165ºF (75ºC).
4. Serve with steamed rice or naan, over zoodles, or with a mixed salad.

## Peruvian-Style Chicken with Green Herb Sauce

**Prep time: 15 minutes | Cook time: 15 minutes | Serves 4**

| | |
|---|---|
| For the Chicken: | oregano, crushed |
| 1½ pounds (680 g) boneless, skinless chicken thighs | ½ teaspoon kosher salt |
| | For the Sauce: |
| 2 teaspoons grated lemon zest | 1 cup fresh cilantro leaves |
| 2 tablespoons fresh lemon juice | 1 jalapeño, seeded and coarsely chopped |
| 1 tablespoon extra-virgin olive oil | 1 garlic clove, minced |
| | 1 tablespoon extra-virgin olive oil |
| 1 serrano chile, seeded and minced | 2½ teaspoons fresh lime juice |
| 1 teaspoon ground cumin | ¼ teaspoon kosher salt |
| ½ teaspoon dried | ⅓ cup mayonnaise |

Make the Chicken
1. Use a fork to pierce the chicken all over to allow the marinade to penetrate better. In a small bowl, combine the lemon zest, lemon juice, olive oil, serrano, cumin, oregano, and salt. Place the chicken in a large bowl or large resealable plastic bag. Pour the marinade over the chicken. Toss to coat. Marinate at room temperature for 30 minutes, or cover and refrigerate for up to 24 hours.
2. Place the chicken in the air-fryer cooking tray. (Discard remaining marinade.) Select Roast. Set temperature to 350ºF (175ºC), and set time to 15 minutes, turning halfway through the cooking time.

Make the Sauce
3. Meanwhile, combine the cilantro, jalapeño, garlic, olive oil, lime juice, and salt in a blender. Blend until combined. Add the mayonnaise and blend until pureed. Transfer to a small bowl. Cover and chill until ready to serve.
4. At the end of the cooking time, use a meat thermometer to ensure the chicken has reached an internal temperature of 165ºF (75ºC). Serve the chicken with the sauce.

## Honey-Lime Glazed Cornish Hens

**Prep time: 5 minutes | Cook time: 25 minutes | Serves 2 to 3**

| | |
|---|---|
| 1 (1½- to 2-pound / 680- to 907-g) Cornish game hen | 1 teaspoon poultry seasoning |
| 1 tablespoon honey | Salt and pepper, to taste |
| 1 tablespoon lime juice | Cooking spray |

1. To split the hen into halves, cut through breast bone and down one side of the backbone.
2. Mix the honey, lime juice, and poultry seasoning together and brush or rub onto all sides of the hen. Season to taste with salt and pepper.
3. Spray air fryer cooking tray with cooking spray and place hen halves in the cooking tray, skin-side down.
4. Select Roast. Set temperature to 330ºF (165ºC), and set time to 25 to 30 minutes. Hen will be done when juices run clear and can be pierced at leg joint with a fork. Let hen rest for 5 to 10 minutes.

## Coconut Chicken with Apricot-Ginger Sauce

**Prep time: 15 minutes | Cook time: 14 minutes | Serves 4**

| | |
|---|---|
| 1½ pounds (680 g) boneless, skinless chicken tenders, cut in large chunks (1¼ inches) | For the Apricot-Ginger Sauce: |
| Salt and pepper, to taste | ½ cup apricot preserves |
| ½ cup cornstarch | 2 tablespoons white vinegar |
| 2 eggs | ¼ teaspoon ground ginger |
| 1 tablespoon milk | ¼ teaspoon low-sodium soy sauce |
| 3 cups shredded coconut | 2 teaspoons white or yellow onion, grated or finely minced |
| Oil for misting or cooking spray | |

1. Mix all ingredients for the Apricot-Ginger Sauce well and let it sit for flavors to blend while you cook the chicken.
2. Season chicken chunks with salt and pepper to taste.
3. Place cornstarch in a shallow dish.
4. In another shallow dish, beat together eggs and milk.
5. Place coconut in a third shallow dish. (If also using panko breadcrumbs, as suggested below, stir them to mix well.)
6. Spray air fryer cooking tray with oil or cooking spray.
7. Dip each chicken chunk into cornstarch, shake off excess, and dip in egg mixture.

8. Shake off excess egg mixture and roll lightly in coconut or coconut mixture. Spray with oil.
9. Place coated chicken chunks in air fryer cooking tray in a single layer, close together but without sides touching.
10. Select Roast. Set temperature to 360ºF (180ºC), and set time to 4 minutes, stop, and turn chunks over.
11. Cook an additional 3 to 4 minutes or until chicken is done inside and coating is crispy brown.
12. Repeat steps 9 through 11 to cook the remaining chicken chunks.

## Buttermilk Fried Chicken

**Prep time: 10 minutes | Cook time: 47 minutes | Serves 4**

| | |
|---|---|
| 1 (4-pound / 1.8-kg) chicken, cut into 8 pieces | 1 teaspoon salt |
| 2 cups buttermilk | Freshly ground black pepper, to taste |
| Hot sauce (optional) | 2 eggs, lightly beaten |
| 1½ cups flour | Vegetable oil, in a spray bottle |
| 2 teaspoons paprika | |

1. Cut the chicken into 8 pieces and submerge them in the buttermilk and hot sauce, if using. A zipper-sealable plastic bag works well for this. Let the chicken soak in the buttermilk for at least one hour or even overnight in the refrigerator.
2. Set up a dredging station. Mix the flour, paprika, salt and black pepper in a clean zipper-sealable plastic bag. Whisk the eggs and place them in a shallow dish. Remove four pieces of chicken from the buttermilk and transfer them to the bag with the flour. Shake them around to coat on all sides. Remove the chicken from the flour, shaking off any excess flour, and dip them into the beaten egg. Return the chicken to the bag of seasoned flour and shake again. Set the coated chicken aside and repeat with the remaining four pieces of chicken.
3. Preheat the oven to 370ºF (190ºC).
4. Spray the chicken on all sides with the vegetable oil and then transfer one batch to the air fryer cooking tray. Select Air Fry. Set temperature to 370ºF (190ºC), and set time to 20 minutes, flipping the pieces over halfway through the cooking process, taking care not to knock off the breading. Transfer the chicken to a plate, but do not cover it. Repeat with the second batch of chicken.
5. Lower the temperature on the air fryer to 340ºF (170ºC). Flip the chicken back over and place the first batch of chicken on top of the second batch already in the cooking tray. Air-fry for another 7 minutes and serve warm.

## Chicken Drumsticks with a Sweet Rub

**Prep time: 10 minutes | Cook time: 20 minutes | Serves 4**

| | |
|---|---|
| ¼ cup brown sugar | paprika |
| 1 tablespoon salt | 1 teaspoon dry mustard |
| ½ teaspoon freshly ground black pepper | 1 teaspoon garlic powder |
| 1 teaspoon chili powder | 1 teaspoon onion powder |
| 1 teaspoon smoked | 4 to 6 chicken drumsticks |
| | 2 tablespoons olive oil |

1. In a small mixing bowl, combine the brown sugar, salt, pepper, chili powder, paprika, mustard, garlic powder, and onion powder.
2. Using a paper towel, wipe any moisture off the chicken.
3. Put the chicken drumsticks into a large resealable plastic bag, then pour in the dry rub. Seal the bag.
4. Shake the bag to coat the chicken.
5. Place the drumsticks in the air fryer cooking tray. Brush the drumsticks with olive oil.
6. Select Roast. Set temperature to 390ºF (200ºC). Set the timer and air fry for 10 minutes.
7. Using tongs, flip the drumsticks, and brush them with olive oil.
8. Reset the timer and bake for 10 minutes more.
9. Check that the chicken has reached an internal temperature of 165ºF (75ºC). Add cooking time if needed.
10. Once the chicken is fully cooked, transfer it to a platter and serve.

## Light and Airy Breaded Chicken Breasts

**Prep time: 5 minutes | Cook time: 14 minutes | Serves 2**

| | |
|---|---|
| 2 large eggs | 4 to 5 tablespoons vegetable oil |
| 1 cup bread crumbs or panko bread crumbs | 2 (8-ounce / 227-g) boneless, skinless chicken breasts |
| 1 teaspoon Italian seasoning | |

1. Preheat the air fryer oven to 370ºF (190ºC). Spray the air fryer cooking tray (or an air fryer–size baking sheet) with olive oil or cooking spray.
2. In a small mixing bowl, beat the eggs until frothy.
3. In a separate small mixing bowl, mix together the bread crumbs, Italian seasoning, and oil.
4. Dip the chicken in the egg mixture, then in the bread crumb mixture.
5. Place the chicken directly into the greased air fryer cooking tray, or on the greased baking sheet set into the cooking tray.
6. Spray the chicken generously and thoroughly with olive oil to avoid powdery, uncooked breading.
7. Select Air Fry. Set temperature to 370ºF (190ºC), and set time to 7 minutes.
8. Using tongs, flip the chicken and generously spray it with olive oil.
9. Reset the timer and fry for 7 minutes more.
10. Check that the chicken has reached an internal temperature of 165ºF (75ºC). Add cooking time if needed.
11. Once the chicken is fully cooked, use tongs to remove it from the oven and serve.

## Peanut Chicken

**Prep time: 15 minutes | Cook time: 20 minutes | Serves 4**

| | |
|---|---|
| ¼ cup creamy peanut butter | ½ cup hot water |
| 2 tablespoons sweet chili sauce | 1 pound (454 g) bone-in chicken thighs |
| 2 tablespoons fresh lime juice | 2 tablespoons chopped fresh cilantro, for garnish |
| 1 tablespoon sriracha | ¼ cup chopped green onions, for garnish |
| 1 tablespoon soy sauce | 2 to 3 tablespoons crushed roasted and salted peanuts, for garnish |
| 1 teaspoon minced fresh ginger | |
| 1 clove garlic, minced | |
| ½ teaspoon kosher salt | |

1. In a small bowl, combine the peanut butter, sweet chili sauce, lime juice, sriracha, soy sauce, ginger, garlic, and salt. Add the hot water and whisk until smooth.
2. Place the chicken in a resealable plastic bag and pour in half of the sauce. (Reserve the remaining sauce for serving.) Seal the bag and massage until all of the chicken is well coated. Marinate at room temperature for 30 minutes or in the refrigerator for up to 24 hours.
3. Remove the chicken from the bag and discard the marinade. Place the chicken in the air fryer cooking tray. Select Roast. Set temperature to 350ºF (175ºC), and set time to 20 minutes. Use a meat thermometer to ensure the chicken has reached an internal temperature of 165ºF (75ºC).
4. Transfer the chicken to a serving platter. Sprinkle with the cilantro, green onions, and peanuts. Serve with the reserved sauce for dipping.

## Turkey Burgers

**Prep time: 10 minutes | Cook time: 10 minutes | Serves 4**

1 pound (454 g) ground turkey
¼ cup diced red onion
1 tablespoon grilled chicken seasoning
½ teaspoon dried parsley
½ teaspoon salt
4 slices provolone cheese
4 whole-grain sandwich buns
Suggested toppings: lettuce, sliced tomatoes, dill pickles, and mustard

1. Combine the turkey, onion, chicken seasoning, parsley, and salt and mix well.
2. Shape into 4 patties.
3. Select Roast. Set temperature to 360ºF (180ºC), and set time to 9 to 11 minutes or until turkey is well done and juices run clear.
4. Top each burger with a slice of cheese and cook 1 to 2 minutes to melt.
5. Serve on buns with your favorite toppings.

## Greek Chicken Souvlaki

**Prep time: 10 minutes | Cook time: 15 minutes | Serves 3 or 4**

For the Chicken:
Grated zest and juice of 1 lemon
2 tablespoons extra-virgin olive oil
1 tablespoon Greek souvlaki seasoning
1 pound (454 g) boneless, skinless chicken breast, cut into
2-inch chunks
Vegetable oil spray
For Serving:
Warm pita bread or hot cooked rice
Sliced ripe tomatoes
Sliced cucumbers
Thinly sliced red onion
Kalamata olives
Tzatziki

1. In a small bowl, combine the lemon zest, lemon juice, olive oil, and souvlaki seasoning. Place the chicken in a gallon-size resealable plastic bag. Pour the marinade over chicken. Seal bag and massage to coat. Place the bag in a large bowl and marinate for 30 minutes, or cover and refrigerate up to 24 hours, turning the bag occasionally.
2. Place the chicken a single layer in the air-fryer cooking tray. Select Roast. Set temperature to 350ºF (175ºC), and set time to 10 minutes, turning the chicken and spraying with a little vegetable oil spray halfway through the cooking time. Increase the air-fryer temperature to 400ºF (205ºC), and set time to 5 minutes to allow the chicken to crisp and brown a little.

3. Transfer the chicken to a serving platter and serve with pita bread or rice, tomatoes, cucumbers, onion, olives and tzatziki.

## Coconut Curried Chicken with Coconut Rice

**Prep time: 15 minutes | Cook time: 1¼ hours | Serves 4**

1 (14-ounce / 397-g) can coconut milk
2 tablespoons green or red curry paste
Zest and juice of one lime
1 clove garlic, minced
1 tablespoon grated fresh ginger
1 teaspoon ground cumin
1 (3- to 4-pound / 1.4- to 1.8-kg) chicken, cut into 8 pieces
Vegetable or olive oil
Salt and freshly ground black pepper, to taste
Fresh cilantro leaves
For the Rice:
1 cup basmati or jasmine rice
1 cup water
1 cup coconut milk
½ teaspoon salt
Freshly ground black pepper, to taste

1. Make the marinade by combining the coconut milk, curry paste, lime zest and juice, garlic, ginger and cumin. Coat the chicken on all sides with the marinade and marinate the chicken for 1 hour to overnight in the refrigerator.
2. Preheat the air fryer to 380ºF (195ºC).
3. Brush the bottom of the air fryer cooking tray with oil. Transfer the chicken thighs and drumsticks from the marinade to the air fryer cooking tray, letting most of the marinade drip off. Season to taste with salt and freshly ground black pepper.
4. Select Roast. Set temperature to 380ºF (195ºC), and set time to 12 minutes. Flip the chicken over and continue to air fry for another 12 minutes. Set aside and air fry the chicken breast pieces at 380ºF (195ºC), and set time to 15 minutes. Turn the chicken breast pieces over and air fry for another 12 minutes. Return the chicken thighs and drumsticks to the air fryer and air fry for an additional 5 minutes.
5. While the chicken is cooking, make the coconut rice. Rinse the rice kernels with water and drain well. Place the rice in a medium saucepan with a tight-fitting lid, along with the water, coconut milk, salt and freshly ground black pepper. Bring the mixture to a boil and then cover, reduce the heat and let it cook gently for 20 minutes without lifting the lid. When the time is up, lift the lid, fluff with a fork and set aside.
6. Remove the chicken from the oven and serve warm with the coconut rice and fresh cilantro scattered around.

## Super Cheesy Chicken Breast

**Prep time: 10 minutes | Cook time: 9 minutes | Serves 4**

½ cup keto marinara
6 tablespoons Mozzarella cheese
1 tablespoon melted ghee
2 tablespoons grated
Parmesan cheese
6 tablespoons gluten-free seasoned breadcrumbs
2 (8-ounce / 227-g) chicken breasts

1. Ensure air fryer oven is preheated to 360ºF (180ºC). Spray the cooking tray with olive oil.
2. Mix Parmesan cheese and breadcrumbs together. Melt ghee.
3. Brush melted ghee onto the chicken and dip into breadcrumb mixture.
4. Place coated chicken in the oven and top with olive oil.
5. Select Roast. Set temperature to 360ºF (180ºC), and set time to 6 minutes and top each breast with a tablespoon of sauce and 1½ tablespoons of Mozzarella cheese. Select Broil for another 3 minutes to melt cheese.
6. Keep cooked pieces warm as you repeat the process with remaining breasts.

## Mozzarella Chicken Parmesan

**Prep time: 10 minutes | Cook time: 14 minutes | Serves 4**

2 (8-ounce / 227-g) boneless, skinless chicken breasts
2 large eggs
1 cup Italian-style bread crumbs
¼ cup shredded Parmesan cheese
½ cup marinara sauce
½ cup shredded Mozzarella cheese

1. Preheat the air fryer oven to 360ºF (180ºC). Spray an air fryer–size baking sheet with olive oil or cooking spray.
2. Using a mallet or rolling pin, flatten the chicken breasts to about ¼ inch thick.
3. In a small mixing bowl, beat the eggs until frothy. In another small mixing bowl, mix together the bread crumbs and Parmesan cheese.
4. Dip the chicken in the egg, then in the bread crumb mixture.
5. Place the chicken on the greased baking sheet. Set the baking sheet into the air fryer cooking tray.
6. Spray the chicken generously with olive oil to avoid powdery, uncooked breading.
7. Select Roast. Set temperature to 360ºF (180ºC), and set time to 7 minutes, or until cooked through and the juices run clear.
8. Flip the chicken and pour the marinara sauce over the chicken. Sprinkle with the Mozzarella cheese. Select Broil. Set temperature to for another 7 minutes.
9. Once the chicken Parmesan is fully cooked, use tongs to remove it from the oven and serve.

## French Garlic Chicken Thighs

**Prep time: 10 minutes | Cook time: 27 minutes | Serves 4**

2 tablespoons extra-virgin olive oil
1 tablespoon Dijon mustard
1 tablespoon apple cider vinegar
3 cloves garlic, minced
2 teaspoons herbes de Provence
½ teaspoon kosher salt
1 teaspoon black pepper
1 pound (454 g) boneless, skinless chicken thighs, halved crosswise
2 tablespoons butter
8 cloves garlic, chopped
¼ cup heavy whipping cream

1. In a small bowl, combine the olive oil, mustard, vinegar, minced garlic, herbes de Provence, salt, and pepper. Use a wire whisk to emulsify the mixture.
2. Pierce the chicken all over with a fork to allow the marinade to penetrate better. Place the chicken in a resealable plastic bag, pour the marinade over, and seal. Massage until the chicken is well coated. Marinate at room temperature for 30 minutes or in the refrigerator for up to 24 hours.
3. When you are ready to cook, place the butter and chopped garlic in a 7 × 3-inch round heatproof pan and place it in the air fryer cooking tray. Select Roast. Set temperature to 400ºF (205ºC), and set time to 5 minutes, or until the butter has melted and the garlic is sizzling.
4. Add the chicken and the marinade to the seasoned butter. Select Roast. Set temperature to 350ºF (175ºC), and set time to 15 minutes. Use a meat thermometer to ensure the chicken has reached an internal temperature of 165ºF (75ºC). Transfer the chicken to a plate and cover lightly with foil to keep warm.
5. Add the cream to the pan, stirring to combine with the garlic, butter, and cooking juices. Place the pan in the air fryer cooking tray. Select Air Fry. Set temperature to 350ºF (175ºC), and set time to 7 minutes.
6. Pour the thickened sauce over the chicken and serve.

Buttermilk-Fried Drumsticks, page 31

Panko-Crusted Chicken Nuggets, page 33

Turkey Burgers, page 39

Gochujang Chicken Wings, page 46

## Spicy Chicken Stir-Fry

**Prep time: 10 minutes | Cook time: 13 minutes | Serves 4**

2 boneless, skinless chicken breasts
2 tablespoons cornstarch
2 tablespoons peanut oil
1 onion, sliced
1 jalapeño pepper, sliced
1 red bell pepper, chopped
1 cup frozen corn
½ cup salsa

1.  Cut the chicken breasts into 1-inch cubes. Put the cornstarch on a shallow plate and toss the chicken in it to coat. Set the chicken aside.
2.  In a 6-inch metal bowl, combine the oil and onion. Cook for 2 to 3 minutes or until crisp and tender.
3.  Add the chicken to the bowl. Cook for 7 to 8 minutes or until almost cooked. Stir in the jalapeño pepper, red bell pepper, corn, and salsa.
4.  Select Air Fry for 4 to 5 minutes or until the chicken is cooked to 165ºF (75ºC) and the vegetables are crisp and tender. Serve over hot rice.

## Chicken with Nashville Hot Sauce

**Prep time: 15 minutes | Cook time: 47 minutes | Serves 4**

1 (4-pound / 1.8-kg) chicken, cut into 6 pieces (2 breasts, 2 thighs and 2 drumsticks)
2 eggs
1 cup buttermilk
2 cups all-purpose flour
2 tablespoons paprika
1 teaspoon garlic powder
1 teaspoon onion powder
2 teaspoons salt
1 teaspoon freshly
ground black pepper
Vegetable oil, in a spray bottle
For the Nashville Hot Sauce:
1 tablespoon cayenne pepper
1 teaspoon salt
¼ cup vegetable oil
4 slices white bread
Dill pickle slices

1.  Cut the chicken breasts into 2 pieces so that you have a total of 8 pieces of chicken.
2.  Set up a two-stage dredging station. Whisk the eggs and buttermilk together in a bowl. Combine the flour, paprika, garlic powder, onion powder, salt and black pepper in a zipper-sealable plastic bag. Dip the chicken pieces into the egg-buttermilk mixture, then toss them in the seasoned flour, coating all sides. Repeat this procedure (egg mixture and then flour mixture) one more time. This can be a little messy, but make sure all sides of the chicken are completely covered. Spray the chicken with vegetable oil and set aside.
3.  Preheat the oven to 370ºF (190ºC). Spray or brush the bottom of the air-fryer cooking tray with a little vegetable oil.
4.  Select Roast. Set temperature to 370ºF (190ºC), and set time to 20 minutes, cook the chicken in two batches, flipping the pieces over halfway through the cooking process. Transfer the chicken to a plate, but do not cover it. Repeat with the second batch of chicken.
5.  Lower the temperature on the oven to 340ºF (170ºC). Flip the chicken back over and place the first batch of chicken on top of the second batch already in the cooking tray. Air fry for another 7 minutes.
6.  While the chicken is air-frying, combine the cayenne pepper and salt in a bowl. Heat the vegetable oil in a small saucepan and when it is very hot, add it to the spice mix, whisking until smooth. It will sizzle briefly when you add it to the spices. Place the fried chicken on top of the white bread slices and brush the hot sauce all over chicken. Top with the pickle slices and serve warm. Enjoy the heat and the flavor!

## Thai Turkey and Zucchini Meatballs

**Prep time: 15 minutes | Cook time: 10 minutes | Serves 4 to 6**

1½ cups grated zucchini, squeezed dry in a clean kitchen towel
3 scallions, finely chopped
2 cloves garlic, minced
1 tablespoon grated fresh ginger
1 tablespoon finely chopped fresh cilantro
Zest of 1 lime
1 teaspoon salt
Freshly ground black pepper, to taste
1½ pounds (680 g) ground turkey (a mix of light and dark meat)
2 eggs, lightly beaten
1 cup Thai sweet chili sauce (spring roll sauce)
Lime wedges, for serving

1.  Combine the zucchini, scallions, garlic, ginger, cilantro, lime zest, salt, pepper, ground turkey and eggs in a bowl and mix the ingredients together. Gently shape the mixture into 24 balls, about the size of golf balls.
2.  Preheat the air fryer oven to 380ºF (195ºC).
3.  Working in batches, select Roast. Set temperature to 380ºF (195ºC), and set time to 10 to 12 minutes, turning the meatballs over halfway through the cooking time. As soon as the meatballs have finished cooking, toss them in a bowl with the Thai sweet chili sauce to coat.
4.  Serve the meatballs over rice noodles or white rice with the remaining Thai sweet chili sauce and lime wedges to squeeze over the top.

## Cumin Chicken Tender

**Prep time: 5 minutes | Cook time: 8 minutes | Makes 2½ cups**

| | |
|---|---|
| 1 pound (454 g) chicken tenders, skinless and boneless | cumin |
| ½ teaspoon ground | ½ teaspoon garlic powder |
| | Cooking spray |

1. Sprinkle raw chicken tenders with seasonings.
2. Spray air fryer cooking tray lightly with cooking spray to prevent sticking.
3. Place chicken in air fryer cooking tray in single layer.
4. Select Roast. Set temperature to 390ºF (200ºC), and set time to 4 minutes, turn chicken strips over, and cook for an additional 4 minutes.
5. Test for doneness. Thick tenders may require an additional minute or two.

## General Tso's Chicken

**Prep time: 15 minutes | Cook time: 25 minutes | Serves 4**

| | |
|---|---|
| 2 pounds (907 g) boneless, skinless chicken breast, cut into bite-size cubes | 1 tablespoon grated fresh ginger |
| ½ cup soy sauce, divided | 12 dried red chiles |
| ½ cup mirin or rice wine, divided | ¼ cup rice vinegar |
| ½ cup plus ½ tablespoon cornstarch | ¼ cup granulated sugar |
| 2 tablespoons vegetable or canola oil plus additional oil for spraying | 2 teaspoons hoisin sauce (optional) |
| 2 cloves garlic, minced | 2 scallions, white and light green part only, sliced |
| | 1 teaspoon sesame seeds |

1. Toss the chicken with ¼ cup of the soy sauce and ¼ cup of the mirin in a glass bowl or baking dish. Cover and refrigerate for at least 15 and up to 30 minutes.
2. Spread ½ cup of cornstarch on a plate. Take 2 pieces of chicken and dredge them in the cornstarch, then tap them against each other to remove any excess. Repeat until you have dredged one-third of the chicken in the cornstarch. Spray the cooking tray of the air fryer with oil. Arrange the dredged chicken pieces in the cooking tray in a single layer. Spray with oil. Select Roast. Set temperature to 400ºF (205ºC), and set time to 8 minutes, turning once, spraying with additional oil if there are dry patches of cornstarch. Set aside.
3. While the first batch of chicken is cooking, dredge the second third of the chicken in the cornstarch. Spray the cooking tray of the oven with oil and cook the second batch of chicken in the same manner. While the second batch is cooking, dredge the remaining chicken in the cornstarch. Cook the last third of the chicken in the same manner as the others. Set the cooked chicken aside.
4. Whisk together the remaining ½ tablespoon of cornstarch with ½ tablespoon of water to create a slurry and set aside. Heat the 2 tablespoons of oil in a large, deep skillet over medium heat. Add the garlic, ginger, and dried red chiles and sauté for 1 minute until fragrant but not browned. Add the remaining soy sauce, mirin, rice vinegar, sugar, and hoisin sauce, if using, and bring to a boil, stirring to dissolve the sugar. Add the cornstarch slurry and cook until the mixture begins to thicken, for 1 to 2 minutes.
5. Add the chicken to the sauce in the pan and toss to coat. Cook until the chicken is heated through. Remove the chicken and sauce to a platter and garnish with scallions and sesame seeds. Serve immediately.

## Chicken Fajita Roll-Ups

**Prep time: 10 minutes | Cook time: 24 minutes | Serves 6 to 8**

| | |
|---|---|
| ½ teaspoon oregano | ½ yellow bell pepper, sliced into strips |
| ½ teaspoon cayenne pepper | ½ green bell pepper, sliced into strips |
| 1 teaspoon cumin | ½ red bell pepper, sliced into strips |
| 1 teaspoon garlic powder | |
| 2 teaspoons paprika | 3 chicken breasts |
| ½ sliced red onion | |

1. Mix oregano, cayenne pepper, garlic powder, cumin and paprika along with a pinch or two of pepper and salt. Set to the side.
2. Slice chicken breasts lengthwise into 2 slices.
3. Between two pieces of parchment paper, add breast slices and pound till they are ¼-inch thick. With seasoning, liberally season both sides of chicken slices.
4. Put 2 strips of each color of bell pepper and a few onion slices onto chicken pieces.
5. Roll up tightly and secure with toothpicks.
6. Repeat with remaining ingredients and sprinkle and rub mixture that is left over the chicken rolls.
7. Lightly grease your air fryer cooking tray and place 3 rollups into the fryer. Select Roast. Set temperature to 400ºF (205ºC), and set time to 12 minutes.
8. Repeat with the remaining rollups.
9. Serve with salad!

## Buffalo Chicken Wings

**Prep time: 5 minutes | Cook time: 30 minutes | Serves 6 to 8**

| | |
|---|---|
| 1 teaspoon salt | ½ cup vegan butter |
| 1 to 2 tablespoons brown sugar | ½ cup cayenne pepper sauce |
| 1 tablespoon Worcestershire sauce | 4 pounds (1.8 kg) chicken wings |

1. Whisk salt, brown sugar, Worcestershire sauce, butter, and hot sauce together and set to the side.
2. Dry wings and add to air fryer cooking tray.
3. Select Air Fry. Set temperature to 380ºF (195ºC), and set time to 25 minutes, tossing halfway through.
4. When timer sounds, shake wings and bump up the temperature to 400ºF (205ºC) and cook for another 5 minutes.
5. Take out the wings and place them into a big bowl. Add sauce and toss well.
6. Serve alongside celery sticks!

## Black Bean and Turkey Burgers

**Prep time: 15 minutes | Cook time: 21 minutes | Serves 2**

| | |
|---|---|
| 1 cup canned black beans, drained and rinsed | 2 slices pepper jack cheese |
| ¾ pound (340.2 g) lean ground turkey | Toasted burger rolls, sliced tomatoes, lettuce leaves |
| 2 tablespoons minced red onion | For the Cumin-Avocado Spread: |
| 1 Jalapeño pepper, seeded and minced | 1 ripe avocado |
| 2 tablespoons plain breadcrumbs | Juice of 1 lime |
| ½ teaspoon chili powder | 1 teaspoon ground cumin |
| ¼ teaspoon cayenne pepper | ½ teaspoon salt |
| Salt, to taste | 1 tablespoon chopped fresh cilantro |
| Olive or vegetable oil | Freshly ground black pepper, to taste |

1. Place the black beans in a large bowl and smash them slightly with the back of a fork. Add the ground turkey, red onion, Jalapeño pepper, breadcrumbs, chili powder and cayenne pepper. Season with salt. Mix with your hands to combine all the ingredients and then shape them into 2 patties. Brush both sides of the burger patties with a little olive or vegetable oil.
2. Preheat the oven to 380ºF (195ºC).

3. Transfer the burgers to the air fryer cooking tray and select Roast. Set temperature to 380ºF (195ºC), and set time to 20 minutes, flipping them over halfway through the cooking process. Top the burgers with the pepper jack cheese (securing the slices to the burgers with a toothpick) for the last 2 minutes of the cooking process.
4. While the burgers are cooking, make the cumin avocado spread. Place the avocado, lime juice, cumin and salt in food processor and process until smooth. (For a chunkier spread, you can mash this by hand in a bowl.) Stir in the cilantro and season with freshly ground black pepper. Chill the spread until you are ready to serve.
5. When the burgers have finished cooking, remove them from the oven and let them rest on a plate, covered gently with aluminum foil. Brush a little olive oil on the insides of the burger rolls. Place the rolls, cut side up, into the air fryer cooking tray and air fry at 400ºF (205ºC), and set time to 1 minute to toast and warm them.
6. Spread the cumin-avocado spread on the rolls and build your burgers with lettuce and sliced tomatoes and any other ingredient you like. Serve warm with a side of sweet potato fries.

## Chicken Breast with Pineapple

**Prep time: 10 minutes | Cook time: 11 minutes | Serves 4**

| | |
|---|---|
| 2 boneless, skinless chicken breasts | 1 red bell pepper, chopped |
| 2 tablespoons cornstarch | 1 (8-ounce / 227-g) can pineapple tidbits, drained, juice reserved |
| 1 egg white, lightly beaten | |
| 1 tablespoon olive or peanut oil | 2 tablespoons reduced-sodium soy sauce |
| 1 onion, sliced | |

1. Cut the chicken breasts into cubes and put into a medium bowl. Add the cornstarch and egg white and mix together thoroughly. Set aside.
2. In a 6-inch metal bowl, combine the oil and the onion. Select Roast, set time to 2 to 3 minutes, until the onion is crisp and tender.
3. Drain the chicken and add to the bowl with the onions; stir well. Cook for 7 to 9 minutes or until the chicken is thoroughly cooked to 165ºF (75ºC).
4. Stir the chicken mixture, then add the pepper, pineapple tidbits, 3 tablespoons of the reserved pineapple liquid, and the soy sauce, and stir again. Cook for 2 to 3 minutes or until the food is cooked and the sauce is slightly thickened.

# Honey Garlic Chicken Wings

**Prep time: 10 minutes | Cook time: 55 minutes | Serves 8**

⅛ cup water
½ teaspoon salt
4 tablespoons minced garlic
¼ cup vegan butter
¼ cup raw honey
¾ cup almond flour
16 chicken wings

1. Rinse off and dry chicken wings well.
2. Spray air fryer cooking tray with olive oil.
3. Coat chicken wings with almond flour and add coated wings to air fryer. Select Air Fry. Set temperature to 380ºF (193ºC), and set time to 25 minutes, shaking every 5 minutes.
4. When the timer goes off, cook for 5 to 10 minutes at 400ºF (204ºC) till skin becomes crispy and dry.
5. As chicken cooks, melt butter in a saucepan and add garlic. Sauté garlic 5 minutes. Add salt and honey, simmer for 20 minutes. Make sure to stir every so often, so the sauce does not burn. Add a bit of water after 15 minutes to ensure sauce does not harden.
6. Take out chicken wings from air fryer and coat in sauce. Enjoy!

# Chicken Breast Parmesan

**Prep time: 10 minutes | Cook time: 12 minutes | Serves 4**

1 egg
1 tablespoon mayonnaise
1 cup panko bread crumbs
½ cup freshly grated Parmesan cheese
1 teaspoon Italian seasoning
1 pound (454 g)
boneless, skinless hand-filleted chicken breasts or regular breasts sliced in half crosswise to create 4 thin breasts
Vegetable oil for spraying
¼ cup Marinara Sauce
6 tablespoons grated Mozzarella cheese

1. Mix the egg and mayonnaise in a shallow bowl until smooth. In another bowl, combine the panko, Parmesan cheese, and Italian seasoning. Dip each piece of chicken in the mayonnaise mixture, shaking off any excess, then dredge in the panko mixture until both sides are coated. Place the breaded chicken on a plate or rack.
2. Preheat the oven to 350ºF (175ºC), and set time to 3 minutes. Spray the cooking tray of the oven with oil and place 2 pieces of chicken in the cooking tray. Spray the chicken cutlets with oil. Select Roast. Set the temperature to 350ºF (175ºC), and set time to

6 minutes, then turn them over. Top each piece of chicken with 1 tablespoon of marinara sauce and 1½ tablespoons of grated Mozzarella cheese. Cook the chicken until the cheese is melted, about 3 additional minutes.
3. Remove the cooked chicken to a serving dish and keep warm. Cook the remaining pieces of chicken in the same manner. Serve warm with pasta on the side.

# Turkey Breast with Cherry Glaze

**Prep time: 10 minutes | Cook time: 42 minutes | Serves 6 to 8**

1 (5-pound / 2.3-kg) turkey breast
2 teaspoons olive oil
1 teaspoon dried thyme
½ teaspoon dried sage
1 teaspoon salt
½ teaspoon freshly
ground black pepper
½ cup cherry preserves
1 tablespoon chopped fresh thyme leaves
1 teaspoon soy sauce
Freshly ground black pepper, to taste

1. All turkeys are built differently, so depending on the turkey breast and how your butcher has prepared it, you may need to trim the bottom of the ribs in order to get the turkey to sit upright in the air fryer cooking tray without touching the heating element. The key to this recipe is getting the right size turkey breast. Once you've managed that, the rest is easy, so make sure your turkey breast fits into the air fryer cooking tray before you preheat the oven.
2. Preheat the oven to 350ºF (175ºC).
3. Brush the turkey breast all over with the olive oil. Combine the thyme, sage, salt and pepper and rub the outside of the turkey breast with the spice mixture.
4. Transfer the seasoned turkey breast to the air fryer cooking tray, breast side up, and select Roast. Set temperature to 350ºF (175ºC), and set time to 25 minutes. Turn the turkey breast on its side and air fry for another 12 minutes. Turn the turkey breast on the opposite side and air fry for 12 more minutes. The internal temperature of the turkey breast should reach 165ºF (75ºC) when fully cooked.
5. While the turkey is air-frying, make the glaze by combining the cherry preserves, fresh thyme, soy sauce and pepper in a small bowl. When the cooking time is up, return the turkey breast to an upright position and brush the glaze all over the turkey. Air fry for a final 5 minutes, until the skin is nicely browned and crispy. Let the turkey rest, loosely tented with foil, for at least 5 minutes before slicing and serving.

## Mozzarella Chicken Fritters

**Prep time: 15 minutes | Cook time: 20 minutes | Make 16 to 18 fritters**

For the Chicken Fritters:
½ teaspoon salt
⅛ teaspoon pepper
1½ tablespoons fresh dill
1⅓ cups shredded Mozzarella cheese
⅓ cup coconut flour
⅓ cup vegan mayo
2 eggs

1½ pounds (680 g) chicken breasts
For the Garlic Dip:
⅛ teaspoon pepper
¼ teaspoon salt
½ tablespoon lemon juice
1 pressed garlic cloves
⅓ cup vegan mayo

1. Slice chicken breasts into ⅓ pieces and place in a bowl. Add all the remaining fritter ingredients to the bowl and stir well. Cover and chill for 2 hours or overnight.
2. Ensure your oven is preheated to 350ºF (175ºC). Spray cooking tray with a bit of olive oil.
3. Add marinated chicken to the oven and select Roast for 20 minutes, making sure to turn halfway through cooking process.
4. To make the dipping sauce, combine all the dip ingredients until smooth.

## Gochujang Chicken Wings

**Prep time: 15 minutes | Cook time: 25 minutes | Serves 4**

For the Wings:
2 pounds (907 g) chicken wings
1 teaspoon kosher salt
1 teaspoon black pepper or gochugaru (Korean red pepper)
For the Sauce:
2 tablespoons gochujang (Korean chile paste)
1 tablespoon mayonnaise
1 tablespoon toasted

sesame oil
1 tablespoon minced fresh ginger
1 tablespoon minced garlic
1 teaspoon sugar
1 teaspoon agave nectar or honey
For Serving:
1 teaspoon sesame seeds
¼ cup chopped scallions

Make the Wings
1. Season the wings with the salt and pepper and place in the air-fryer cooking tray. Select Air Fry. Set temperature to 400ºF (205ºC), and set time to 20 minutes, turning the wings halfway through the cooking time.

Make the Sauce
2. In a small bowl, combine the gochujang, mayonnaise, sesame oil, ginger, garlic, sugar, and agave; set aside.
3. As you near the 20-minute mark, use a meat thermometer to check the meat. When the wings reach 160ºF (70ºC), transfer them to a large bowl. Pour about half the sauce on the wings; toss to coat (serve the remaining sauce as a dip).
4. Return the wings to the air-fryer cooking tray and cook for 5 minutes, until the sauce has glazed.
5. Transfer the wings to a serving platter. Sprinkle with the sesame seeds and scallions. Serve with the reserved sauce on the side for dipping.

## Lemon Sage Roast Chicken

**Prep time: 5 minutes | Cook time: 1 hour | Serves 4**

1 (4-pound / 1.8-kg) chicken
1 bunch sage, divided

1 lemon, zest and juice
Salt and freshly ground black pepper, to taste

1. Preheat the oven to 350ºF (175ºC) and pour a little water into the bottom of the air fryer drawer. (This will help prevent the grease that drips into the bottom drawer from burning and smoking.)
2. Run your fingers between the skin and flesh of the chicken breasts and thighs. Push a couple of sage leaves up underneath the skin of the chicken on each breast and each thigh.
3. Push some of the lemon zest up under the skin of the chicken next to the sage. Sprinkle some of the zest inside the chicken cavity, and reserve any leftover zest. Squeeze the lemon juice all over the chicken and in the cavity as well.
4. Season the chicken, inside and out, with the salt and freshly ground black pepper. Set a few sage leaves aside for the final garnish. Crumple up the remaining sage leaves and push them into the cavity of the chicken, along with one of the squeezed lemon halves.
5. Place the chicken breast side up into the air fryer cooking tray and select Roast. Set temperature to 350ºF (175ºC), and set time to 20 minutes. Flip the chicken over so that it is breast-side down and continue to air fry for another 20 minutes. Return the chicken to breast side up and finish air-frying for 20 more minutes. The internal temperature of the chicken should register 165ºF (75ºC) in the thickest part of the thigh when fully cooked. Remove the chicken from the oven and let it rest on a cutting board for at least 5 minutes.
6. Cut the rested chicken into pieces, sprinkle with the reserved lemon zest and garnish with the reserved sage leaves.

## Chicken Breast with Buttermilk Waffles

**Prep time: 20 minutes | Cook time: 32 minutes | Serves 4**

For the Fried Chicken:
4 (2-pound / 907-g) small boneless, skinless chicken breasts
½ cup all-purpose flour
1 teaspoon kosher salt
½ teaspoon cayenne pepper
1 egg
2 tablespoons buttermilk
Dash hot sauce
1½ cups panko bread crumbs
Vegetable oil for spraying

For the Buttermilk Waffles:
1¾ cups all-purpose flour
2 teaspoons baking powder
1 teaspoon granulated sugar
1 teaspoon baking soda
1 teaspoon kosher salt
1¾ cups buttermilk
2 eggs
½ cup unsalted butter, melted and cooled
Maple syrup or honey to serve

Make the Chicken
1. To make the chicken, cut each chicken breast in half lengthwise to make 2 long chicken tenders. Whisk together the flour, salt, and cayenne pepper on a large plate. Beat the egg with the buttermilk and hot sauce in a large, shallow bowl. Place the panko in a separate shallow bowl or pie plate.
2. Dredge the chicken tenders in the flour, shake off any excess, and then dip them in the egg mixture. Dredge the chicken tenders in the panko, making sure to coat them completely. Shake off any excess panko. Place the battered chicken tenders on a plate.
3. Preheat the oven to 375ºF (190ºC). Spray the cooking tray lightly with oil. Arrange half the chicken tenders in the cooking tray of the oven and spray the tops with oil. Select Roast. Set the temperature to 375ºF (190ºC) until the top side of the tenders is browned and crispy, for 8 to 10 minutes. Flip the tenders and spray the second side with oil. Cook until the second side is browned and crispy and the internal temperature reaches 165ºF (75ºC), for another 8 to 10 minutes. Remove the first batch of tenders and keep it warm. Cook the second batch in the same manner.

Make the Waffles
4. While the tenders are cooking, make the waffles. In a large bowl, whisk together the flour, baking powder, sugar, baking soda, and salt. In a separate bowl, whisk together the buttermilk, eggs, and melted butter, reserving a small amount of butter to brush on the waffle iron. Add the wet ingredients to the dry ingredients and stir with a fork until just combined. Allow the batter to rest for at least 5 minutes. Brush the waffle iron with reserved melted butter and preheat according to the manufacturer's instructions. Scoop ⅓ to ½ cup of batter into each grid of the waffle iron and cook according to your waffle iron's instructions. (You should be able to make 8 waffles.)
5. To serve, place 2 chicken tenders on top of 1 or 2 waffles, depending on the person's appetite. Serve with maple syrup or honey and additional hot sauce.

## Asian-Style Duck Breast

**Prep time: 5 minutes | Cook time: 30 minutes | Serves 3**

1 pound (454 g) duck breast
1 tablespoon Hoisin sauce
1 tablespoon Five-spice powder
Sea salt and black pepper, to taste
¼ teaspoon ground cinnamon

1. Pat the duck breasts dry with paper towels. Toss the duck breast with the remaining ingredients.
2. Select Roast. Set temperature to 330ºF (165ºC), and set time to 15 minutes, turning them over halfway through the cooking time.
3. Turn the heat to 350ºF (175ºC); continue to cook for about 15 minutes or until cooked through.
4. Let it rest for 10 minutes before carving and serving. Bon appétit!

## Marinaded Chicken Strips

**Prep time: 10 minutes | Cook time: 12 minutes | Serves 4**

1 pound (454 g) chicken tenders
For the Marinade:
¼ cup olive oil
2 tablespoons water
2 tablespoons honey
2 tablespoons white vinegar
½ teaspoon salt
½ teaspoon crushed red pepper
1 teaspoon garlic powder
1 teaspoon onion powder
½ teaspoon paprika

1. Combine all marinade ingredients and mix well.
2. Add chicken and stir to coat. Cover tightly and let marinate in refrigerator for 30 minutes.
3. Remove tenders from marinade and place them in a single layer in the air fryer cooking tray.
4. Select Roast. Set temperature to 390ºF (200ºC), and set time to 3 minutes. Turn tenders over and cook for 3 to 5 minutes longer or until chicken is done and juices run clear.
5. Repeat step 4 to cook the remaining tenders.

## Mustard Chicken Tenders

**Prep time: 5 minutes | Cook time: 10 minutes | Serves 4 to 6**

| | |
|---|---|
| pepper and salt to taste | 2 beaten eggs |
| ½ cup coconut flour | 1 pound (454 g) of |
| 1 tablespoon spicy brown mustard | chicken tenders |

1. Season tenders with pepper and salt.
2. Place a thin layer of mustard onto tenders and then dredge in flour and dip in egg.
3. Add to the oven and select Air Fry. Set temperature to 390ºF (200ºC), and set time to 10 to 15 minutes or till crispy.

## Italian Herbed Turkey Breasts

**Prep time: 5 minutes | Cook time: 1 hour | Serves 4**

| | |
|---|---|
| 1 tbsp. butter, room temperature | 1 tsp.cayenne pepper |
| Kosher salt and ground black pepper, to taste | 1 tsp. Italian herb mix |
| | 1 pound (454 g) turkey breast, bone-in |

1. In a mixing bowl, thoroughly combine the butter, salt, black pepper, cayenne pepper, and herb mix.
2. Rub the mixture all over the turkey breast.
3. Select Roast. Set temperature to 350ºF (175ºC), and set time to 1 hour, turning them over every 20 minutes.
4. Bon appétit!

## Cornish Hen with Montreal Chicken Seasoning

**Prep time: 5 minutes | Cook time: 30 minutes | Serves 2**

2 tablespoons Montreal chicken seasoning
1 (1½- to 2-pound / 680- to 907-g) Cornish hen

1. Preheat the air fryer oven to 390ºF (200ºC).
2. Rub the seasoning over the chicken, coating it thoroughly.
3. Place the chicken in the Rotisserie Spit. Set the timer and Roast for 15 minutes.
4. Flip the chicken and roast for another 15 minutes.
5. Check that the chicken has reached an internal temperature of 165ºF (75ºC). Add cooking time if needed.

## Chinese Spicy Chicken Patties

**Prep time: 5 minutes | Cook time: 17 minutes | Serves 4**

| | |
|---|---|
| 1 pound (454 g) chicken, ground | 1 teaspoon garlic, minced |
| 1 tablespoon olive oil | 1 tablespoon chili sauce |
| 1 small onion, chopped | Kosher salt and ground black pepper, to taste |

1. Mix all ingredients until everything is well combined. Form the mixture into four patties.
2. Select Roast. Set temperature to 380ºF (195ºC), and set time to about 17 minutes or until cooked through; make sure to turn them over halfway through the cooking time.
3. Bon appétit!

## Smoked Paprika Chicken Cutlets

**Prep time: 5 minutes | Cook time: 12 minutes | Serves 4**

| | |
|---|---|
| 1 pound (454 g) chicken breasts, boneless, skinless, cut into 4 pieces | 1 teaspoon smoked paprika |
| 1 tablespoon butter, melted | Kosher salt and ground black pepper, to taste |
| | 1 teaspoon garlic powder |

1. Flatten the chicken breasts to ¼-inch thickness.
2. Toss the chicken breasts with the remaining ingredients.
3. Select Roast. Set temperature to 380ºF (195ºC), and set time to 12 minutes, turning them over halfway through the cooking time.
4. Bon appétit!

## Chinese Spiced Chicken Drumsticks

**Prep time: 5 minutes | Cook time: 22 minutes | Serves 3**

| | |
|---|---|
| 3 chicken drumsticks | 1 tablespoon soy sauce |
| 2 tablespoons sesame oil | 1 teaspoon Five-spice |
| Kosher salt and ground black pepper, to taste | powder |

1. Pat the chicken drumsticks dry with paper towels. Toss the chicken drumsticks with the remaining ingredients.
2. Select Roast. Set temperature to 370ºF (190ºC), and set time to 22 minutes, turning them over halfway through the cooking time.
3. Bon appétit!

## Barbecued Chicken Thighs

**Prep time: 5 minutes | Cook time: 15 minutes | Serves 4**

6 boneless, skinless chicken thighs
¼ cup gluten-free barbecue sauce

2 cloves garlic, minced
2 tablespoons lemon juice

1. In a medium bowl, combine the chicken, barbecue sauce, cloves, and lemon juice, and mix well. Marinate for 10 minutes.
2. Remove the chicken thighs from the bowl and shake off excess sauce. Put the chicken pieces in the oven, leaving a bit of space between each one.
3. Select Roast for 15 to 18 minutes or until the chicken is 165ºF (75ºC) on an instant-read meat thermometer.

## Teriyaki Orange Chicken Legs

**Prep time: 5 minutes | Cook time: 18 minutes | Serves 2**

4 tablespoons teriyaki sauce
1 tablespoon orange juice

1 teaspoon smoked paprika
4 chicken legs
Cooking spray

1. Mix together the teriyaki sauce, orange juice, and smoked paprika. Brush on all sides of chicken legs.
2. Spray air fryer cooking tray with nonstick cooking spray and place chicken in cooking tray.
3. Select Roast. Set temperature to 360ºF (180ºC), and set time to 6 minutes. Turn and baste with sauce. Cook for 6 more minutes, turn and baste. Cook for 6 to 8 minutes more, until juices run clear when chicken is pierced with a fork.

## Chicken and Carrot Salad

**Prep time: 5 minutes | Cook time: 12 minutes | Serves 3**

1 pound (454 g) chicken breast
2 tablespoons scallions, chopped
1 carrot, shredded

½ cup mayonnaise
1 tablespoon mustard
Sea salt and ground black pepper, to taste
a salad bowl for serve

1. Pat the chicken dry with kitchen towels. Place the chicken in a lightly oiled cooking tray.
2. Select Roast. Set temperature to 380ºF (195ºC), and set time to 12 minutes, turning them over halfway through the cooking time.
3. Chop the chicken breasts and transfer them to a salad bowl; add in the remaining ingredients and toss to combine well. Bon appétit!

## Breaded Chicken Breast

**Prep time: 10 minutes | Cook time: 12 minutes | Serves 4**

1 pound (454 g) chicken breasts, boneless and skinless
1 tablespoon butter, room temperature
1 egg, whisked

1 teaspoon cayenne pepper
1 teaspoon garlic powder
Kosher salt and ground black pepper, to taste
½ cup breadcrumbs

1. Pat the chicken dry with paper towels.
2. In a bowl, thoroughly combine the butter, egg, cayenne pepper, garlic powder, kosher salt, black pepper.
3. Dip the chicken breasts into the egg mixture. Then, roll the chicken breasts over the breadcrumbs.
4. Select Roast. Set temperature to 380ºF (195ºC), and set time to 12 minutes, turning them over halfway through the cooking time.
5. Bon appétit!

## Southern Fried Chicken Drumsticks

**Prep time: 10 minutes | Cook time: 25 minutes | Serves 4**

cayenne pepper and salt to taste
2 tablespoons mustard powder
2 tablespoons oregano
2 tablespoons thyme

3 tablespoons coconut milk
1 beaten egg
¼ cup cauliflower
¼ cup gluten-free oats
8 chicken drumsticks

1. Ensure air fryer oven is preheated to 350ºF (175ºC).
2. Lay out chicken and season with pepper and salt on all sides.
3. Add all other ingredients to a blender, blending till a smooth-like breadcrumb mixture is created. Place in a bowl and add a beaten egg to another bowl.
4. Dip chicken into breadcrumbs, then into egg, and into breadcrumbs once more.
5. Place coated drumsticks into the oven and select Air Fry. Set temperature to 350ºF (175ºC), and set time to 20 minutes. Bump up the temperature to 390ºF (200ºC) and cook for another 5 minutes till crispy.

## Greek Chicken Salad

**Prep time: 10 minutes | Cook time: 12 minutes | Serves 4**

1 pound (454 g) chicken breasts, boneless, skinless
1 red onion, thinly sliced
1 bell pepper, sliced
4 Kalamata olives, pitted and minced
1 small Greek cucumber, grated and squeezed

4 tablespoons Greek yogurt
4 tablespoons mayonnaise
1 tablespoon fresh lemon juice
Coarse sea salt and red pepper flakes, to taste

1. Pat the chicken dry with paper towels. Place the chicken breasts in a lightly oiled Air Fryer cooking tray.
2. Select Roast. Set temperature to 380ºF (195ºC), and set time to 12 minutes, turning them over halfway through the cooking time.
3. Chop the chicken breasts and transfer it to a salad bowl; add in the remaining ingredients and toss to combine well.
4. Serve well-chilled and enjoy!

## Spinach and Feta Cheese Stuffed Chicken

**Prep time: 10 minutes | Cook time: 20 minutes | Serves 4**

1 pound (454 g) chicken breasts, skinless, boneless and cut into pieces
2 tablespoons olives, chopped
1 garlic clove, minced

2 cups spinach, torn into pieces
2 ounces (57 g) Feta cheese
Sea salt and ground black pepper, to taste
2 tablespoons olive oil

1. Flatten the chicken breasts with a mallet.
2. Stuff each piece of chicken with olives, garlic, spinach, and cheese. Roll them up and secure with toothpicks.
3. Sprinkle the chicken with the salt, black pepper, and olive oil.
4. Place the stuffed chicken breasts in the Air Fryer cooking tray. Select Roast. Set temperature to 400ºF (205ºC), and set time to about 20 minutes, turning them over halfway through the cooking time.
5. Bon appétit!

## The Best Chicken Burgers Ever

**Prep time: 10 minutes | Cook time: 17 minutes | Serves 3**

¾ pound (340.2 g) chicken, ground
¼ cup tortilla chips, crushed
¼ cup Parmesan cheese, grated

1 egg, beaten
2 tablespoons onion, minced
2 garlic cloves, minced
1 tablespoon BBQ sauce

1. Mix all ingredients until everything is well combined. Form the mixture into three patties.
2. Select Roast. Set temperature to 380ºF (195ºC), and set time to about 17 minutes or until cooked through; make sure to turn them over halfway through the cooking time.
3. Bon appétit!

## Panko-Crusted Chicken Chunks

**Prep time: 5 minutes | Cook time: 16 minutes | Serves 4**

1 pound (454 g) chicken tenders cut in large chunks, about 1½ inches
Salt and pepper, to taste
½ cup cornstarch

2 eggs, beaten
1 cup panko breadcrumbs
Oil for misting or cooking spray

1. Season chicken chunks to your liking with salt and pepper.
2. Dip chicken chunks in cornstarch. Then dip in egg and shake off excess. Then roll in panko crumbs to coat well.
3. Spray all sides of chicken chunks with oil or cooking spray.
4. Place chicken in air fryer cooking tray in single layer and select Air Fry. Set temperature to 390ºF (199ºC), and set time to 5 minutes. Spray with oil, turn chunks over, and spray another side.
5. Air fry for an additional 3 to 5 minutes or until chicken juices run clear and the outside is golden brown.
6. Repeat steps 4 and 5 to cook the remaining chicken.

# Chapter 5 Beef

## Pulled Beef

**Prep time: 10 minutes | Cook time: 1¼ hours | Serves 4**

1½ pounds (680 g) beef brisket
2 tablespoons olive oil
3 garlic cloves, pressed
Sea salt and ground black pepper, to taste
1 teaspoon red pepper flakes, crushed
2 tablespoons tomato ketchup
2 tablespoons Dijon mustard

1. Toss the beef brisket with the olive oil, garlic, salt, black pepper, and red pepper; now, place the beef brisket in the Air Fryer cooking tray.
2. Select Roast. Set temperature to 390ºF (200ºC), and set time to 15 minutes. Turn the beef over and reduce the temperature to 360ºF (180ºC).
3. Continue to cook the beef brisket for approximately 55 minutes or until cooked through.
4. Shred the beef with two forks; add in the ketchup and mustard and stir to combine well. Bon appétit!

## Thai-Style Curry Beef Meatballs

**Prep time: 5 minutes | Cook time: 15 minutes | Serves 4**

1 pound (454 g) ground beef
1 tablespoon sesame oil
2 teaspoons chopped lemongrass
1 teaspoon red Thai curry paste
1 teaspoon Thai seasoning blend
Juice and zest of ½ lime
Cooking spray

1. Spritz the air fryer cooking tray with cooking spray.
2. In a medium bowl, combine all the ingredients until well blended.
3. Shape the meat mixture into 24 meatballs and arrange them in the air fryer cooking tray. Select Roast. Set temperature to 380ºF (195ºC), and set time to 15 minutes, or until well browned. Flip halfway through to ensure even cooking.
4. Transfer the meatballs to plates. Cool for 5 minutes before serving.

## Cheddar Roasted Stuffed Peppers

**Prep time: 10 minutes | Cook time: 18 minutes | Serves 4**

4 ounces (113 g) shredded Cheddar cheese
½ teaspoon pepper
½ teaspoon salt
1 teaspoon Worcestershire sauce
½ cup tomato sauce
8 ounces (227 g) lean ground beef
1 teaspoon olive oil
1 minced garlic clove
½ chopped onion
2 green bell peppers

1. Ensure your air fryer oven is preheated to 390ºF (200ºC). Spray with olive oil.
2. Cut stems off bell peppers and remove seeds. Cook in boiling salted water for 3 minutes.
3. Sauté garlic and onion together in a skillet until golden in color.
4. Take skillet off the heat. Mix pepper, salt, Worcestershire sauce, ¼ cup of tomato sauce, half of cheese and beef together.
5. Divide meat mixture into pepper halves. Top filled peppers with remaining cheese and tomato sauce.
6. Place filled peppers in air fryer and select Roast, and set time to 15 to 20 minutes.

## Beef Cheese Cups with Glaze

**Prep time: 10 minutes | Cook time: 25 minutes | Serves 4**

For the Meatloaves:
1 pound (454 g) ground beef
¼ cup seasoned breadcrumbs
¼ cup Parmesan cheese, grated
1 small onion, minced
2 garlic cloves, pressed
1 egg, beaten
Sea salt and ground black pepper, to taste
For the Glaze:
4 tablespoons tomato sauce
1 tablespoon brown sugar
1 tablespoon Dijon mustard

1. Thoroughly combine all ingredients for the meatloaves until everything is well combined.
2. Scrape the beef mixture into lightly oiled silicone cups and transfer them to the Air Fryer cooking tray.
3. Select Roast. Set temperature to 380ºF (195ºC), and set time to 20 minutes.
4. In the meantime, mix the remaining ingredients for the glaze. Then, spread the glaze on top of each muffin; continue to cook for another 5 minutes.
5. Bon appétit!

## Beef and Brown Rice Stuffed Bell Peppers

**Prep time: 10 minutes | Cook time: 15 minutes | Serves 4**

4 medium bell peppers, any colors, rinsed, tops removed
1 medium onion, chopped
½ cup grated carrot
2 teaspoons olive oil
2 medium beefsteak tomatoes, chopped
1 cup cooked brown rice
1 cup chopped cooked low-sodium roast beef
1 teaspoon dried marjoram

1. Remove the stems from the bell pepper tops and chop the tops.
2. In a 6-by-2-inch pan, combine the chopped bell pepper tops, onion, carrot, and olive oil. Cook for 2 to 4 minutes, or until the vegetables are crisp-tender.
3. Transfer the vegetables to a medium bowl. Add the tomatoes, brown rice, roast beef, and marjoram. Stir to mix.
4. Stuff the vegetable mixture into the bell peppers. Place the bell peppers in the air fryer cooking tray. Select Roast, and set time to 11 to 16 minutes, or until the peppers are tender and the filling is hot. Serve immediately.

## Beef and Fruit Stir-Fry

**Prep time: 10 minutes | Cook time: 8 minutes | Serves 4**

12 ounces (340 g) sirloin tip steak, thinly sliced
1 tablespoon freshly squeezed lime juice
1 cup canned mandarin orange segments, drained, juice reserved
1 cup canned pineapple chunks, drained, juice
reserved
1 teaspoon low-sodium soy sauce
1 tablespoon cornstarch
1 teaspoon olive oil
2 scallions, white and green parts, sliced
Brown rice, cooked (optional)

1. In a medium bowl, mix the steak with the lime juice. Set aside.
2. In a small bowl, thoroughly mix 3 tablespoons of reserved mandarin orange juice, 3 tablespoons of reserved pineapple juice, the soy sauce, and cornstarch.
3. Drain the beef and transfer it to a medium metal bowl, reserving the juice. Stir the reserved juice into the mandarin-pineapple juice mixture. Set aside.
4. Add the olive oil and scallions to the steak. Place the metal bowl in the oven and select Roast, and set time

to 3 to 4 minutes, or until the steak is almost cooked, shaking the cooking tray once during cooking.
5. Stir in the mandarin oranges, pineapple, and juice mixture. Select Roast, and set time to for 3 to 7 minutes or more, or until the sauce is bubbling and the beef is tender and reaches at least 145ºF (65ºC) on a meat thermometer.
6. Stir and serve over hot cooked brown rice, if desired.

## Low-Carb Cheesy Lasagna

**Prep time: 15 minutes | Cook time: 20 minutes | Serves 4**

For the Meat Layer:
Extra-virgin olive oil
1 pound (454 g) 85% lean ground beef
1 cup prepared marinara sauce
¼ cup diced celery
¼ cup diced red onion
½ teaspoon minced garlic
Kosher salt and black pepper, to taste
For the Cheese Layer:
8 ounces (227 g)ricotta cheese
1 cup shredded Mozzarella cheese
½ cup grated Parmesan cheese
2 large eggs
1 teaspoon dried Italian seasoning, crushed
½ teaspoon each minced garlic, garlic powder, and black pepper

Make the Meat Layer
1. Grease a 7½-inch barrel cake pan with 1 teaspoon of olive oil.
2. In a large bowl, combine the ground beef, marinara, celery, onion, garlic, salt, and pepper. Place the seasoned meat in the pan.
3. Place the pan in the air-fryer cooking tray. Select Roast. Set temperature to 375ºF (190ºC), and set time to 10 minutes.

Make the Cheese Layer
4. Meanwhile, in a medium bowl, combine the ricotta, half the Mozzarella, the Parmesan, lightly beaten eggs, Italian seasoning, minced garlic, garlic powder, and pepper. Stir until well blended.
5. At the end of the cooking time, spread the cheese mixture over the meat mixture. Sprinkle with the remaining ½ cup Mozzarella. Select Roast. Set temperature to 375ºF (190ºC), and set time to 10 minutes, or until the cheese is browned and bubbling.
6. At the end of the cooking time, use a meat thermometer to ensure the meat has reached an internal temperature of 160ºF (70ºC).
7. Drain the fat and liquid from the pan. Let it stand for 5 minutes before serving.

## Beef Burgers

**Prep time: 10 minutes | Cook time: 10 minutes | Serves 4**

| | |
|---|---|
| 1 pound (454 g) lean ground beef | powder |
| 1 teaspoon dried parsley | ½ teaspoon garlic powder |
| ½ teaspoon dried oregano | Few drops of liquid smoke |
| ½ teaspoon pepper | 1 teaspoon Worcestershire sauce |
| ½ teaspoon salt | |
| ½ teaspoon onion | |

1. Ensure your air fryer oven is preheated to 350ºF (175ºC).
2. Mix all seasonings together till combined.
3. Place beef in a bowl and add seasonings. Mix well, but do not overmix.
4. Make 4 patties from the mixture and using your thumb, make an indent in the center of each patty.
5. Add patties to air fryer cooking tray and select Roast, and set time to 10 minutes. No need to turn!

## Beef, Broccoli, and Mushroom

**Prep time: 10 minutes | Cook time: 15 minutes | Serves 4**

| | |
|---|---|
| 2 tablespoons cornstarch | 2½ cups broccoli florets |
| ½ cup low-sodium beef broth | 1 onion, chopped |
| 1 teaspoon low-sodium soy sauce | 1 cup sliced cremini mushrooms |
| 12 ounces (340 g) sirloin strip steak, cut into 1-inch cubes | 1 tablespoon grated fresh ginger |
| | Brown rice, cooked (optional) |

1. In a medium bowl, stir together the cornstarch, beef broth, and soy sauce.
2. Add the beef and toss to coat. Let it stand for 5 minutes at room temperature.
3. With a slotted spoon, transfer the beef from the broth mixture into a medium metal bowl. Reserve the broth.
4. Add the broccoli, onion, mushrooms, and ginger to the beef. Place the bowl into the oven and select Roast, and set the time to 12 to 15 minutes, or until the beef reaches at least 145ºF (65ºC) on a meat thermometer and the vegetables are tender.
5. Add the reserved broth and roast for 2 to 3 minutes or more, or until the sauce boils.
6. Serve immediately over hot cooked brown rice, if desired.

## Sicilian Beef Stuffed Peppers

**Prep time: 15 minutes | Cook time: 31 minutes | Serves 4**

| | |
|---|---|
| 2 tablespoons extra-virgin olive oil | ¼ cup pine nuts |
| 1 yellow onion, diced | ¼ cup raisins |
| 3 cloves garlic, minced | 3 tablespoons red wine vinegar |
| ¾ pound (340.2 g) ground beef | 1 cup cooked rice |
| 2 teaspoons kosher salt | 4 red bell peppers |
| Pinch red pepper flakes | Vegetable oil for spraying |
| 2 medium tomatoes or 1 large tomato | 1 cup grated Mozzarella cheese |

1. Heat the olive oil in a large, deep skillet over medium heat. When the oil is shimmering, add the onion and sauté until softened, about 5 minutes. Add the garlic and sauté for an additional minute. Add the ground beef, salt, and red pepper flakes and cook until the meat is no longer pink, about 6 minutes. If the meat has given off a lot of greases, carefully remove it from the pan with a spoon.
2. Slice off the stem end of the tomatoes and grate them using the coarse side of a box grater. Discard the skin. Add the tomato pulp, pine nuts, raisins, and vinegar to the meat mixture and sauté a few additional minutes to thicken. Add the cooked rice and stir to combine. Remove from the heat and set aside.
3. If you have a drawer-style oven with a deep cooking tray, cut off the top third of the peppers and remove the seeds and inner membranes. Divide the meat mixture evenly among the 4 peppers. Place the tops back on the peppers and place them carefully in the cooking tray of the oven. Spray or brush the outsides and tops of the peppers with oil. Select Roast. Set temperature to 375ºF (190ºC), and set time to 15 minutes, roasting the peppers halfway through. Remove the tops and add ¼ cup grated Mozzarella to each pepper. Select Broil, until the cheese is melted and browned, about 4 minutes.
4. If you have a toaster oven–style air fryer, cut the peppers in half through the stem. Brush the bottoms of the peppers with oil. Arrange the peppers in a single layer in the cooking tray of the oven. Divide the meat mixture evenly among the pepper halves. Select Roast. Set temperature to 350ºF (175ºC) until the peppers are tender, about 10 minutes. Sprinkle 2 tablespoons of grated cheese on top of each pepper half and cook until the cheese is melted and brown, for 2 to 3 minutes. Serve immediately.

## Peruvian Stir-Fried Beef with Fries

**Prep time: 10 minutes | Cook time: 32 minutes | Serves 4**

2 russet potatoes
1 pound (454 g) beef sirloin
2 cloves garlic, minced
2 tablespoons soy sauce plus more for serving
Juice of 1 lime
2 teaspoons aji amarillo (Peruvian yellow chile powder or paste)
½ red onion, sliced
2 tomatoes, cut into wedges
1 tablespoon vegetable oil plus more for spraying
Kosher salt and pepper, to taste

1. Peel the potatoes and cut them into ¼-inch slices. Cut each slice into 4 or 5 thick fries. (Halve any especially long pieces. You're looking for fries the size of your finger.) Place the cut potatoes into a bowl of cold water and let them soak for at least 30 minutes to get rid of excess starch.
2. While the potatoes are soaking, marinate the beef. Cut the beef sirloin into strips approximately ½ to 1 inch wide and 4 to 5 inches long. Whisk together the garlic, soy sauce, lime juice, and aji amarillo in a medium bowl. Add the beef and toss to combine. Marinate at room temperature for 15 minutes.
3. While the beef is marinating, cook the onion and tomatoes. Preheat the air fryer oven to 375ºF (190ºC). Spray the cooking tray of the oven with oil. Arrange the vegetables in a single layer in the cooking tray and spray with oil. Season with salt and pepper. Select Roast, until the vegetables begin to char and soften, for 9 to 10 minutes. Remove the vegetables to a large bowl.
4. Remove the beef from the marinade and, work in batches if necessary, and arrange the beef in a single layer in the cooking tray of the oven. Select Roast. Set temperature to 375ºF (190ºC) until the meat is browned on the outside but pink inside, for about 3 to 4 minutes. Place the beef in the bowl with the vegetables.
5. Drain the potatoes and dry them well. Toss the potatoes with the tablespoon of oil and salt. Arrange the potatoes in a single layer in the cooking tray of the oven. (Depending on the size of your machine, you may have to work in 2 batches. Do not overcrowd the cooking tray.) Select Roast, and set time to 10 minutes. Open the oven and shake the cooking tray to redistribute the potatoes. Roast for an additional 10 to 12 minutes until all the potatoes are browned and crisp. Repeat with the remaining potatoes if necessary.
6. Quickly reheat the meat and vegetables in a large skillet over medium heat. If desired, add the fries to the skillet and stir to combine. (You can also serve the fries on the side if you prefer. Both ways are common in Peru.) Taste and adjust the seasoning, adding more soy sauce, salt, and pepper if necessary. Serve immediately with rice.

## T-Bone Steak Salad

**Prep time: 10 minutes | Cook time: 12 minutes | Serves 5**

2 pounds (907 g) T-bone steak
1 teaspoon garlic powder
Sea salt and ground black pepper, to taste
2 tablespoons lime juice
¼ cup extra-virgin olive oil
1 bell pepper, seeded and sliced
1 red onion, sliced
1 tomato, diced

1. Toss the steak with the garlic powder, salt, and black pepper; place the steak in the Air Fryer cooking tray.
2. Select Roast. Set temperature to 400ºF (205ºC), and set time to 12 minutes, turning it over halfway through the cooking time.
3. Cut the steak into slices and add in the remaining ingredients. Serve at room temperature or well-chilled.
4. Bon appétit!

## Copycat Taco Bell Crunch Wraps

**Prep time: 10 minutes | Cook time: 2 minutes | Serves 6**

6 wheat tostadas
2 cups sour cream
2 cups Mexican blend cheese
2 cups shredded lettuce
12 ounces (340 g) low-sodium nacho cheese
3 Roma tomatoes
6 (12-inch) wheat tortillas
1⅓ cups water
2 packets low-sodium taco seasoning
2 pounds (907 g) of lean ground beef

1. Ensure your air fryer oven is preheated to 400ºF (205ºC).
2. Make beef according to taco seasoning packets.
3. Place ⅔ cup prepared beef, 4 tablespoons nacho cheese, 1 tostada, ⅓ cup sour cream, ⅓ cup lettuce, ⅙ of tomatoes and ⅓ cup Mexican cheese on each tortilla.
4. Fold up tortillas' edges and repeat with the remaining ingredients.
5. Lay the folded sides of tortillas down into the oven and spray with olive oil.
6. Select Roast. Set temperature to 400ºF (205ºC), and set time to 2 minutes.

## Brandy Rump Roast

**Prep time: 5 minutes | Cook time: 50 minutes | Serves 4**

| | |
|---|---|
| 1½ pounds (680 g) rump roast | 1 teaspoon paprika |
| | 2 tablespoons olive oil |
| Ground black pepper and kosher salt, to taste | ¼ cup brandy |
| | 2 tablespoons cold butter |

1. Toss the rump roast with the black pepper, salt, paprika, olive oil, and brandy; place the rump roast in a lightly oiled Air Fryer cooking tray.
2. Select Roast. Set temperature to 390ºF (200ºC), and set time to 50 minutes, turning it over halfway through the cooking time.
3. Serve with the cold butter and enjoy!

## Coulotte Roast

**Prep time: 5 minutes | Cook time: 55 minutes | Serves 5**

| | |
|---|---|
| 2 pounds (907 g) Coulotte roast | 1 tablespoon fresh cilantro, finely chopped |
| 2 tablespoons olive oil | 2 garlic cloves, minced |
| 1 tablespoon fresh parsley, finely chopped | Kosher salt and ground black pepper, to taste |

1. Toss the roast beef with the remaining ingredients; place the roast beef in the Air Fryer cooking tray.
2. Select Roast. Set temperature to 390ºF (200ºC), and set time to 55 minutes, turning over halfway through the cooking time.
3. Enjoy!

## Chinese Spiced Beef Tenderloin

**Prep time: 10 minutes | Cook time: 20 minutes | Serves 4**

| | |
|---|---|
| 1½ pounds (680 g) beef tenderloin, sliced | 2 garlic cloves, minced |
| 2 tablespoons sesame oil | 1 teaspoon fresh ginger, peeled and grated |
| 1 teaspoon Five-spice powder | 2 tablespoons soy sauce |

1. Toss the beef tenderloin with the remaining ingredients; place the beef tenderloin in the Air Fryer cooking tray.
2. Select Roast. Set temperature to 400ºF (205ºC), and set time to 20 minutes, turning it over halfway through the cooking time.
3. Enjoy!

## Mediterranean Filet Mignon

**Prep time: 10 minutes | Cook time: 14 minutes | Serves 4**

| | |
|---|---|
| 1½ pounds (680 g) filet mignon | 1 teaspoon dried rosemary |
| Sea salt and ground black pepper, to taste | 1 teaspoon dried thyme |
| | 1 teaspoon dried basil |
| 2 tablespoons olive oil | 2 cloves garlic, minced |

1. Toss the beef with the remaining ingredients; place the beef in the Air Fryer cooking tray.
2. Select Roast. Set temperature to 400ºF (205ºC), and set time to 14 minutes, turning it over halfway through the cooking time.
3. Enjoy!

## New York Strip Steak

**Prep time: 5 minutes | Cook time: 15 minutes | Serves 4**

| | |
|---|---|
| 1½ pounds (680 g) New York strip steak | black pepper, to taste |
| | 1 teaspoon paprika |
| 2 tablespoons butter, melted | 1 teaspoon dried thyme |
| Sea salt and ground | 1 teaspoon dried rosemary |

1. Toss the beef with the remaining ingredients; place the beef in the Air Fryer cooking tray.
2. Select Roast. Set temperature to 400ºF (205ºC), and set time to 15 minutes, turning it over halfway through the cooking time.
3. Enjoy!

## Italian Herbed Filet Mignon

**Prep time: 5 minutes | Cook time: 14 minutes | Serves 4**

| | |
|---|---|
| 1½ pounds (680 g) filet mignon | 1 teaspoon cayenne pepper |
| 2 tablespoons olive oil | Kosher salt and freshly ground black pepper, to taste |
| 2 cloves garlic, pressed | |
| 1 tablespoon Italian herb mix | |

1. Toss the beef with the remaining ingredients; place the beef in the Air Fryer cooking tray.
2. Select Roast. Set temperature to 400ºF (205ºC), and set time to 14 minutes, turning it over halfway through the cooking time.
3. Enjoy!

## Barbecue Beef Brisket

**Prep time: 5 minutes | Cook time: 1¼ hours | Serves 4**

1½ pounds (680 g) beef brisket

¼ cup barbecue sauce
2 tablespoons soy sauce

1. Toss the beef with the remaining ingredients; place the beef in the Air Fryer cooking tray.
2. Select Roast. Set temperature to 390ºF (200ºC), and set time to 15 minutes, turn the beef over and turn the temperature to 360ºF (180ºC).
3. Continue to cook the beef for 55 minutes or more. Bon appétit!

## Paprika Flank Steak

**Prep time: 5 minutes | Cook time: 12 minutes | Serves 5**

2 pounds (907 g) flank steak
2 tablespoons olive oil

1 teaspoon paprika
Sea salt and ground black pepper, to taste

1. Toss the steak with the remaining ingredients; place the steak in the Air Fryer cooking tray.
2. Select Roast. Set temperature to 400ºF (205ºC), and set time to 12 minutes, turning over halfway through the cooking time.
3. Bon appétit!

## Italian Rump Roast

**Prep time: 10 minutes | Cook time: 55 minutes | Serves 4**

1½ pounds (680 g) rump roast
2 tablespoons olive oil
Sea salt and ground black pepper, to taste

1 teaspoon Italian seasoning mix
1 onion, sliced
2 cloves garlic, peeled
¼ cup red wine

1. Toss the rump roast with the rest of the ingredients; place the rump roast in a lightly oiled Air Fryer cooking tray.
2. Select Roast. Set temperature to 390ºF (200ºC), and set time to 55 minutes, turning it over halfway through the cooking time.
3. Bon appétit!

## Oregano Roast Beef

**Prep time: 10 minutes | Cook time: 50 minutes | Serves 4**

1½ pounds (680 g) bottom round roast
2 tablespoons olive oil
2 garlic cloves, minced
1 teaspoon rosemary

1 teaspoon parsley
1 teaspoon oregano
Sea salt and freshly ground black pepper, to taste

1. Toss the beef with the spices, garlic, and olive oil; place the beef in the Air Fryer cooking tray.
2. Select Roast. Set temperature to 390ºF (200ºC), and set time to 50 minutes, turning it over halfway through the cooking time.
3. Cut the beef into slices and serve them with dinner rolls. Bon appétit!

## Mustard Skirt Steak Sliders

**Prep time: 10 minutes | Cook time: 15 minutes | Serves 4**

1½ pounds (680 g) skirt steak
1 teaspoon steak dry rub
½ teaspoon cayenne pepper
Sea salt and ground

black pepper, to taste
2 tablespoons olive oil
2 tablespoons Dijon mustard
8 Hawaiian buns

1. Toss the beef with the spices and olive oil; place the beef in the Air Fryer cooking tray.
2. Select Roast. Set temperature to 400ºF (205ºC), and set time to 15 minutes, turning it over halfway through the cooking time.
3. Cut the beef into slices and serve them with mustard and Hawaiian buns. Bon appétit!

## Rosemary Top Round Roast

**Prep time: 10 minutes | Cook time: 55 minutes | Serves 5**

2 pounds (907 g) top round roast
2 tablespoons extra-virgin olive oil
2 cloves garlic, pressed
1 tablespoon fresh rosemary, chopped

1 tablespoon fresh parsley, chopped
1 teaspoon red chili powder
Kosher salt and freshly ground black pepper, to taste

1. Toss the beef with the remaining ingredients; place the beef in the Air Fryer cooking tray.
2. Select Roast. Set temperature to 390ºF (200ºC), and set time to 55 minutes, turning it over halfway through the cooking time.
3. Enjoy!

## Easy Beef Sliders

**Prep time: 5 minutes | Cook time: 15 minutes | Serves 4**

1 pound (454 g) ground beef
½ teaspoon garlic powder
½ teaspoon onion powder
1 teaspoon paprika
Sea salt and ground black pepper, to taste
8 dinner rolls

1.  Mix all ingredients, except for the dinner rolls. Shape the mixture into four patties.
2.  Select Roast. Set temperature to 380ºF (195ºC), and set time to about 15 minutes or until cooked through; make sure to turn them over halfway through the cooking time.
3.  Serve your burgers on the prepared dinner rolls and enjoy!

## Christmas Corned Beef Brisket

**Prep time: 10 minutes | Cook time: 1¼ hours | Serves 4**

1½ pounds (680 g) beef brisket
2 tablespoons olive oil
1 tablespoon smoked paprika
1 tablespoon English mustard powder
1 teaspoon ground
1 teaspoon chili pepper flakes
2 garlic cloves, pressed

1.  Toss the beef with the remaining ingredients; place the beef in the Air Fryer cooking tray.
2.  Select Roast. Set temperature to 390ºF (200ºC), and set time to 15 minutes, turn the beef over and reduce the temperature to 360ºF (180ºC).
3.  Continue to cook the beef for 55 minutes more. Bon appétit!

## Beef Shoulder with Onion

**Prep time: 10 minutes | Cook time: 55 minutes | Serves 4**

1½ pounds (680 g) beef shoulder
Sea salt and ground black pepper, to taste
1 teaspoon cayenne pepper
½ teaspoon ground cumin
2 tablespoons olive oil
2 cloves garlic, minced
1 teaspoon Dijon mustard
1 onion, cut into slices

1.  Toss the beef with the spices, garlic, mustard, and olive oil; place the beef in a lightly oiled Air Fryer cooking tray.
2.  Select Roast. Set temperature to 390ºF (200ºC), and set time to 45 minutes, turning it over halfway through the cooking time.
3.  Add in the onion and continue to cook for an additional 10 minutes.
4.  Bon appétit!

## Garlicky Chuck Roast

**Prep time: 10 minutes | Cook time: 55 minutes | Serves 5**

½ cup red wine
1 tablespoon Dijon mustard
1 tablespoon fresh garlic, minced
1 teaspoon red pepper
flakes, crushed
Sea salt and ground black pepper, to taste
2 pounds (907 g) chuck roast
1 tablespoon corn flour

1.  Place the wine, mustard, garlic, red pepper, salt, black pepper, and chuck roast in a ceramic bowl. Cover the bowl and let the meat marinate for 3 hours in your refrigerator.
2.  Toss the roast beef with the corn flour; place the roast beef in the Air Fryer cooking tray.
3.  Select Roast. Set temperature to 390ºF (200ºC), and set time to 55 minutes, turning them over halfway through the cooking time.
4.  Enjoy!

## Mushroom and Beef Patties

**Prep time: 10 minutes | Cook time: 15 minutes | Serves 4**

1 pound (454 g) ground chuck
2 garlic cloves, minced
1 small onion, chopped
1 cup mushrooms, chopped
1 teaspoon cayenne pepper
Sea salt and ground black pepper, to taste
4 brioche rolls

1.  Mix the ground chuck, garlic, onion, mushrooms, cayenne pepper, salt, and black pepper until everything is well combined. Form the mixture into four patties.
2.  Select Roast. Set temperature to 380ºF (195ºC), and set time to about 15 minutes or until cooked through; make sure to turn them over halfway through the cooking time.
3.  Serve your patties on the prepared brioche rolls and enjoy!

New York Strip Steak, page 56

Rosemary Ribeye Steak, page 62

Barbecue Beef Brisket, page 57

Light Herbed Meatballs, page 66

## BBQ Cheeseburgers

**Prep time: 5 minutes | Cook time: 15 minutes | Serves 3**

¾ pound (340.2 g) ground chuck
1 teaspoon garlic, minced
2 tablespoons BBQ sauce
Sea salt and ground black pepper, to taste
3 slices cheese
3 hamburger buns

1. Mix the ground chuck, garlic, BBQ sauce, salt, and black pepper until everything is well combined. Form the mixture into four patties.
2. Select Roast. Set temperature to 380ºF (195ºC), and set time to about 15 minutes or until cooked through; make sure to turn them over halfway through the cooking time.
3. Top each burger with cheese. Serve your burgers on the prepared buns and enjoy!

## Marinated London Broil

**Prep time: 10 minutes | Cook time: 28 minutes | Serves 4**

1 pound (454 g) London broil
Kosher salt and ground black pepper, to taste
2 tablespoons olive oil
1 small lemon, freshly squeezed
3 cloves garlic, minced
1 tablespoon fresh parsley, chopped
1 tablespoon fresh coriander, chopped

1. Toss the beef with the remaining ingredients and let it marinate for an hour.
2. Place the beef in a lightly oiled Air Fryer cooking tray and discard the marinade.
3. Select Roast. Set temperature to 400ºF (205ºC), and set time to 28 minutes, turning it over halfway through the cooking time.
4. Bon appétit!

## Mexican Carnitas

**Prep time: 5 minutes | Cook time: 1¼ hours | Serves 4**

1½ pounds (680 g) beef brisket
2 tablespoons olive oil
Sea salt and ground
black pepper, to taste
1 teaspoon chili powder
4 medium-sized flour tortillas

1. Toss the beef brisket with the olive oil, salt, black pepper, and chili powder; now, place the beef brisket in the Air Fryer cooking tray.
2. Select Roast. Set temperature to 390ºF (200ºC), and set time to 15 minutes, turn the beef over and reduce the temperature to 360ºF (180ºC).
3. Continue to cook the beef brisket for approximately 55 minutes or until cooked through.
4. Shred the beef with two forks and serve with tortillas and toppings of choice. Bon appétit!

## Roast Beef with Carrots and Herbs

**Prep time: 10 minutes | Cook time: 55 minutes | Serves 5**

2 pounds (907 g) top sirloin roast
2 tablespoons olive oil
Sea salt and ground black pepper, to taste
2 carrots, sliced
1 tablespoon fresh coriander
1 tablespoon fresh thyme
1 tablespoon fresh rosemary

1. Toss the beef with the olive oil, salt, and black pepper; place the beef in the Air Fryer cooking tray.
2. Select Roast. Set temperature to 390ºF (200ºC), and set time to 45 minutes, turning it over halfway through the cooking time.
3. Top the beef with the carrots and herbs. Continue to cook for an additional 10 minutes.
4. Enjoy!

## Beef Risotto

**Prep time: 10 minutes | Cook time: 20 minutes | Serves 4**

2 teaspoons olive oil
1 onion, finely chopped
3 garlic cloves, minced
½ cup chopped red bell pepper
¾ cup short-grain rice
1¼ cups low-sodium beef broth
½ cup chopped cooked roast beef
3 tablespoons grated Parmesan cheese

1. In a 6-by-2-inch pan, combine the olive oil, onion, garlic, and red bell pepper. Place the pan in the oven for 2 minutes, or until the vegetables are crisp-tender. Remove from the oven.
2. Add the rice, beef broth, and roast beef. Return the pan to the oven and select Roast, and set time to 18 to 22 minutes, stirring once during cooking, until the rice is tender and the beef reaches at least 145ºF (65ºC) on a meat thermometer. Remove the pan from the oven.
3. Stir in the Parmesan cheese and serve immediately.

## Spicy Beef Burgers

**Prep time: 10 minutes | Cook time: 15 minutes | Serves 3**

¾ pound (340.2 g) ground beef
2 tablespoons onion, minced
1 teaspoon garlic, minced
1 teaspoon cayenne pepper
Sea salt and ground black pepper, to taste
1 teaspoon red chili powder
3 hamburger buns

1. Mix the beef, onion, garlic, cayenne pepper, salt, black pepper, and red chili powder until everything is well combined. Form the mixture into three patties.
2. Select Roast. Set temperature to 380ºF (195ºC), and set time to about 15 minutes or until cooked through; make sure to turn them over halfway through the cooking time.
3. Serve your burgers on the prepared buns and enjoy!

## Thyme Roast Beef

**Prep time: 10 minutes | Cook time: 20 minutes | Serves 10 to 12**

½ teaspoon fresh rosemary
1 teaspoon dried thyme
¼ teaspoon pepper
1 teaspoon salt
4 pounds (1.8 kg) top round roast beef
2 teaspoons olive oil

1. Ensure your air fryer oven is preheated to 360ºF (180ºC).
2. Rub olive oil all over the beef.
3. Mix rosemary, thyme, pepper, and salt together and proceed to rub all sides of the beef with spice mixture.
4. Place the seasoned beef into air fryer and select Roast. Set temperature to 360ºF (180ºC), and set time to 20 minutes.
5. Allow it to rest for 10 minutes before slicing to serve.

## Beef Satay

**Prep time: 15 minutes | Cook time: 8 minutes | Serves 4**

1 pound (454 g) beef flank steak, thinly sliced into long strips
2 tablespoons vegetable oil
1 tablespoon fish sauce
1 tablespoon soy sauce
1 tablespoon minced fresh ginger
1 tablespoon minced garlic
1 tablespoon sugar
1 teaspoon sriracha or other hot sauce
1 teaspoon ground coriander
½ cup chopped fresh cilantro
¼ cup chopped roasted peanuts
Peanut sauce, for serving

1. Place the beef strips in a large bowl or resealable plastic bag. Add the vegetable oil, fish sauce, soy sauce, ginger, garlic, sugar, sriracha, coriander, and ¼ cup of the cilantro to the bag. Seal and massage the bag to thoroughly coat and combine. Marinate at room temperature for 30 minutes, or cover and refrigerate for up to 24 hours.
2. Using tongs, remove the beef strips from the bag and lay them flat in the air-fryer cooking tray, minimizing overlap as much as possible; discard the marinade. Select Roast. Set temperature to 400ºF (205ºC), and set time to 8 minutes, turning the beef strips halfway through the cooking time.
3. Transfer the meat to a serving platter. Sprinkle with the remaining ¼ cup cilantro and the peanuts. Serve with peanut sauce.

## Carne Asada

**Prep time: 15 minutes | Cook time: 16 minutes | Serves 4**

Juice of 2 limes
1 orange, peeled and seeded
1 cup fresh cilantro leaves
1 jalapeño, diced
2 tablespoons vegetable oil
2 tablespoons apple cider vinegar
2 teaspoons ancho chile powder
2 teaspoons sugar
1 teaspoon kosher salt
1 teaspoon cumin seeds
1 teaspoon coriander seeds
1½ pounds (680 g) skirt steak, cut into 3 pieces

1. In a blender, combine the lime juice, orange, cilantro, jalapeño, vegetable oil, vinegar, chile powder, sugar, salt, cumin, and coriander. Blend until smooth.
2. Place the steak in a resealable plastic bag. Pour the marinade over the steak and seal the bag. Let it stand at room temperature for 30 minutes or cover and refrigerate for up to 24 hours.
3. Place the steak pieces in the air-fryer cooking tray (depending on the size of your oven, you may have to do this in two batches). Discard marinade. Select Roast. Set temperature to 400ºF (205ºC), and set time to 8 minutes. Use a meat thermometer to ensure the steak has reached an internal temperature of 145ºF (65ºC). (It is critical to not overcook skirt steak to avoid toughening the meat.)
4. Transfer the steak to a cutting board and let it rest for 10 minutes. Slice across the grain and serve.

## Juicy Peppery Tomahawk Steaks

**Prep time: 10 minutes | Cook time: 14 minutes | Serves 4**

1½ pounds (680 g) Tomahawk steaks
2 bell peppers, sliced
2 tablespoons butter, melted

2 teaspoons Montreal steak seasoning
2 tablespoons fish sauce
Sea salt and ground black pepper, to taste

1. Toss all ingredients in the Air Fryer cooking tray.
2. Select Roast. Set temperature to 400ºF (205ºC), and set time to about 14 minutes, turning it over halfway through the cooking time.
3. Bon appétit!

## Classic Beef Brisket

**Prep time: 10 minutes | Cook time: 1¼ hours | Serves 4**

1½ pounds (680 g) beef brisket
2 tablespoons olive oil
1 teaspoon onion powder
1 teaspoon garlic powder

Sea salt and ground black pepper, to taste
1 teaspoon dried parsley flakes
1 teaspoon dried thyme

1. Toss the beef with the remaining ingredients; place the beef in the Air Fryer cooking tray.
2. Select Roast. Set temperature to 390ºF (200ºC), and set time to 15 minutes, turn the beef over and turn the temperature to 360ºF (180ºC).
3. Continue to cook the beef for 55 minutes or more. Bon appétit!

## Rosemary Ribeye Steak

**Prep time: 5 minutes | Cook time: 15 minutes | Serves 4**

1 pound (454 g) ribeye steak, bone-in
2 tablespoons butter, room temperature
2 garlic cloves, minced

Sea salt and ground black pepper, to taste
2 rosemary sprigs, leaves picked, chopped

1. Toss the ribeye steak with the butter, garlic, salt, black pepper, and rosemary; place the steak in the Air Fryer cooking tray.
2. Select Roast. Set temperature to 400ºF (205ºC), and set time to 15 minutes, turning it over halfway through the cooking time.
3. Bon appétit!

## Ribeye Steak

**Prep time: 5 minutes | Cook time: 13 minutes | Serves 4**

1 tablespoon olive oil
Pepper and salt, to taste

2 pounds (907 g) of ribeye steak

1. Season meat on both sides with pepper and salt.
2. Rub all sides of meat with olive oil.
3. Preheat air fryer oven to 356ºF (180ºC) and spritz with olive oil.
4. Select Roast, and set time to 7 minutes. Flip and roast an additional 6 minutes.
5. Let the meat sit for 2 to 5 minutes to rest. Slice and serve with salad.

## French Chateaubriand

**Prep time: 5 minutes | Cook time: 14 minutes | Serves 4**

1 pound (454 g) beef filet mignon
Sea salt and ground black pepper, to taste
1 teaspoon cayenne pepper

3 tablespoons olive oil
1 tablespoon Dijon mustard
4 tablespoons dry French wine

1. Toss the filet mignon with the rest of the ingredients; place the filet mignon in the Air Fryer cooking tray.
2. Select Roast. Set temperature to 400ºF (205ºC), and set time to 14 minutes, turning it over halfway through the cooking time.
3. Enjoy!

## Traditional Skirt Steak

**Prep time: 5 minutes | Cook time: 12 minutes | Serves 4**

1½ pounds (680 g) skirt steak
Kosher salt and freshly cracked black pepper, to taste
1 teaspoon cayenne

pepper
¼ teaspoon cumin powder
2 tablespoons olive oil
2 garlic cloves, minced

1. Toss the steak with the other ingredients; place the steak in the Air Fryer cooking tray.
2. Select Roast. Set temperature to 400ºF (205ºC), and set time to 12 minutes, turning it over halfway through the cooking time.
3. Bon appétit!

## Buttery Filet Mignon

**Prep time: 5 minutes | Cook time: 14 minutes | Serves 4**

1½ pounds (680 g) filet mignon
2 tablespoons soy sauce
2 tablespoons butter, melted
1 teaspoon mustard powder
1 teaspoon garlic powder
Sea salt and ground black pepper, to taste

1. Toss the filet mignon with the remaining ingredients; place the filet mignon in the Air Fryer cooking tray.
2. Select Roast. Set temperature toat 400ºF (205ºC), and set time to 14 minutes, turning it over halfway through the cooking time.
3. Enjoy!

## Ritzy Steak with Mushroom Gravy

**Prep time: 20 minutes | Cook time: 33 minutes | Serves 2**

For the Mushroom Gravy:
¾ cup sliced button mushrooms
¼ cup thinly sliced onions
¼ cup unsalted butter, melted
½ teaspoon fine sea salt
¼ cup beef broth
For the Steaks:
½ pound (227 g) ground beef (85% lean)
1 tablespoon dry mustard
2 tablespoons tomato paste
¼ teaspoon garlic powder
½ teaspoon onion powder
½ teaspoon fine sea salt
¼ teaspoon ground black pepper
Chopped fresh thyme leaves, for garnish

1. Toss the mushrooms and onions with butter in a baking pan to coat well, and then sprinkle with salt.
2. Place the baking pan in the oven and select Roast. Set temperature to 390ºF (200ºC), and set time to 8 minutes or until the mushrooms are tender. Stir the mixture halfway through.
3. Pour the broth in the baking pan and cook for 10 more minutes to make the gravy.
4. Meanwhile, combine all the ingredients for the steaks, except for the thyme leaves, in a large bowl. Stir to mix well. Shape the mixture into two oval steaks.
5. Arrange the steaks over the gravy and cook for 15 minutes or until the patties are browned. Flip the steaks halfway through.
6. Transfer the steaks onto a plate and pour the gravy over. Sprinkle with fresh thyme and serve immediately.

## Dijon London Broil

**Prep time: 10 minutes | Cook time: 28 minutes | Serves 4**

1½ pounds (680 g) London broil
Kosher salt and ground black pepper, to taste
¼ teaspoon ground bay leaf
3 tablespoons butter,
cold
1 tablespoon Dijon mustard
1 teaspoon garlic, pressed
1 tablespoon fresh parsley, chopped

1. Toss the beef with the salt and black pepper; place the beef in a lightly oiled Air Fryer cooking tray.
2. Select Roast. Set temperature to 400ºF (205ºC), and set time to 28 minutes, turning over halfway through the cooking time.
3. In the meantime, mix the butter with the remaining ingredients and place it in the refrigerator until well-chilled.
4. Serve warm beef with the chilled garlic butter on the side. Bon appétit!

## Beef with Fajita Veggie

**Prep time: 10 minutes | Cook time: 18 minutes | Serves 4 to 6**

For the Beef:
⅛ cup carne asada seasoning
2 pounds (907 g) beef flap meat
Diet 7-Up (soda)
For the Fajita Veggies:
1 teaspoon chili powder
1 to 2 teaspoons pepper
1 to 2 teaspoons salt
2 bell peppers, your choice of color
1 onion
4 wheat tortillas

1. Slice flap meat into manageable pieces and place into a bowl. Season meat with carne seasoning and pour diet soda over meat. Cover and chill overnight.
2. Ensure your air fryer oven is preheated to 380ºF (195ºC).
3. Place a parchment liner into air fryer cooking tray and spray with olive oil. Place beef in layers into the cooking tray.
4. Cook for 8 to 10 minutes, making sure to flip halfway through. Remove and set to the side.
5. Slice up veggies and spray air fryer cooking tray. Add veggies to the fryer and season with pepper and salt. Select Roast. Set temperature to 400ºF (205ºC), and set time to 10 minutes, shaking 1 to 2 times during cooking process.
6. Serve meat and veggies on wheat tortillas and top with favorite keto fillings!

## Mexican-Style Meatloaf

**Prep time: 10 minutes | Cook time: 25 minutes | Serves 4**

| | |
|---|---|
| 1½ pounds (680 g) ground chuck | crushed |
| ½ onion, chopped | 1 teaspoon garlic, minced |
| 1 teaspoon habanero pepper, minced | Sea salt and ground black pepper, to taste |
| ¼ cup tortilla chips, | 2 tablespoons olive oil |
| | 1 egg, whisked |

1. Thoroughly combine all ingredients until everything is well combined.
2. Scrape the beef mixture into a lightly oiled baking pan and transfer it to the Air Fryer cooking tray.
3. Select Roast. Set temperature to 390ºF (200ºC), and set time to 25 minutes. Bon appétit!

## Blue Cheese Ribeye Steak

**Prep time: 10 minutes | Cook time: 15 minutes | Serves 4**

| | |
|---|---|
| 1 pound (454 g) ribeye steak, bone-in | ½ teaspoon onion powder |
| Sea salt and ground black pepper, to taste | 1 teaspoon garlic powder |
| 2 tablespoons olive oil | 1 cup blue cheese, crumbled |

1. Toss the ribeye steak with the salt, black pepper, olive oil, onion powder, and garlic powder; place the ribeye steak in the Air Fryer cooking tray.
2. Select Roast. Set temperature to 400ºF (205ºC), and set time to 15 minutes, turning it over halfway through the cooking time.
3. Top the ribeye steak with the cheese and serve warm. Bon appétit!

## Old-Fashioned Rosemary Meatloaf

**Prep time: 10 minutes | Cook time: 25 minutes | Serves 4**

| | |
|---|---|
| 1½ pounds (680 g) ground chuck | 2 garlic cloves, minced |
| 1 egg, beaten | 1 tablespoon fresh rosemary, chopped |
| 2 tablespoons olive oil | 1 tablespoon fresh thyme, chopped |
| 4 tablespoons crackers, crushed | Sea salt and ground black pepper, to taste |
| ½ cup shallots, minced | |

1. Thoroughly combine all ingredients until everything is well combined.

2. Scrape the beef mixture into a lightly oiled baking pan and transfer it to the Air Fryer cooking tray.
3. Select Roast. Set temperature to 390ºF (200ºC), and set time to 25 minutes. Bon appétit!

## Sherry Beef and Broccoli

**Prep time: 10 minutes | Cook time: 12 minutes | Serves 4**

| | |
|---|---|
| 1 minced garlic clove | soy sauce |
| 1 sliced ginger root | ⅓ cup sherry |
| 1 tablespoon olive oil | 2 teaspoons sesame oil |
| 1 teaspoon almond flour | ⅓ cup oyster sauce |
| 1 teaspoon sweetener of choice | 1 pound of broccoli |
| 1 teaspoon low-sodium | ¾ pound (340.2 g) round steak |

1. Remove the stems from broccoli and slice into florets. Slice steak into thin strips.
2. Combine sweetener, soy sauce, sherry, almond flour, sesame oil, and oyster sauce together, stirring till sweetener dissolves.
3. Put strips of steak into the mixture and allow to marinate for 45 minutes to 2 hours.
4. Add broccoli and marinated steak to the oven. Place garlic, ginger, and olive oil on top.
5. Select Roast. Set temperature to 400ºF (205ºC), and set time to 12 minutes. Serve with cauliflower rice!

## Tenderloin Steaks with Cremini Mushrooms

**Prep time: 10 minutes | Cook time: 15 minutes | Serves 4**

| | |
|---|---|
| 1½ pounds (680 g) tenderloin steaks | 1 teaspoon cayenne pepper |
| 2 tablespoons butter, melted | Sea salt and ground black pepper, to taste |
| 1 teaspoon garlic powder | ½ pound (227 g) cremini mushrooms, sliced |
| ½ teaspoon mustard powder | |

1. Toss the beef with 1 tablespoon of the butter and spices; place the beef in the Air Fryer cooking tray.
2. Select Roast. Set temperature to 400ºF (205ºC), and set time to 10 minutes, turning it over halfway through the cooking time.
3. Add in the mushrooms along with the remaining 1 tablespoon of the butter. Continue to cook for an additional 5 minutes. Serve warm.
4. Bon appétit!

## Montreal Ribeye Steak

**Prep time: 5 minutes | Cook time: 15 minutes | Serves 4**

1½ pounds (680 g) ribeye steak, bone-in
2 tablespoons butter
1 Montreal seasoning mix
Sea salt and ground black pepper, to taste

1. Toss the ribeye steak with the remaining ingredients; place the ribeye steak in a lightly oiled Air Fryer cooking tray.
2. Select Roast. Set temperature to 400ºF (205ºC), and set time to 15 minutes, turning it over halfway through the cooking time.
3. Bon appétit!

## Smoked Beef Sausage with Bell Peppers

**Prep time: 10 minutes | Cook time: 15 minutes | Serves 4**

1 pound (454 g) smoked beef sausage
2 bell peppers, sliced
2 garlic cloves, pressed
2 tablespoons olive oil
1 teaspoon sage
1 teaspoon thyme
Sea salt and red pepper, to season

1. Toss all ingredients in a lightly oiled Air Fryer cooking tray.
2. Select Roast. Set temperature to 380ºF (195ºC), and set time to 15 minutes, tossing the cooking tray halfway through the cooking time.
3. Serve warm and enjoy!

## Beef Empanadas

**Prep time: 5 minutes | Cook time: 32 minutes | Serves 8**

1 teaspoon water
1 egg white
1 cup picadillo
8 Goya empanada discs (thawed)

1. Ensure your air fryer oven is preheated to 320ºF (160ºC)
2. Spray cooking tray with olive oil.
3. Place 2 tablespoons of picadillo into the center of each disc. Fold disc in half and use a fork to seal edges. Repeat with all ingredients.
4. Whisk egg white with water and brush tops of empanadas with egg wash.
5. Add 2 to 3 empanadas to the oven. Select Roast. Set temperature to 320ºF (160ºC), and set time to 8 minutes. Repeat till you cook all filled empanadas.

## Chuck Eye Roast with Tomatoes

**Prep time: 5 minutes | Cook time: 55 minutes | Serves 4**

1½ pounds (680 g) chuck eye roast
Sea salt and ground black pepper, to taste
1 teaspoon red pepper flakes, crushed
2 tablespoons olive oil, melted
1 jalapeno pepper, chopped
1 large-sized tomato, sliced

1. Toss the roast beef with the salt, black pepper, red pepper flakes, and olive oil; place the roast beef in a lightly oiled Air Fryer cooking tray.
2. Select Roast. Set temperature to 390ºF (200ºC), and set time to 45 minutes, turning it over halfway through the cooking time.
3. Top the roast beef with the tomato and jalapeno pepper. Continue to cook for 10 minutes or more. Enjoy!

## Spicy Sirloin Tip Steak

**Prep time: 10 minutes | Cook time: 12 minutes | Serves 4**

2 tablespoons low-sodium salsa
1 tablespoon minced chipotle pepper
1 tablespoon apple cider vinegar
1 teaspoon ground cumin
⅛ teaspoon freshly
ground black pepper
⅛ teaspoon red pepper flakes
¾ pound (340.2 g) sirloin tip steak, cut into 4 pieces and gently pounded to about ⅓ inch thick

1. In a small bowl, thoroughly mix the salsa, chipotle pepper, cider vinegar, cumin, black pepper, and red pepper flakes. Rub this mixture into both sides of each steak piece. Let it stand for 15 minutes at room temperature.
2. Select Roast. Roast the steaks in the oven, two at a time, for 6 to 9 minutes, or until they reach at least 145ºF (65ºC) on a meat thermometer.
3. Remove the steaks to a clean plate and cover with aluminum foil to keep warm. Repeat with the remaining steaks.
4. Slice the steaks thinly against the grain and serve.

# Greek Pulled Beef

**Prep time: 10 minutes | Cook time: 1¼ hours | Serves 4**

1½ pounds (680 g) beef brisket
2 tablespoons olive oil
Sea salt and freshly ground black pepper, to season
1 teaspoon dried oregano
1 teaspoon mustard powder

½ teaspoon ground cumin
2 cloves garlic, minced
2 tablespoons chives, chopped
2 tablespoons cilantro, chopped

1. Toss the beef brisket with the rest of the ingredients; now, place the beef brisket in the Air Fryer cooking tray.
2. Select Roast. Set temperature to 390ºF (200ºC), and set time to 15 minutes, turn the beef over and reduce the temperature to 360ºF (180ºC).
3. Continue to roast the beef brisket for approximately 55 minutes or until cooked through.
4. Shred the beef with two forks and serve with toppings of choice. Bon appétit!

# Light Herbed Meatballs

**Prep time: 10 minutes | Cook time: 15 minutes | Makes 24 meatballs**

1 medium onion, minced
2 garlic cloves, minced
1 teaspoon olive oil
1 slice low-sodium whole-wheat bread, crumbled

3 tablespoons 1 percent milk
1 teaspoon dried marjoram
1 teaspoon dried basil
1 pound (454 g) 96 percent lean ground beef

1. In a 6-by-2-inch pan, combine the onion, garlic, and olive oil. Air fry for 2 to 4 minutes, or until the vegetables are crisp-tender.
2. Transfer the vegetables to a medium bowl, and add the bread crumbs, milk, marjoram, and basil. Mix well.
3. Add the ground beef. With your hands, work the mixture gently but thoroughly until combined. Form the meat mixture into about 24 (1-inch) meatballs.
4. Select Roast. Roast the meatballs, in batches, in the air fryer cooking tray for 12 to 17 minutes, or until they reach 160ºF (70ºC) on a meat thermometer. Serve immediately.

# Mongolian Beef

**Prep time: 15 minutes | Cook time: 12 minutes | Serves 6 to 10**

½ cup almond flour
2 pounds (907 g) beef tenderloin or beef chuck, sliced into strips
For the Sauce:
½ cup chopped green onion
1 teaspoon red chili flakes
1 teaspoon almond flour
½ cup brown sugar

1 teaspoon hoisin sauce
½ cup water
½ cup rice vinegar
½ cup low-sodium soy sauce
1 tablespoon chopped garlic
1 tablespoon finely chopped ginger
2 tablespoons olive oil

1. Toss strips of beef in almond flour, ensuring they are coated well.
2. Select Roast. Set temperature to 300ºF (150ºC), and set time to 10 minutes.
3. Meanwhile, add all sauce ingredients to the pan and bring to a boil. Mix well.
4. Add beef strips to the sauce and cook for 2 minutes.
5. Serve over cauliflower rice!

# Chapter 6 Pork

## Cuban Pork Sandwich

**Prep time: 10 minutes | Cook time: 55 minutes | Serves 4**

1½ pounds (680 g) pork butt
1 teaspoon stone-ground mustard
½ teaspoon ground cumin
2 cloves garlic, crushed
Kosher salt and freshly ground black pepper, to

season
½ teaspoon ground allspice
2 tablespoons fresh pineapple juice
2 ounces Swiss cheese, sliced
16 ounces (454 g) Cuban bread loaf, sliced

1. Toss all ingredients, except for the cheese and bread, in a lightly greased Air Fryer cooking tray.
2. Select Roast. Set temperature to 360ºF (180ºC), and set time to 55 minutes, turning it over halfway through the cooking time.
3. Using two forks, shred the pork; assemble your sandwiches with cheese and bread. Serve warm and enjoy!

## Breaded Sirloin Chops

**Prep time: 10 minutes | Cook time: 15 minutes | Serves 3**

1 pound (454 g) sirloin chops
1 egg
2 tablespoons butter, at room temperature
Sea salt and ground

black pepper, to taste
3 tablespoons Pecorino cheese, grated
½ cup breadcrumbs
1 teaspoon paprika
1 teaspoon garlic powder

1. Pat the pork sirloin chops dry with kitchen towels.
2. In a shallow bowl, whisk the egg until pale and frothy.
3. In another shallow bowl, thoroughly combine the remaining ingredients. Dip the pork chops into the egg, then the cheese/crumb mixture.
4. Place the pork sirloin chops in a lightly oiled Air Fryer cooking tray.
5. Select Roast. Set temperature to 400ºF (205ºC), and set time to 15 minutes, turning them over halfway through the cooking time.
6. Bon appétit!

## Pork Tenderloin and Fruit Kebabs

**Prep time: 10 minutes | Cook time: 10 minutes | Serves 4**

⅓ cup apricot jam
2 tablespoons freshly squeezed lemon juice
2 teaspoons olive oil
½ teaspoon dried tarragon
1 (1-pound / 227-g) pork

tenderloin, cut into 1-inch cubes
4 plums, pitted and quartered
4 small apricots, pitted and halved

1. In a large bowl, mix the jam, lemon juice, olive oil, and tarragon.
2. Add the pork and stir to coat. Let it stand for 10 minutes at room temperature.
3. Alternating the items, thread the pork, plums, and apricots onto 4 metal skewers that fit into the oven. Brush with any remaining jam mixture. Discard any remaining marinade.
4. Select Roast, and set time to 9 to 12 minutes, or until the pork reaches 145ºF (65ºC) on a meat thermometer and the fruit is tender. Serve immediately.

## Pork and Creamer Potatoes

**Prep time: 10 minutes | Cook time: 25 minutes | Serves 4**

2 cups creamer potatoes, rinsed and dried
2 teaspoons olive oil
1 (1-pound / 227-g) pork tenderloin, cut into 1-inch cubes
1 onion, chopped

1 red bell pepper, chopped
2 garlic cloves, minced
½ teaspoon dried oregano
2 tablespoons low-sodium chicken broth

1. In a medium bowl, toss the potatoes and olive oil to coat.
2. Transfer the potatoes to the air fryer cooking tray. Select Roast, and set time to 15 minutes.
3. In a medium metal bowl, mix the potatoes, pork, onion, red bell pepper, garlic, and oregano.
4. Drizzle with the chicken broth. Put the bowl in the air fryer cooking tray. Select Roast, and set time about 10 minutes or more, shaking the cooking tray once during cooking, until the pork reaches at least 145ºF (65ºC) on a meat thermometer and the potatoes are tender. Serve immediately.

## Country-Style Pork Belly

**Prep time: 10 minutes | Cook time: 17 minutes | Serves 6**

| | |
|---|---|
| 1½ pounds (680 g) pork belly, cut into pieces | 2 tablespoons dark brown sugar |
| ¼ cup tomato sauce | 1 teaspoon garlic, minced |
| 1 tablespoon tamari sauce | Sea salt and ground black pepper, to season |

1. Toss all ingredients in your Air Fryer cooking tray.
2. Select Roast. Set temperature to 400ºF (205ºC), and set time to about 17 minutes, shaking the cooking tray halfway through the cooking time.
3. Bon appétit!

## Rosemary Pork Butt

**Prep time: 5 minutes | Cook time: 55 minutes | Serves 4**

| | |
|---|---|
| 1½ pounds (680 g) pork butt | rosemary, chopped |
| 1 teaspoon butter, melted | Coarse sea salt and freshly ground black |
| 2 garlic cloves, pressed | pepper, to taste |
| 2 tablespoons fresh | |

1. Toss all ingredients in a lightly greased Air Fryer cooking tray.
2. Select Roast. Set temperature to 360ºF (180ºC), and set time to 55 minutes, turning it over halfway through the cooking time.
3. Serve warm and enjoy!

## Pork Spareribs

**Prep time: 10 minutes | Cook time: 35 minutes | Serves 4**

| | |
|---|---|
| 2 pounds (907 g) pork spareribs | sugar |
| 1 teaspoon coarse sea salt | 1 teaspoon cayenne pepper |
| ⅓ teaspoon freshly ground black pepper | 1 teaspoon garlic powder |
| 1 tablespoon brown | 1 teaspoon mustard powder |

1. Toss all ingredients in a lightly greased Air Fryer cooking tray.
2. Select Roast. Set temperature to 350ºF (175ºC), and set time to 35 minutes, turning them over halfway through the cooking time.
3. Bon appétit!

## Smoked Paprika Pork Loin Chops

**Prep time: 5 minutes | Cook time: 15 minutes | Serves 4**

| | |
|---|---|
| 1 pound (454 g) pork loin chops | black pepper, to taste |
| 1 tablespoon olive oil | 1 tablespoon smoked paprika |
| Sea salt and ground | |

1. Place all ingredients in a lightly greased Air Fryer cooking tray.
2. Select Roast. Set temperature to 400ºF (205ºC), and set time to 15 minutes, turning them over halfway through the cooking time.
3. Bon appétit!

## Pork Sausage with Brussels Sprouts

**Prep time: 10 minutes | Cook time: 15 minutes | Serves 4**

| | |
|---|---|
| 1 pound (454 g) sausage links, uncooked | 1 teaspoon dried rosemary |
| 1 pound (454 g) Brussels sprouts, halved | 1 teaspoon dried parsley flakes |
| 1 teaspoon dried thyme | 1 teaspoon garlic powder |

1. Place all the ingredients in a lightly greased Air Fryer cooking tray.
2. Select Roast. Set temperature to 380ºF (195ºC), and set time to approximately 15 minutes tossing the cooking tray halfway through the cooking time.
3. Bon appétit!

## Hot Center Cut Rib Roast

**Prep time: 10 minutes | Cook time: 55 minutes | Serves 4**

| | |
|---|---|
| 1½ pounds (680 g) pork center cut rib roast | 1 teaspoon garlic powder |
| 2 teaspoons butter, melted | ½ teaspoon onion powder |
| 1 teaspoon red chili powder | Sea salt and ground black pepper, to taste |
| 1 teaspoon paprika | 2 tablespoons tamari sauce |

1. Toss all ingredients in a lightly greased Air Fryer cooking tray.
2. Select Roast. Set temperature to 360ºF (180ºC), and set time to 55 minutes, turning it over halfway through the cooking time.
3. Serve warm and enjoy!

## Chinese Back Ribs

**Prep time: 10 minutes | Cook time: 35 minutes | Serves 4**

| | |
|---|---|
| 1 tablespoon sesame oil | 1 tablespoon soy sauce |
| 1½ pounds (680 g) back ribs | 2 tablespoons agave syrup |
| ½ cup tomato sauce | 2 tablespoons rice wine |

1. Toss all ingredients in a lightly greased Air Fryer cooking tray.
2. Select Roast. Set temperature to 350ºF (175ºC), and set time to 35 minutes, turning them over halfway through the cooking time.
3. Bon appétit!

## Hot St. Louis-Style Ribs

**Prep time: 5 minutes | Cook time: 35 minutes | Serves 4**

| | |
|---|---|
| 1½ pounds (680 g) St. Louis-style ribs | Kosher salt and ground black pepper, to taste |
| 1 teaspoon hot sauce | 2 garlic cloves, minced |
| 1 tablespoon canola oil | |

1. Toss all ingredients in a lightly greased Air Fryer cooking tray.
2. Select Roast. Set temperature to 350ºF (175ºC), and set time to 35 minutes, turning them over halfway through the cooking time.
3. Bon appétit!

## Pork Loin Chops with Onions

**Prep time: 5 minutes | Cook time: 15 minutes | Serves 4**

| | |
|---|---|
| 1½ pounds (680 g) pork loin chops, boneless | 1 teaspoon garlic powder |
| 2 tablespoons olive oil | Sea salt and ground black pepper, to taste |
| ½ teaspoon cayenne pepper | 1 onion, cut into wedges |

1. Place all ingredients in a lightly greased Air Fryer cooking tray.
2. Select Roast. Set temperature to 400ºF (205ºC), and set time to 15 minutes, turning them over halfway through the cooking time.
3. Bon appétit!

## Mix-Herb Pork Butt

**Prep time: 10 minutes | Cook time: 55 minutes | Serves 4**

| | |
|---|---|
| 1½ pounds (680 g) pork butt | 1 teaspoon dried oregano |
| 1 teaspoon olive oil | 1 teaspoon dried basil |
| 1 teaspoon dried rosemary | 1 teaspoon cayenne pepper |
| 1 teaspoon dried thyme | Sea salt and ground black pepper, to taste |

1. Toss all ingredients in a lightly greased Air Fryer cooking tray.
2. Select Roast. Set temperature to 360ºF (180ºC), and set time to 55 minutes, turning it over halfway through the cooking time.
3. Serve warm and enjoy!

## Mexican-Style Pork Tacos

**Prep time: 10 minutes | Cook time: 55 minutes | Serves 4**

| | |
|---|---|
| 2 ancho chiles, seeded and minced | season |
| 2 garlic cloves, chopped | 1 teaspoon dried Mexican oregano |
| 1 tablespoon olive oil | 1½ pounds (680 g) pork butt |
| Kosher salt and freshly ground black pepper, to | 4 corn tortillas, warmed |

1. Toss all ingredients, except for the tortillas, in a lightly greased Air Fryer cooking tray.
2. Select Roast. Set temperature to 360ºF (180ºC), and set time to 55 minutes, turning it over halfway through the cooking time.
3. Using two forks, shred the pork and serve in tortillas with toppings of choice. Serve immediately!

## Dijon Mustard Pork Loin Roast

**Prep time: 5 minutes | Cook time: 15 minutes | Serves 4**

| | |
|---|---|
| 1½ pounds (680 g) top loin roasts, sliced into four pieces | black pepper |
| 2 tablespoons olive oil | 1 tablespoon Dijon mustard |
| 1 teaspoon hot paprika | 1 teaspoon garlic, pressed |
| Sea salt and ground | |

1. Place all ingredients in a lightly greased Air Fryer cooking tray.
2. Select Roast. Set temperature to 400ºF (205ºC), and set time to 15 minutes, turning it over halfway through the cooking time.
3. Bon appétit!

## Sriracha Spareribs

**Prep time: 5 minutes | Cook time: 35 minutes | Serves 5**

2 pounds (907 g) spareribs
¼ cup Sriracha sauce

1 teaspoon paprika
Sea salt and ground black pepper, to taste

1. Toss all ingredients in a lightly greased Air Fryer cooking tray.
2. Select Roast. Set temperature to 350ºF (175ºC), and set time to 35 minutes, turning them over halfway through the cooking time.
3. Bon appétit!

## Pork Sausage with Onions Rings

**Prep time: 5 minutes | Cook time: 15 minutes | Serves 4**

1 pound (454 g) pork sausage, smoked
4 ounces (113 g) onion rings

1. Place the sausage in a lightly greased Air fryer cooking tray.
2. Select Roast. Set temperature to 370ºF (190ºC), and set time to approximately 7 minutes, tossing the cooking tray halfway through the cooking time.
3. Add in the onion rings and continue to cook for 8 minutes more. Bon appétit!

## Buttery Rosemary Pork Loin Roast

**Prep time: 5 minutes | Cook time: 55 minutes | Serves 4**

1½ pounds (680 g) pork loin roast
2 tablespoons butter, melted
Sea salt and ground black pepper, to taste

1 teaspoon cayenne pepper
1 teaspoon garlic, pressed
1 teaspoon dried rosemary

1. Toss all ingredients in a lightly greased Air Fryer cooking tray.
2. Select Roast. Set temperature to 360ºF (180ºC), and set time to 55 minutes, turning it over halfway through the cooking time.
3. Serve warm and enjoy!

## Center Cut Pork Roast

**Prep time: 10 minutes | Cook time: 55 minutes | Serves 4**

1½ pounds (680 g) center-cut pork roast
1 tablespoon olive oil
Sea salt and freshly ground black pepper, to taste

1 teaspoon garlic powder
1 teaspoon hot paprika
½ teaspoon dried parsley flakes
½ teaspoon dried rosemary

1. Toss all ingredients in a lightly greased Air Fryer cooking tray.
2. Select Roast. Set temperature to 360ºF (180ºC), and set time to 55 minutes, turning it over halfway through the cooking time.
3. Serve warm and enjoy!

## Pork Chops with Bell Peppers

**Prep time: 10 minutes | Cook time: 15 minutes | Serves 4**

1½ pounds (680 g) center-cut rib chops
2 bell peppers, seeded and sliced
2 tablespoons olive oil
½ teaspoon mustard powder

Kosher salt and freshly ground black pepper, to taste
1 teaspoon fresh rosemary, chopped
1 teaspoon fresh basil, chopped

1. Toss all ingredients in a lightly greased Air Fryer cooking tray.
2. Select Roast. Set temperature to 400ºF (205ºC), and set time to 15 minutes, turning them over halfway through the cooking time.
3. Bon appétit!

## Chinese Pork Loin Porterhouse

**Prep time: 10 minutes | Cook time: 15 minutes | Serves 4**

1½ pounds (680 g) pork loin porterhouse, cut into four slices
1½ tablespoons sesame oil
½ teaspoon Five-spice powder

2 garlic cloves, crushed
1 tablespoon soy sauce
1 tablespoon hoisin sauce
2 tablespoons Shaoxing wine

1. Place all ingredients in a lightly greased Air Fryer cooking tray.
2. Select Roast. Set temperature to 400ºF (205ºC), and set time to 15 minutes, turning them over halfway through the cooking time.
3. Bon appétit!

## Pork Sausage with Fennel

**Prep time: 5 minutes | Cook time: 15 minutes | Serves 4**

1 pound (454 g) pork sausage
1 pound (454 g) fennel, quartered

1 teaspoon garlic powder
½ teaspoon onion powder
2 teaspoons mustard

1. Place all ingredients in a lightly greased Air Fryer cooking tray.
2. Select Roast. Set temperature to 370ºF (190ºC), and set time to approximately 15 minutes, tossing the cooking tray halfway through the cooking time.
3. Bon appétit!

## Barbecue Pork Butt

**Prep time: 5 minutes | Cook time: 55 minutes | Serves 5**

2 pounds (907 g) pork butt
1 tablespoon olive oil
Kosher salt and ground

black pepper, to taste
1 teaspoon ground cumin
½ cup BBQ sauce

1. Toss all ingredients in a lightly greased Air Fryer cooking tray.
2. Select Roast. Set temperature to 360ºF (180ºC), and set time to 55 minutes, turning it over halfway through the cooking time.
3. Serve warm and enjoy!

## Beer Pork Loin

**Prep time: 5 minutes | Cook time: 55 minutes | Serves 5**

4 tablespoons beer
1 tablespoon garlic, crushed
1 teaspoon paprika

Sea salt and ground black pepper, to taste
2 pounds (907 g) pork loin

1. Toss all ingredients in a lightly greased Air Fryer cooking tray.
2. Select Roast. Set temperature to 360ºF (180ºC), and set time to 55 minutes, turning it over halfway through the cooking time.
3. Serve warm and enjoy!

## Sriracha Country-Style Ribs

**Prep time: 5 minutes | Cook time: 35 minutes | Serves 5**

2 pounds (907 g) Country-style ribs
¼ cup Sriracha sauce
2 tablespoons bourbon

1 tablespoon honey
1 teaspoon stone-ground mustard

1. Toss all ingredients in a lightly greased Air Fryer cooking tray.
2. Select Roast. Set temperature to 350ºF (175ºC), and set time to 35 minutes, turning them over halfway through the cooking time.
3. Bon appétit!

## Coconut Pork Chops

**Prep time: 5 minutes | Cook time: 15 minutes | Serves 4**

2 teaspoons parsley
2 teaspoons grated garlic cloves
1 tablespoon coconut oil

1 tablespoon coconut butter
4 pork chops
olive oil and green salad

1. Ensure your air fryer oven is preheated to 350ºF (175ºC).
2. Mix butter, coconut oil, and all seasoning together. Then rub seasoning mixture over all sides of pork chops. Place in foil, seal, and chill for 1 hour.
3. Remove pork chops from foil and place into the oven.
4. Select Roast, and set time to 7 minutes on one side and 8 minutes on the other.
5. Drizzle with olive oil and serve alongside a green salad.

## Pork Dinner Rolls

**Prep time: 10 minutes | Cook time: 15 minutes | Serves 4**

1 pound (454 g) ground pork
Sea salt and freshly ground black pepper, to taste
1 teaspoon red pepper

flakes, crushed
½ cup scallions, chopped
2 garlic cloves, minced
1 tablespoon olive oil
1 tablespoon soy sauce
8 dinner rolls, split

1. In a mixing bowl, thoroughly combine the pork, salt, pepper, pepper flakes, scallions, garlic, olive oil, and soy sauce. Form the mixture into four patties.
2. Select Roast. Set temperature to 380ºF (195ºC), and set time to about 15 minutes or until cooked through; make sure to turn them over halfway through the cooking time.
3. Serve the patties in dinner rolls and enjoy!

## Vietnamese Grilled Pork Shoulder

**Prep time: 10 minutes | Cook time: 20 minutes | Serves 6**

¼ cup minced yellow onion
2 tablespoons sugar
2 tablespoons vegetable oil
1 tablespoon minced garlic
1 tablespoon fish sauce
1 tablespoon minced fresh lemongrass
2 teaspoons dark soy

sauce
½ teaspoon black pepper
1½ pounds (680 g) boneless pork shoulder, cut into ½-inch-thick slices
¼ cup chopped salted roasted peanuts
2 tablespoons chopped fresh cilantro or parsley

1. In a large bowl, combine the onion, sugar, vegetable oil, garlic, fish sauce, lemongrass, soy sauce, and pepper. Add the pork and toss to coat. Marinate at room temperature for 30 minutes, or cover and refrigerate for up to 24 hours.
2. Arrange the pork slices in the air-fryer cooking tray; discard the marinade. Select Roast. Set temperature to 400ºF (205ºC), and set time to 20 minutes, turning the pork halfway through the cooking time.
3. Transfer the pork to a serving platter. Sprinkle with the peanuts and cilantro and serve.

## Pork Bulgogi

**Prep time: 15 minutes | Cook time: 15 minutes | Serves 4**

1 onion, thinly sliced
2 tablespoons gochujang (Korean red chile paste)
1 tablespoon minced fresh ginger
1 tablespoon minced garlic
1 tablespoon soy sauce
1 tablespoon Shaoxing wine (rice cooking wine)
1 tablespoon toasted sesame oil

1 teaspoon sugar
¼ to 1 teaspoon cayenne pepper or gochugaru (Korean ground red pepper)
1 pound (454 g) boneless pork shoulder, cut into ½-inch-thick slices
1 tablespoon sesame seeds
¼ cup sliced scallions

1. In a large bowl, combine the onion, gochujang, ginger, garlic, soy sauce, wine, sesame oil, sugar, and cayenne. Add the pork and toss to coat. Marinate at room temperature for 30 minutes, or cover and refrigerate for up to 24 hours.
2. Arrange the pork and onion slices in the air-fryer cooking tray; discard the marinade. Select Roast.

Set temperature to 400ºF (205ºC), and set time to 15 minutes, turning the pork halfway through the cooking time.
3. Arrange the pork on a serving platter. Sprinkle with the sesame seeds and scallions and serve.

## Vietnamese Pork Sausages

**Prep time: 15 minutes | Cook time: 15 minutes | Serves 4**

For the Sausages:
1 heaping tablespoon jasmine rice
2 tablespoons fish sauce
2 garlic cloves, minced
1 tablespoon sugar
½ teaspoon black pepper
½ teaspoon kosher salt
½ teaspoon baking powder
1 pound (454 g) finely

ground pork
For Serving:
Hot cooked rice or rice noodles
Shredded lettuce
Fresh mint and basil leaves
Sliced cucumber
Sliced scallions
Dipping Sauce

Make the Sausages
1. Place the rice in a small heavy-bottomed skillet. Toast over medium heat, stirring continuously, until it turns a deep golden yellow color, for 5 to 8 minutes. Pour the rice onto a plate to cool completely. Grind in a spice or coffee grinder to a fine powder.
2. In a large bowl, stir together the rice powder, fish sauce, garlic, sugar, pepper, salt, and baking powder until thoroughly combined. Add the pork and mix gently until the seasonings are incorporated.
3. Divide the meat mixture into eight equal pieces. Roll each into a 3-inch-long log. Cover lightly with plastic wrap. Refrigerate for at least 30 minutes or up to 24 hours.
4. Arrange the sausages in the air-fryer cooking tray. Select Roast. Set temperature to 375ºF (190ºC), and set time to 15 minutes. Use a meat thermometer to ensure the sausages have reached an internal temperature of 160ºF (70ºC).
5. Arrange the sausages, lettuce, mint, basil, cucumbers, and scallions over the rice. Serve with the dipping sauce.

## Chinese-Style Slab Baby Back Ribs

**Prep time: 10 minutes | Cook time: 30 minutes | Serves 4**

| | |
|---|---|
| 1 tablespoon toasted sesame oil | 1 tablespoon agave nectar or honey |
| 1 tablespoon fermented black bean paste | 1 teaspoon minced garlic |
| 1 tablespoon Shaoxing wine (rice cooking wine) | 1 teaspoon minced fresh ginger |
| 1 tablespoon dark soy sauce | 1 (1½-pound / 680-g) slab baby back ribs, cut into individual ribs |

1. In a large bowl, stir together the sesame oil, black bean paste, wine, soy sauce, agave, garlic, and ginger. Add the ribs and toss well to coat. Marinate at room temperature for 30 minutes, or cover and refrigerate for up to 24 hours.
2. Place the ribs in the air-fryer cooking tray; discard the marinade. Select Roast. Set temperature to 350ºF (175ºC), and set time to 30 minutes.

## Sweet and Sour Pork Chunks

**Prep time: 15 minutes | Cook time: 10 minutes | Serves 4 to 6**

| | |
|---|---|
| 3 tablespoons olive oil | Sauce: |
| ⅙ teaspoon Chinese Five Spice | ¼ teaspoon sea salt |
| ¼ teaspoon pepper | ½ teaspoon garlic powder |
| ½ teaspoon sea salt | 1 tablespoon low-sodium soy sauce |
| 1 teaspoon pure sesame oil | ½ cup rice vinegar |
| 2 eggs | 5 tablespoons tomato paste |
| 1 cup almond flour | ⅛ teaspoon water |
| 2 pounds (907 g) pork, sliced into chunks | ½ cup sweetener of choice |
| For the Sweet and Sour | |

1. To make the dipping sauce, whisk all sauce ingredients together over medium heat, stirring 5 minutes. Simmer for uncovered 5 minutes till thickened.
2. Meanwhile, combine almond flour, five spice, pepper, and salt.
3. In another bowl, mix eggs with sesame oil.
4. Dredge pork in flour mixture and then in egg mixture. Shake any excess off before adding to air fryer cooking tray.
5. Select Roast. Set temperature to 340ºF (170ºC), and set time to 8 to 12 minutes.
6. Serve with sweet and sour dipping sauce!

## Italian-Style Pork Burgers

**Prep time: 10 minutes | Cook time: 15 minutes | Serves 4**

| | |
|---|---|
| 1 pound (454 g) ground pork | grated |
| Sea salt and ground black pepper, to taste | ¼ cup seasoned breadcrumbs |
| 1 tablespoon Italian herb mix | 1 egg |
| 1 small onion, chopped | 4 hamburger buns |
| 1 teaspoon garlic, minced | 4 teaspoons Dijon mustard |
| ¼ cup Parmesan cheese, | 4 tablespoons mayonnaise |

1. In a mixing bowl, thoroughly combine the pork, salt, pepper, herb, onion, garlic, Parmesan, breadcrumbs, and egg. Form the mixture into four patties.
2. Select Roast. Set temperature to 380ºF (195ºC), and set time to about 15 minutes or until cooked through; make sure to turn them over halfway through the cooking time.
3. Serve your burgers with hamburger buns, mustard, and mayonnaise. Enjoy!

## Breaded Pork Chops

**Prep time: 10 minutes | Cook time: 24 minutes | Serves 8**

| | |
|---|---|
| 1 teaspoon salt and pepper, divided | 2 tablespoons grated Parmesan cheese |
| ¼ teaspoon chili powder | ⅓ cup crushed cornflake crumbs |
| ½ teaspoon onion powder | ½ cup panko breadcrumbs |
| ½ teaspoon garlic powder | 1 beaten egg |
| 1¼ teaspoons sweet paprika | 6 center-cut boneless pork chops |

1. Ensure that your air fryer oven is preheated to 400ºF (205ºC). Spray the cooking tray with olive oil.
2. With ½ teaspoon salt and pepper, season both sides of pork chops.
3. Combine ¾ teaspoon salt with pepper, chili powder, onion powder, garlic powder, paprika, cornflake crumbs, panko breadcrumbs and Parmesan cheese.
4. Beat egg in another bowl.
5. Dip pork chops into the egg and then crumb mixture.
6. Add pork chops to the oven and spritz with olive oil. Select Roast, and set time to 12 minutes, making sure to flip over halfway through cooking process.
7. Only add 3 chops in at a time and repeat the process with the remaining pork chops.

Breaded Sirloin Chops, page 68

Country-Style Pork Belly, page 69

Pork Taquitos, page 79

Pork Chops with Orange Glaze, page 77

## Italian Herbed Pork Center Cut

**Prep time: 5 minutes | Cook time: 55 minutes | Serves 5**

2 pounds (907 g) pork center cut
2 tablespoons olive oil
1 tablespoon Italian herb mix

1 teaspoon red pepper flakes, crushed
Sea salt and freshly ground black pepper, to taste

1. Toss all ingredients in a lightly greased Air Fryer cooking tray.
2. Select Roast. Set temperature to 360ºF (180ºC), and set time to 55 minutes, turning it over halfway through the cooking time.
3. Serve warm and enjoy!

## Holiday Pork Belly

**Prep time: 5 minutes | Cook time: 20 minutes | Serves 5**

1 pound (454 g) pork belly
1 tablespoon tomato sauce
2 tablespoons rice

vinegar
1 teaspoon dried thyme
1 teaspoon dried rosemary

1. Toss all ingredients in a lightly greased Air Fryer cooking tray.
2. Select Roast. Set temperature to 320ºF (160ºC), and set time to 20 minutes. Now, turn it over and continue cooking for a further 25 minutes.
3. Serve warm and enjoy!

## Roasted Pork Loin

**Prep time: 10 minutes | Cook time: 25 minutes | Serves 6 to 8**

Balsamic vinegar
1 teaspoon parsley
½ teaspoon red pepper flakes
½ teaspoon garlic

powder
1 teaspoon pepper
1 teaspoon salt
2 pounds (907 g) pork loin

1. Sprinkle pork loin with seasonings and brush with vinegar.
2. Place pork in your air fryer oven. Select Roast. Set temperature to 340ºF (170ºC), and set time to 25 minutes.
3. Remove from air fryer and let it rest 10 minutes before slicing.

## Dijon Pork Loin

**Prep time: 10 minutes | Cook time: 55 minutes | Serves 4**

1½ pounds (680 g) pork top loin
1 tablespoon olive oil
1 tablespoon Dijon mustard
2 cloves garlic, crushed

1 tablespoon parsley
1 tablespoon coriander
½ teaspoon red pepper flakes, crushed
Kosher salt and ground black pepper, to taste

1. Toss all ingredients in a lightly greased Air Fryer cooking tray.
2. Select Roast. Set temperature to 360ºF (180ºC), and set time to 55 minutes, turning it over halfway through the cooking time.
3. Serve warm and enjoy!

## Rosemary Pork Shoulder Chops

**Prep time: 5 minutes | Cook time: 15 minutes | Serves 4**

1½ pounds (680 g) pork shoulder chops
2 tablespoons olive oil
Kosher salt and ground black pepper, to taste

2 sprigs rosemary, leaves picked and chopped
1 teaspoon garlic, pressed

1. Toss all ingredients in a lightly greased Air Fryer cooking tray.
2. Select Roast. Set temperature to 400ºF (205ºC), and set time to 15 minutes, turning them over halfway through the cooking time.
3. Bon appétit!

## Tortilla Chips Coated Pork Cutlets

**Prep time: 5 minutes | Cook time: 15 minutes | Serves 4**

1½ pounds (680 g) pork cutlets
Salt and ground black pepper, to taste
1 cup tortilla chips,

crushed
½ teaspoon cayenne pepper
2 tablespoons olive oil

1. Toss the pork cutlets with the remaining ingredients; place them in a lightly oiled Air Fryer cooking tray.
2. Select Roast. Set temperature to 400ºF (205ºC), and set time to 15 minutes, turning them over halfway through the cooking time.
3. Bon appétit!

## Bratwurst with Brussels Sprouts

**Prep time: 10 minutes | Cook time: 15 minutes | Serves 4**

1 pound (454 g) bratwurst wedges
1 pound (454 g) Brussels 1 teaspoon garlic, minced
sprouts 1 tablespoon mustard
1 large onion, cut into 2 tablespoons honey

1. Toss all ingredients in a lightly greased Air Fryer cooking tray.
2. Select Roast. Set temperature to 380ºF (195ºC), and set time to approximately 15 minutes, tossing the cooking tray halfway through the cooking time.
3. Bon appétit!

## Pork Chops with Orange Glaze

**Prep time: 5 minutes | Cook time: 15 minutes | Serves 3**

1 pound (454 g) rib pork juice, freshly squeezed
chops 1 teaspoon rosemary,
½ tablespoon butter, chopped
melted Sea salt and cayenne
2 tablespoons orange pepper, to taste

1. Toss all ingredients in a lightly greased Air Fryer cooking tray.
2. Select Roast. Set temperature to 400ºF (205ºC), and set time to 15 minutes, turning them over halfway through the cooking time.
3. Bon appétit!

## Buttery Country-Style Ribs

**Prep time: 10 minutes | Cook time: 35 minutes | Serves 5**

2 pounds (907 g) 1 teaspoon mustard
Country-style ribs powder
Coarse sea salt and 1 tablespoon butter,
ground black pepper, to melted
taste 1 teaspoon chili sauce
1 teaspoon smoked 4 tablespoons dry red
paprika wine

1. Toss all ingredients in a lightly greased Air Fryer cooking tray.
2. Select Roast. Set temperature to 350ºF (175ºC), and set time to 35 minutes, turning them over halfway through the cooking time.
3. Bon appétit!

## Bacon Salad with Croutons

**Prep time: 10 minutes | Cook time: 16 minutes | Serves 5**

1 pound (454 g) bacon, 2 tablespoons freshly
cut into thick slices squeezed lemon juice
1 head lettuce, torn into 2 garlic cloves, minced
leaves Coarse sea salt and
1 tablespoon fresh chive, ground black pepper, to
chopped taste
1 tablespoon fresh 1 teaspoon red pepper
tarragon, chopped flakes, crushed
1 tablespoon fresh 2 cups bread cubes
parsley, chopped

1. Place the bacon in the Air Fryer cooking tray. Then, cook the bacon at 400ºF (205ºC), and set time to approximately 10 minutes, tossing the cooking tray halfway through the cooking time; reserve.
2. Select Roast. Set temperature tot 390ºF (200ºC), and set time to approximately 6 minutes or until the bread is toasted.
3. Toss the remaining ingredients in a salad bowl; top your salad with the bacon and croutons. Bon appétit!

## Pork Tenderloin and Mixed Greens Salad

**Prep time: 10 minutes | Cook time: 5 minutes | Serves 4**

2 pounds (907 g) pork 6 cups mixed salad
tenderloin, cut into 1-inch greens
slices 1 red bell pepper, sliced
1 teaspoon olive oil 1 (8 ounce / 227g)
1 teaspoon dried package button
marjoram mushrooms, sliced
⅛ teaspoon freshly ⅓ cup low-sodium low-fat
ground black pepper vinaigrette dressing

1. In a medium bowl, mix the pork slices and olive oil. Toss to coat.
2. Sprinkle with the marjoram and pepper and rub these into the pork.
3. Select Roast. Roast the pork in the oven, in batches, for about 4 to 6 minutes, or until the pork reaches at least 145ºF (65ºC) on a meat thermometer.
4. Meanwhile, in a serving bowl, mix the salad greens, red bell pepper, and mushrooms. Toss gently.
5. When the pork is cooked, add the slices to the salad. Drizzle with the vinaigrette and toss gently. Serve immediately.

## Greek Souvlaki

**Prep time: 10 minutes | Cook time: 15 minutes | Serves 4**

1 tablespoon olive oil
½ teaspoon sweet paprika
1 pound (454 g) pork tenderloin, cubed
1 small lemon, freshly

juiced
1 eggplant, diced
2 bell peppers, diced
½ pound (227 g) fennel, diced

1. Toss all ingredients in a mixing bowl until well coated on all sides.
2. Thread the ingredients onto skewers and place them in the Air Fryer cooking tray.
3. Then, select Roast. Set temperature to 400ºF (205ºC), and set time to approximately 15 minutes, turning them over halfway through the cooking time.
4. Bon appétit!

## Pork Chops with Worcestershire Sauce

**Prep time: 5 minutes | Cook time: 16 minutes | Serves 2**

2 (10 ounce / 283-g) bone-in, center-cut pork chops, 1-inch thick
2 teaspoons

Worcestershire sauce
Salt and pepper, to taste
Cooking spray

1. Rub the Worcestershire sauce into both sides of pork chops.
2. Season with salt and pepper to taste.
3. Spray air fryer cooking tray with cooking spray and place the chops in cooking tray side by side.
4. Select Roast. Set temperature to 360ºF (180ºC), and set time to 16 to 20 minutes or until well done. Let it rest for 5 minutes before serving.

## Fall-Off-The-Bone Ribs with Zucchini

**Prep time: 10 minutes | Cook time: 37 minutes | Serves 4**

1½ pounds (680 g) pork loin ribs
2 cloves garlic, minced
1 tablespoon olive oil
4 tablespoons whiskey

1 teaspoon onion powder
Sea salt and ground black pepper, to taste
½ pound (227 g) zucchini, sliced

1. Toss the pork ribs with the garlic, olive oil, whiskey

and spices; place the ingredients in a lightly greased Air Fryer cooking tray.
2. Select Roast. Set temperature to 350ºF (175ºC), and set time to 25 minutes, turning them over halfway through the cooking time.
3. Top the pork ribs with the sliced zucchini and continue cooking for an additional 12 minutes. Serve immediately.
4. Bon appétit!

## Brown Sugar Pulled Pork Sliders

**Prep time: 10 minutes | Cook time: 55 minutes | Serves 4**

1 pound (454 g) pork shoulder
1 tablespoon olive oil
2 cloves garlic, minced
1 teaspoon cayenne pepper
1 tablespoon fresh sage, chopped

1 tablespoon fresh thyme, chopped
1 tablespoon brown sugar
2 tablespoons fish sauce
Kosher salt and freshly ground pepper, to taste
8 dinner rolls

1. Toss all ingredients, except for the dinner rolls, in a lightly greased Air Fryer cooking tray.
2. Select Roast. Set temperature to 360ºF (180ºC), and set time to 55 minutes, turning it over halfway through the cooking time.
3. Serve on dinner rolls and enjoy!

## Mustard Pork Tenderloin with Walnut

**Prep time: 10 minutes | Cook time: 14 minutes | Serves 4**

3 tablespoons low-sodium grainy mustard
2 teaspoons olive oil
¼ teaspoon dry mustard powder
1 (1-pound / 227-g) pork tenderloin, silverskin and

excess fat trimmed and discarded
2 slices low-sodium whole-wheat bread, crumbled
¼ cup ground walnuts
2 tablespoons cornstarch

1. In a small bowl, stir together the mustard, olive oil, and mustard powder. Spread this mixture over the pork.
2. On a plate, mix the bread crumbs, walnuts, and cornstarch. Dip the mustard-coated pork into the crumb mixture to coat.
3. Select Roast. Roast the pork for 12 to 16 minutes, or until it registers at least 145ºF (65ºC) on a meat thermometer. Slice to serve.

## Smoked Paprika Baby Back Ribs

**Prep time: 10 minutes | Cook time: 35 minutes | Serves 4**

1½ pounds (680 g) baby back ribs
2 tablespoons olive oil
1 teaspoon smoked paprika
1 teaspoon garlic powder
1 teaspoon onion powder
½ teaspoon ground

cumin
1 teaspoon mustard powder
1 teaspoon dried thyme
Coarse sea salt and freshly cracked black pepper, to season

1. Toss all ingredients in a lightly greased Air Fryer cooking tray.
2. Select Roast. Set temperature to 350ºF (175ºC), and set time to 35 minutes, turning them over halfway through the cooking time.
3. Bon appétit!

## Pork Loin Filets with Blue Cheese

**Prep time: 5 minutes | Cook time: 15 minutes | Serves 4**

1½ pounds (680 g) pork loin filets
Sea salt and ground black pepper, to taste
2 tablespoons olive oil

1 pound (454 g) mushrooms, sliced
2 ounces (57 g) blue cheese

1. Place the pork, salt, black pepper, and olive oil in a lightly greased Air Fryer cooking tray.
2. Select Roast. Set temperature to 400ºF (205ºC), and set time to 10 minutes, turning them over halfway through the cooking time.
3. Top the pork loin filets with the mushrooms. Continue to cook for about 5 minutes or longer. Top the warm pork with blue cheese.
4. Bon appétit!

## Pork Taquitos

**Prep time: 5 minutes | Cook time: 10 minutes | Serves 8**

1 juiced lime
10 whole-wheat tortillas
2½ cups shredded Mozzarella cheese

30 ounces (850.5 g) of cooked and shredded pork tenderloin

1. Ensure your air fryer oven is preheated to 380ºF (195ºC).
2. Drizzle pork with lime juice and gently mix.
3. Heat up tortillas in the microwave with a dampened paper towel to soften.
4. Add about 3 ounces of pork and ¼ cup of shredded cheese to each tortilla. Tightly roll them up.
5. Spray the air fryer cooking tray with a bit of olive oil.
6. Select Roast, and set time to 7 to 10 minutes till tortillas turn a slight golden color, making sure to flip halfway through cooking process.

## Apple Pork Tenderloin

**Prep time: 10 minutes | Cook time: 15 minutes | Serves 4**

1 (1-pound / 227-g) pork tenderloin, cut into 4 pieces
1 tablespoon apple butter
2 teaspoons olive oil
2 Granny Smith apples or

Jonagold apples, sliced
3 celery stalks, sliced
1 onion, sliced
½ teaspoon dried marjoram
⅓ cup apple juice

1. Rub each piece of pork with the apple butter and olive oil.
2. In a medium metal bowl, mix the pork, apples, celery, onion, marjoram, and apple juice.
3. Place the bowl into the oven and select Roast, and set time to 14 to 19 minutes, or until the pork reaches at least 145ºF (65ºC) on a meat thermometer and the apples and vegetables are tender. Stir once during cooking. Serve immediately.

## Greek Spice Pork Gyros

**Prep time: 10 minutes | Cook time: 55 minutes | Serves 4**

1 pound (454 g) pork shoulder
1 teaspoon smoked paprika
½ teaspoon onion powder
1 teaspoon garlic powder

½ teaspoon ground cumin
½ teaspoon ground bay leaf
Sea salt and ground black pepper, to taste
4 pitta bread, warmed

1. Toss the pork on all sides, top and bottom, with the spices. Place the pork in a lightly greased Air Fryer cooking tray.
2. Select Roast. Set temperature to 360ºF (180ºC), and set time to 55 minutes, turning it over halfway through the cooking time.
3. Shred the pork with two forks and serve on warmed pitta bread and some extra toppings of choice. Enjoy!

## Espresso-Lemon Pork Tenderloin

**Prep time: 10 minutes | Cook time: 10 minutes | Serves 4**

1 tablespoon packed brown sugar
2 teaspoons espresso powder
1 teaspoon ground paprika
½ teaspoon dried marjoram
1 tablespoon honey
1 tablespoon freshly squeezed lemon juice
2 teaspoons olive oil
1 (1-pound / 227-g) pork tenderloin

1. In a small bowl, mix the brown sugar, espresso powder, paprika, and marjoram.
2. Stir in the honey, lemon juice, and olive oil until well mixed.
3. Spread the honey mixture over the pork and let it stand for 10 minutes at room temperature.
4. Select Roast. Roast the tenderloin in the air fryer cooking tray for 9 to 11 minutes, or until the pork registers at least 145ºF (65ºC) on a meat thermometer. Slice the meat to serve.

## Ham and Cheese Roll-Ups

**Prep time: 10 minutes | Cook time: 15 minutes | Serves 12**

2 teaspoons raw honey
2 teaspoons dried parsley
1 tablespoon poppy seeds
½ cup melted coconut oil
salt and pepper to taste
¼ cup spicy brown mustard
9 slices of provolone cheese
10 ounces (283 g) of thinly sliced Black Forest Ham
1 tube of crescent rolls

1. Roll out dough into a rectangle. Spread 2 to 3 tablespoons of spicy mustard onto dough, then layer provolone cheese and ham slices.
2. Roll the filled dough up as tight as you can and slice into 12 to 15 pieces.
3. Melt coconut oil and mix with a pinch of salt and pepper, parsley, honey, and remaining mustard.
4. Brush mustard mixture over roll-ups and sprinkle with poppy seeds.
5. Grease air fryer cooking tray liberally with olive oil and add rollups.
6. Select Roast. Set temperature to 350ºF (175ºC), and set time to 15 minutes.
7. Serve!

## Caribbean-Style Pork Patties with Brioche

**Prep time: 10 minutes | Cook time: 15 minutes | Serves 4**

1 pound (454 g) ground pork
Kosher salt and ground black pepper, to taste
1 tablespoon fresh parsley, chopped
1 tablespoon fresh coriander, chopped
1 teaspoon habanero pepper, sliced
1 tablespoon teriyaki sauce
1 small onion, chopped
1 clove garlic, minced
4 brioche hamburger buns, lightly toasted

1. In a mixing bowl, thoroughly combine the pork and other ingredients except brioche hamburger buns. Then, roll the mixture into four patties.
2. Select Roast. Set temperature to 380ºF (195ºC), and set time to about 15 minutes or until cooked through; make sure to turn them over halfway through the cooking time.
3. Serve the patties with the brioche hamburger buns. Enjoy!

## Wiener Lemony Schnitzel

**Prep time: 10 minutes | Cook time: 14 minutes | Serves 4**

4 thin boneless pork loin chops
2 tablespoons lemon juice
½ cup flour
1 teaspoon salt
¼ teaspoon marjoram
1 cup plain breadcrumbs
2 eggs, beaten
Oil for misting or cooking spray
lemon wedges

1. Rub the lemon juice into all sides of pork chops.
2. Mix together the flour, salt, and marjoram.
3. Place flour mixture on a sheet of wax paper.
4. Place breadcrumbs on another sheet of wax paper.
5. Roll pork chops in flour, dip in beaten eggs, then roll in breadcrumbs. Mist all sides with oil or cooking spray.
6. Spray air fryer cooking tray with nonstick cooking spray and place pork chops in cooking tray.
7. Select Roast. Set temperature to 390ºF (200ºC), and set time to 7 minutes. Turn, mist again, and cook for another 7 or 8 minutes, until well done. Serve with lemon wedges.

# Pork and Veggie Skewers

**Prep time: 10 minutes | Cook time: 15 minutes | Serves 4**

1 pound (454 g) pork tenderloin, cubed
1 pound (454 g) bell peppers, diced
1 pound (454 g) eggplant, diced
1 tablespoon olive oil

1 tablespoon parsley, chopped
1 tablespoon cilantro, chopped
Sea salt and ground black pepper, to taste

1. Toss all ingredients in a mixing bowl until well coated on all sides.
2. Thread the ingredients onto skewers and place them in the Air Fryer cooking tray.
3. Then, select Roast. Set temperature to 400ºF (205ºC), and set time to approximately 15 minutes, turning them over halfway through the cooking time.
4. Bon appétit!

# Picnic Ham with Rice Vinegar

**Prep time: 5 minutes | Cook time: 45 minutes | Serves 4**

1½ pounds (680 g) picnic ham
2 tablespoons olive oil
2 garlic cloves, minced

2 tablespoons rice vinegar
1 tablespoon tamari sauce

1. Preheat your Air Fryer to 400ºF (205ºC), and set time to about 13 minutes.
2. Toss the ham with the remaining ingredients; wrap the ham in a piece of aluminum foil and lower it into the Air Fryer cooking tray.
3. Reduce the temperature to 375ºF (190ºC) and select Roast. Set time to 30 minutes.
4. Remove the foil, turn the temperature to 400ºF (205ºC), and continue to roast for an additional 15 minutes or until cooked through.
5. Bon appétit!

# Pork Cutlets with Aloha Salsa

**Prep time: 15 minutes | Cook time: 7 minutes | Serves 4**

2 eggs
2 tablespoons milk
¼ cup flour
¼ cup panko breadcrumbs
4 teaspoons sesame seeds
1 pound (454 g) boneless, thin pork cutlets (⅜- to ½-inch thick)
Lemon pepper and salt
¼ cup cornstarch
Oil for misting or cooking spray

For the Aloha Salsa:
1 cup fresh pineapple, chopped into small pieces
¼ cup red onion, finely chopped
¼ cup green or red bell pepper, chopped
½ teaspoon ground cinnamon
1 teaspoon low-sodium soy sauce
⅛ teaspoon crushed red pepper
⅛ teaspoon ground black pepper

1. In a medium bowl, stir together all ingredients for salsa. Cover and refrigerate while cooking pork.
2. Preheat air fryer oven to 390ºF (200ºC).
3. Beat together eggs and milk in shallow dish.
4. In another shallow dish, mix together the flour, panko, and sesame seeds.
5. Sprinkle pork cutlets with lemon pepper and salt to taste. Most lemon pepper seasoning contains salt, so go easy when adding extra.
6. Dip pork cutlets in cornstarch, egg mixture, and then panko coating. Spray both sides with oil or cooking spray.
7. Select Roast. Set temperature to 390ºF (200ºC), and set time to 3 minutes. Turn cutlets over, spraying both sides, and continue cooking for 4 to 6 minutes or until well done.
8. Serve fried cutlets with salsa on the side.

# Chapter 7 Fish and Seafood

## English Muffin Tuna Melts

**Prep time: 10 minutes | Cook time: 14 minutes | Serves 4**

1 pound (454 g) tuna, boneless and chopped
½ cup all-purpose flour
½ cup breadcrumbs
2 tablespoons buttermilk
2 eggs, whisked
Kosher salt and ground

black pepper, to taste
½ teaspoon cayenne pepper
1 tablespoon olive oil
4 Mozzarella cheese slices
4 English muffins

1. Mix all ingredients, except for the cheese and English muffins, in a bowl. Shape the mixture into four patties and place them in a lightly oiled Air Fryer cooking tray.
2. Select Broil. Set temperature to 400ºF (205ºC), and set time to about 14 minutes, turning them over halfway through the cooking time.
3. Place the cheese slices on the warm patties and serve on hamburger buns and enjoy!

## Sea Scallops

**Prep time: 5 minutes | Cook time: 16 minutes | Serves 4**

1½ pounds (680 g) sea scallops
Salt and pepper, to taste
2 eggs

½ cup flour
½ cup plain breadcrumbs
Oil for misting or cooking spray

1. Rinse scallops and remove the tough side muscle. Sprinkle to taste with salt and pepper.
2. Beat eggs together in a shallow dish. Place flour in a second shallow dish and breadcrumbs in a third.
3. Preheat air fryer oven to 390ºF (200ºC).
4. Dip scallops in flour, then eggs, and then roll in breadcrumbs. Mist with oil or cooking spray.
5. Place scallops in air fryer cooking tray in a single layer, leaving some space between. You should be able to cook about a dozen at a time.
6. Select Air Fry. Set temperature to 390ºF (200ºC), and set time to 6 to 8 minutes, watching carefully so as not to overcook. Scallops are done when they turn opaque all the way through. They will feel slightly firm when pressed with tines of a fork.
7. Repeat step 6 to cook the remaining scallops.

## Cod Fish Fingers

**Prep time: 10 minutes | Cook time: 10 minutes | Serves 4**

2 eggs
½ cup all-purpose flour
Sea salt and ground black pepper, to taste
½ teaspoon onion powder

¼ teaspoon garlic powder
¼ cup plain breadcrumbs
1½ tablespoons olive oil
1 pound (454 g) cod fish fillets, slice into pieces

1. In a mixing bowl, thoroughly combine the eggs, flour, and spices. In a separate bowl, thoroughly combine the breadcrumbs and olive oil.
2. Mix to combine well.
3. Now, dip the fish pieces into the flour mixture to coat; roll the fish pieces over the breadcrumb mixture until they are well coated on all sides.
4. Select Broil. Set temperature to 400ºF (205ºC), and set time to 10 minutes, turning them over halfway through the cooking time.
5. Bon appétit!

## Crumb Coated Fish Fillet

**Prep time: 10 minutes | Cook time: 6 minutes | Serves 4**

1 pound (454 g) fish fillets
½ teaspoon hot sauce
1 tablespoon coarse brown mustard
1 teaspoon Worcestershire sauce
Salt, to taste

For the Crumb Coating:
¾ cup panko breadcrumbs
¼ cup stone-ground cornmeal
¼ teaspoon salt
Oil for misting or cooking spray

1. Cut fish fillets crosswise into slices of 1-inch wide.
2. Mix the hot sauce, mustard, and Worcestershire sauce together to make a paste and rub on all sides of the fish. Season to taste with salt.
3. Mix crumb coating ingredients together and spread on a sheet of wax paper.
4. Roll the fish fillets in the crumb mixture.
5. Spray all sides with olive oil or cooking spray and place in air fryer cooking tray in a single layer.
6. Select Broil. Set temperature to 390ºF (200ºC), and set time to 6 to 9 minutes, until fish flakes easily.

## Tandoori Shrimp

**Prep time: 10 minutes | Cook time: 6 minutes | Serves 4**

1 pound (454 g) jumbo raw shrimp, peeled and deveined
1 tablespoon minced fresh ginger
3 cloves garlic, minced
¼ cup chopped fresh cilantro or parsley, plus more for garnish
1 teaspoon ground turmeric
1 teaspoon garam masala
1 teaspoon smoked paprika
1 teaspoon kosher salt
½ to 1 teaspoon cayenne pepper
2 tablespoons olive oil (for Paleo) or melted ghee
2 teaspoons fresh lemon juice

1.  In a large bowl, combine the shrimp, ginger, garlic, cilantro, turmeric, garam masala, paprika, salt, and cayenne. Toss well to coat. Add the oil or ghee and toss again. Marinate at room temperature for 15 minutes, or cover and refrigerate for up to 8 hours.
2.  Place the shrimp in a single layer in the air fryer cooking tray. Select Air Fry. Set temperature to 325ºF (165ºC), and set time to 6 minutes. Transfer the shrimp to a serving platter. Cover and let the shrimp finish cooking in the residual heat, about 5 minutes.
3.  Sprinkle the shrimp with the lemon juice and toss to coat. Garnish with additional cilantro and serve.

## Pesto White Fish Pie

**Prep time: 10 minutes | Cook time: 15 minutes | Serves 4**

2 tablespoons prepared pesto
¼ cup half-and-half
¼ cup grated Parmesan cheese
1 teaspoon kosher salt
1 teaspoon black pepper
Vegetable oil spray
1 (10 ounce / 283 g) package frozen chopped
spinach, thawed and squeezed dry
1 pound (454 g) firm white fish, cut into 2-inch chunks
½ cup cherry tomatoes, quartered
All-purpose flour
½ sheet frozen puff pastry, thawed

1.  In a small bowl, combine the pesto, half-and-half, Parmesan, salt, and pepper. Stir until well combined; set aside.
2.  Spray a 7 × 3-inch round heatproof pan with vegetable oil spray. Arrange the spinach evenly across the bottom of the pan. Top with the fish and tomatoes. Pour the pesto mixture evenly over

everything.

3.  On a lightly floured surface, roll the puff pastry sheet into a circle. Place the pastry on top of the pan and tuck it in around the edges of the pan. (Or, do what I do and stretch it with your hands and then pat it into place.)
4.  Place the pan in the air fryer cooking tray. Select Broil. Set temperature to 400ºF (205ºC), and set time to 15 minutes, or until the pastry is well browned. Let it stand 5 minutes before serving.

## One-Pot Shrimp Fried Rice

**Prep time: 15 minutes | Cook time: 25 minutes | Serves 4**

For the Shrimp:
1 teaspoon cornstarch
½ teaspoon kosher salt
¼ teaspoon black pepper
1 pound (454 g) jumbo raw shrimp, peeled and deveined
For the Rice:
2 cups cold cooked rice
1 cup frozen peas and carrots, thawed
¼ cup chopped green
onions (white and green parts)
3 tablespoons toasted sesame oil
1 tablespoon soy sauce
½ teaspoon kosher salt
1 teaspoon black pepper
For the Eggs:
2 large eggs, beaten
¼ teaspoon kosher salt
¼ teaspoon black pepper

Make the Shrimp
1.  In a small bowl, whisk together the cornstarch, salt, and pepper until well combined. Place the shrimp in a large bowl and sprinkle the seasoned cornstarch over. Toss until well coated; set aside.

Make the Rice
2.  In a 6 × 3-inch round heatproof pan, combine the rice, peas and carrots, green onions, sesame oil, soy sauce, salt, and pepper. Toss and stir until well combined.
3.  Place the pan in the air fryer cooking tray. Select Air Fry. Set temperature to 350ºF (175ºC), and set time to 15 minutes, stirring and tossing the rice halfway through the cooking time.
4.  Place the shrimp on top of the rice. Select Air Fry. Set temperature to 350ºF (175ºC), and set time to 5 minutes.

Make the Eggs
5.  In a medium bowl, beat the eggs with the salt and pepper.
6.  Open the oven and pour the eggs over the shrimp and rice mixture. Select Air Fry. Set temperature to 350ºF (175ºC), and set time to 5 minutes.
7.  Remove the pan from the oven. Stir to break up the rice and mix in the eggs and shrimp.

## Bang Bang Panko-Crusted Shrimp

**Prep time: 10 minutes | Cook time: 8 minutes | Serves 4**

1 teaspoon paprika
Montreal chicken seasoning
¾ cup panko bread crumbs
½ cup almond flour
1 egg white
1 pound (454 g) raw

shrimp (peeled and deveined)
For the Bang Bang Sauce:
¼ cup sweet chili sauce
2 tablespoons sriracha sauce
⅓ cup plain Greek yogurt

1. Ensure your air fryer oven is preheated to 400ºF (205ºC).
2. Season all shrimp with seasonings.
3. Add flour to one bowl, egg white in another, and breadcrumbs to a third.
4. Dip seasoned shrimp in flour, then egg whites, and then breadcrumbs.
5. Spray coated shrimp with olive oil and add to air fryer cooking tray.
6. Select Air Fry. Set temperature to 400ºF (205ºC), and set time to 4 minutes, flip, and cook for an additional 4 minutes.
7. To make the sauce, mix together all sauce ingredients until smooth.

## Bang Bang Shrimp

**Prep time: 10 minutes | Cook time: 14 minutes | Serves 4**

For the Sauce:
½ cup mayonnaise
¼ cup sweet chili sauce
2 to 4 tablespoons sriracha
1 teaspoon minced fresh ginger

For the Shrimp:
1 pound (454 g) jumbo raw shrimp, peeled and deveined
2 tablespoons cornstarch or rice flour
½ teaspoon kosher salt
Vegetable oil spray

Make the Sauce
1. In a large bowl, combine the mayonnaise, chili sauce, sriracha, and ginger. Stir until well combined. Remove half of the sauce to serve as a dipping sauce.
Make the Shrimp
2. Place the shrimp in a medium bowl. Sprinkle the cornstarch and salt over the shrimp and toss until well coated.
3. Place the shrimp in the air fryer cooking tray in a single layer. (If they won't fit in a single layer, set a rack or trivet on top of the bottom layer of shrimp

and place the rest of the shrimp on the rack.) Spray generously with vegetable oil spray. Select Air Fry. Set temperature to 350ºF (175ºC), and set time to 10 minutes, turning and spraying with additional oil spray halfway through the cooking time.
4. Remove the shrimp and toss in the bowl with half of the sauce. Place the shrimp back in the air fryer cooking tray. Select Air Fry. Set temperature to 350ºF (175ºC), and set time to an additional 4 to 5 minutes, or until the sauce has formed a glaze.
5. Serve the hot shrimp with the reserved sauce for dipping.

## Shrimp and Grits

**Prep time: 15 minutes | Cook time: 20 minutes | Serves 4**

1 pound (454 g) raw shelled shrimp, deveined
For the Marinade:
2 tablespoons lemon juice
2 tablespoons Worcestershire sauce
1 tablespoon olive oil
1 teaspoon Old Bay seasoning
½ teaspoon hot sauce
For the Grits:
¾ cup quick cooking grits

(not instant)
3 cups water
½ teaspoon salt
1 tablespoon butter
½ cup chopped green bell pepper
½ cup chopped celery
½ cup chopped onion
½ teaspoon oregano
¼ teaspoon Old Bay seasoning
2 ounces (57 g) sharp Cheddar cheese, grated

1. Stir together all marinade ingredients. Pour marinade over shrimp and set aside.
2. For grits, heat water and salt to boil in saucepan on stovetop. Stir in grits, lower heat to medium-low, and cook about 5 minutes or until thick and done.
3. Place butter, bell pepper, celery, and onion in air fryer cooking tray. Select Roast. Set temperature to 390ºF (200ºC), and set time to 2 minutes and stir. Roast for 6 or 7 minutes longer, until crisp-tender.
4. Add oregano and 1 teaspoon Old Bay to cooked vegetables. Stir in grits and cheese and select Broil. Set temperature to 390ºF (200ºC), and set time to 1 minute. Stir and broil 1 to 2 minutes longer to melt cheese.
5. Remove baking pan from air fryer. Cover with plate to keep warm while shrimp cooks.
6. Drain marinade from shrimp. Place shrimp in air fryer cooking tray and select Air Fry. Set temperature to 360ºF (180ºC), and set time to 3 minutes. Stir or shake cooking tray. Air fry 2 to 4 minutes, until done.
7. To serve, spoon grits onto plates and top with shrimp.

# Honey Mustard Salmon Fillet

**Prep time: 10 minutes | Cook time: 10 minutes | Serves 4**

4 (6 ounce / 170 g) skinless salmon fillets
3 tablespoons honey mustard
½ teaspoon dried thyme
½ teaspoon dried basil
¼ cup panko bread crumbs
⅓ cup crushed potato chips
2 tablespoons olive oil

1. Place the salmon on a plate. In a small bowl, combine the mustard, thyme, and basil, and spread evenly over the salmon.
2. In another small bowl, combine the bread crumbs and potato chips and mix well. Drizzle in the olive oil and mix until combined.
3. Place the salmon in the air fryer cooking tray and gently but firmly press the bread crumb mixture onto the top of each fillet.
4. Select Broil. Set time to 9 to 12 minutes or until the salmon reaches at least 145ºF (65ºC) on a meat thermometer and the topping is browned and crisp.

# Coconut-Shrimp Po' Boys

**Prep time: 10 minutes | Cook time: 12 minutes | Serves 4**

½ cup cornstarch
2 eggs
2 tablespoons milk
¾ cup shredded coconut
½ cup panko breadcrumbs
1 pound (454 g) shrimp, peeled and deveined
Old Bay seasoning, to taste
Oil for misting or cooking spray
2 large hoagie rolls
Honey mustard or light mayonnaise
1½ cups shredded lettuce
1 large tomato, thinly sliced

1. Place cornstarch in a shallow dish or plate.
2. In another shallow dish, beat together eggs and milk.
3. In a third dish mix the coconut and panko crumbs.
4. Sprinkle shrimp with Old Bay seasoning.
5. Dip shrimp in cornstarch to coat lightly, dip in egg mixture, shake off excess, and roll in coconut mixture to coat well.
6. Spray both sides of coated shrimp with oil or cooking spray.
7. Select Air Fry. Set temperature to 390ºF (200ºC), and set time to 5 minutes.
8. Repeat to cook remaining shrimp.
9. Split each hoagie lengthwise, leaving one long edge intact.
10. Place in air fryer cooking tray and cook at 390ºF (200ºC), and set time to 1 to 2 minutes or until heated through.
11. Remove buns, break apart, and place on 4 plates, cut side up.
12. Spread with honey mustard and/or mayonnaise.
13. Top with shredded lettuce, tomato slices, and coconut shrimp.

# Lush Stuffed Shrimp

**Prep time: 15 minutes | Cook time: 24 minutes | Serves 4**

16 tail-on shrimp, peeled and deveined (last tail section intact)
¾ cup crushed panko breadcrumbs
Oil for misting or cooking spray
For the Stuffing:
2 (6-ounce / 170-g) cans lump crabmeat
2 tablespoons chopped shallots
2 tablespoons chopped green onions
2 tablespoons chopped celery
2 tablespoons chopped green bell pepper
½ cup crushed saltine crackers
1 teaspoon Old Bay seasoning
1 teaspoon garlic powder
¼ teaspoon ground thyme
2 teaspoons dried parsley flakes
2 teaspoons fresh lemon juice
2 teaspoons Worcestershire sauce
1 egg, beaten

1. Rinse shrimp. Remove tail section (shell) from 4 shrimp, discard, and chop the meat finely.
2. To prepare the remaining 12 shrimp, cut a deep slit down the back side so that the meat lies open flat. Do not cut all the way through.
3. Preheat air fryer to 360ºF (180ºC).
4. Place chopped shrimp in a large bowl with all of the stuffing ingredients and stir to combine.
5. Divide stuffing into 12 portions, about 2 tablespoons each.
6. Place one stuffing portion onto the back of each shrimp and form into a ball or oblong shape. Press firmly so that stuffing sticks together and adheres to shrimp.
7. Gently roll each stuffed shrimp in panko crumbs and mist with oil or cooking spray.
8. Place 6 shrimp in air fryer cooking tray and select Air Fry. Set temperature to 360ºF (180ºC), and set time to 10 minutes. Mist with oil or spray and cook 2 minutes or longer until stuffing cooks through inside and is crispy outside.
9. Repeat step 8 to cook the remaining shrimp.

## Louisiana Shrimp Po Boy

**Prep time: 15 minutes | Cook time: 10 minutes | Serves 4**

1 teaspoon creole seasoning
8 slices of tomato
Lettuce leaves
¼ cup buttermilk
½ cup Louisiana Fish Fry
1 pound (454 g) deveined shrimp
For the Remoulade Sauce:
1 chopped green onion
1 teaspoon hot sauce
1 teaspoon Dijon mustard
½ teaspoon creole seasoning
1 teaspoon Worcestershire sauce
Juice of ½ a lemon
½ cup vegan mayo

1. Combine all sauce ingredients until well incorporated. Chill them while you cook shrimp.
2. Mix seasonings together and liberally season shrimp.
3. Add buttermilk to a bowl. Dip each shrimp into milk and place in a Ziploc bag. Chill half an hour to marinate.
4. Add fish fry to a bowl. Take shrimp from marinating bag and dip into fish fry, then add to air fryer.
5. Ensure your air fryer oven is preheated to 400ºF (205ºC).
6. Spray shrimp with olive oil. Select Air Fry. Set temperature to 400ºF (205ºC), and set time to 5 minutes, flip and then cook another 5 minutes.
7. Assemble "Keto" Po Boy by adding sauce to lettuce leaves, along with shrimp and tomato.

## Marinaded Crispy Shrimp

**Prep time: 10 minutes | Cook time: 16 minutes | Serves 4**

1 pound (454 g) shrimp, peeled, deveined, and butterflied (last tail section of shell intact)
For the Marinade:
1 can(5 ounce / 142g) evaporated milk
2 eggs, beaten
2 tablespoons white vinegar
1 tablespoon baking
powder
For the Coating:
1 cup crushed panko breadcrumbs
½ teaspoon paprika
½ teaspoon Old Bay seasoning
¼ teaspoon garlic powder
Oil for misting or cooking spray

1. Stir together all marinade ingredients until well mixed. Add shrimp and stir to coat. Refrigerate for 1 hour.
2. When ready to cook, preheat air fryer oven to 390ºF (200ºC).
3. Combine coating ingredients in a shallow dish.
4. Remove shrimp from marinade, roll in crumb mixture, and spray with olive oil or cooking spray.
5. Cooking in two batches, place shrimp in air fryer cooking tray in single layer, close but not overlapping. Select Air Fry. Set temperature to 390ºF (200ºC), and set time to 6 to 8 minutes, until light golden brown and crispy.
6. Repeat step 5 to cook the remaining shrimp.

## Cajun Fried Shrimp with Remoulade

**Prep time: 20 minutes | Cook time: 8 minutes | Serves 4**

For the Remoulade:
½ cup mayonnaise
1 green onion, finely chopped
1 clove garlic, minced
1 tablespoon sweet pickle relish
2 tablespoons Creole mustard
2 teaspoons fresh lemon juice
½ teaspoon hot pepper sauce
½ teaspoon Worcestershire sauce
¼ teaspoon smoked
paprika
¼ teaspoon kosher salt
For the Shrimp:
1½ cups buttermilk
1 large egg
3 teaspoons salt-free Cajun seasoning
1 pound (454 g) jumbo raw shrimp, peeled and deveined
2 cups finely ground cornmeal
Kosher salt and black pepper
Vegetable oil spray

Make the Remoulade
1. In a small bowl, stir together all the ingredients until well combined. Cover the sauce and chill until serving time.

Make the Shrimp
2. In a large bowl, whisk together the buttermilk, egg, and 1 teaspoon of the Cajun seasoning. Add the shrimp and toss gently to combine. Refrigerate for at least 15 minutes, or up to 1 hour.
3. Meanwhile, in a shallow dish, whisk together the remaining 2 teaspoons of Cajun seasoning, cornmeal, and salt and pepper to taste.
4. Spray the air fryer cooking tray with the vegetable oil spray. Dredge the shrimp in the cornmeal mixture until well coated. Shake off any excess and arrange the shrimp in the air fryer cooking tray. Spray with oil spray.
5. Select Air Fry. Set temperature to 350ºF (175ºC), and set time to 8 minutes, carefully turning and spraying the shrimp with the oil spray halfway through the cooking time.
6. Serve the shrimp with the remoulade.

## Butter and Parsley Calamari

**Prep time: 5 minutes | Cook time: 5 minutes | Serves 4**

1 pound (454 g) calamari, sliced into rings
2 tablespoons butter
2 tablespoons parsley, chopped
2 garlic cloves, minced
1 teaspoon cayenne pepper
Sea salt and freshly ground black pepper, to taste

1. Toss all ingredients in a lightly greased Air Fryer cooking tray.
2. Select Air Fry. Set temperature to 400ºF (205ºC), and set time to 5 minutes, tossing the cooking tray halfway through the cooking time.
3. Bon appétit!

## Healthy Tilapia Fillet and Chips

**Prep time: 5 minutes | Cook time: 15 minutes | Serves 3**

Old Bay seasoning
½ cup panko breadcrumbs
1 egg
2 tablespoons almond
flour
2 (4 to 6 ounces / 113 to 170 g) tilapia fillets
Frozen crinkle cut fries

1. Add almond flour to one bowl, beat egg in another bowl, and add panko breadcrumbs to the third bowl, mixed with Old Bay seasoning.
2. Dredge tilapia in flour, then egg, and then breadcrumbs.
3. Place coated fish in air fryer oven along with fries.
4. Select Broil. Set temperature to 390ºF (200ºC), and set time to 15 minutes.

## Breaded Coconut Shrimp

**Prep time: 5 minutes | Cook time: 10 minutes | Serves 3**

1 cup almond flour
1 cup panko breadcrumbs
1 tablespoon coconut flour
1 cup unsweetened, dried coconut
1 egg white
12 raw large shrimp

1. Put shrimp on paper towels to drain.
2. Mix coconut and panko breadcrumbs together. Then mix in coconut flour and almond flour in a different bowl. Set to the side.
3. Dip shrimp into flour mixture, then into egg white, and then into coconut mixture.
4. Place into air fryer cooking tray. Repeat with remaining shrimp.
5. Select Air Fry. Set temperature to 350ºF (175ºC), and set time to 10 minutes. Turn halfway through cooking process.

## Italian Cheesy Squid

**Prep time: 10 minutes | Cook time: 5 minutes | Serves 4**

1½ pounds (680 g) small squid tubes
2 tablespoons butter, melted
1 chili pepper, chopped
2 garlic cloves, minced
1 teaspoon red pepper flakes
Sea salt and ground
black pepper, to taste
¼ cup dry white wine
2 tablespoons fresh lemon juice
1 teaspoon Mediterranean herb mix
2 tablespoons Parmigiano-Reggiano cheese, grated

1. Toss all ingredients, except for the Parmigiano-Reggiano cheese, in a lightly greased Air Fryer cooking tray.
2. Select Air Fry. Set temperature to 400ºF (205ºC), and set time to 5 minutes, tossing the cooking tray halfway through the cooking time.
3. Top the warm squid with the cheese. Bon appétit!

## King Prawn Salad

**Prep time: 10 minutes | Cook time: 6 minutes | Serves 4**

1½ pounds (680 g) king prawns, peeled and deveined
Coarse sea salt and ground black pepper, to taste
1 tablespoon fresh lemon juice
1 cup mayonnaise
1 teaspoon Dijon mustard
1 tablespoon fresh parsley, roughly chopped
1 teaspoon fresh dill, minced
1 shallot, chopped

1. Toss the prawns with the salt and black pepper in a lightly greased Air Fryer cooking tray.
2. Select Air Fry. Set temperature to 400ºF (205ºC), and set time to 6 minutes, tossing the cooking tray halfway through the cooking time.
3. Add the prawns to a salad bowl; add in the remaining ingredients and stir to combine well.
4. Bon appétit!

## Peppercorn Halibut Steaks

**Prep time: 5 minutes | Cook time: 12 minutes | Serves 4**

1 pound (454 g) halibut steaks
¼ cup butter
Sea salt, to taste
2 tablespoons fresh

chives, chopped
1 teaspoon garlic, minced
1 teaspoon mixed peppercorns, ground

1. Toss the halibut steaks with the rest of the ingredients and place them in a lightly oiled Air Fryer cooking tray.
2. Select Broil. Set temperature to 400ºF (205ºC), and set time to about 12 minutes, turning them over halfway through the cooking time.
3. Bon appétit!

## Lemon Shrimp with Broccoli

**Prep time: 10 minutes | Cook time: 6 minutes | Serves 4**

1 pound (454 g) raw shrimp, peeled and deveined
½ pound (227 g) broccoli florets
1 tablespoon olive oil
1 garlic clove, minced

2 tablespoons freshly squeezed lemon juice
Coarse sea salt and ground black pepper, to taste
1 teaspoon paprika

1. Toss all ingredients in a lightly greased Air Fryer cooking tray.
2. Select Air Fry. Set temperature to 400ºF (205ºC), and set time to 6 minutes, tossing the cooking tray halfway through the cooking time.
3. Bon appétit!

## Swordfish Steaks

**Prep time: 10 minutes | Cook time: 10 minutes | Serves 4**

1 pound (454 g) swordfish steaks
2 tablespoons olive oil
2 teaspoons tamari sauce
Salt and freshly ground

pepper, to taste
¼ cup dry red wine
2 sprigs rosemary
1 sprig thyme
1 tablespoon grated lemon rind

1. Toss the swordfish steaks with the remaining ingredients in a ceramic dish; cover and let it marinate in your refrigerator for about 2 hours.

2. Then, discard the marinade and place the fish in a lightly oiled Air Fryer cooking tray.
3. Select Broil. Set temperature to 400ºF (205ºC), and set time to about 10 minutes, turning them over halfway through the cooking time.
4. Bon appétit!

## Tilapia Fillet Nuggets

**Prep time: 10 minutes | Cook time: 10 minutes | Serves 4**

1½ pounds (680 g) tilapia fillets, cut into 1½-inch pieces
1 tablespoon dried thyme
1 tablespoon dried oregano
1 tablespoon Dijon

mustard
2 tablespoons olive oil
1½ cups all-purpose flour
Sea salt and ground black pepper, to taste
½ teaspoon baking powder

1. Pat the fish dry with kitchen towels.
2. In a mixing bowl, thoroughly combine all remaining ingredients until well mixed. Now, dip the fish pieces into the batter to coat.
3. Select Broil. Set temperature to 400ºF (205ºC), and set time to 10 minutes, shaking the cooking tray halfway through the cooking time.
4. Bon appétit!

## Restaurant-Style Fried Calamari Rings

**Prep time: 10 minutes | Cook time: 5 minutes | Serves 4**

1 cup all-purpose flour
½ cup tortilla chips, crushed
1 teaspoon mustard powder
1 tablespoon dried parsley
Sea salt and freshly

ground black pepper, to taste
1 teaspoon cayenne pepper
2 tablespoons olive oil
1 pound (454 g) calamari, sliced into rings

1. In a mixing bowl, thoroughly combine the flour, tortilla chips, spices, and olive oil. Mix to combine well.
2. Now, dip your calamari into the flour mixture to coat.
3. Select Air Fry. Set temperature to 400ºF (205ºC), and set time to 5 minutes, turning them over halfway through the cooking time.
4. Bon appétit!

Sea Scallops, page 83

Marinaded Crispy Shrimp, page 87

Herb Salmon Fillets, page 95

Cod Fish Fingers, page 83

## Halibut Burgers

**Prep time: 10 minutes | Cook time: 14 minutes | Serves 4**

1 pound (454 g) halibut, chopped
2 garlic cloves, crushed
4 tablespoons scallions, chopped
Sea salt and ground
black pepper, to taste
1 teaspoon smoked paprika
A pinch of grated nutmeg
1 tablespoon olive oil
4 hamburger buns

1. Mix all ingredients, except for the hamburger buns, in a bowl. Shape the mixture into four patties and place them in a lightly oiled Air Fryer cooking tray.
2. Select Broil. Set temperature to 400ºF (205ºC), and set time to about 14 minutes, turning them over halfway through the cooking time.
3. Serve on hamburger buns and enjoy!

## Smoked Paprika Pollock

**Prep time: 10 minutes | Cook time: 14 minutes | Serves 4**

1 pound (454 g) pollock, chopped
1 teaspoon chili sauce
Sea salt and ground
black pepper, to taste
4 tablespoons all-
purpose
1 teaspoon smoked paprika
2 tablespoons olive oil
4 ciabatta buns

1. Mix all ingredients, except for the ciabatta buns, in a bowl. Shape the mixture into four patties and place them in a lightly oiled Air Fryer cooking tray.
2. Select Broil. Set temperature to 400ºF (205ºC), and set time to about 14 minutes, turning them over halfway through the cooking time.
3. Serve on ciabatta buns and enjoy!

## Coconut Shrimp

**Prep time: 10 minutes | Cook time: 9 minutes | Serves 4**

½ cup whole-wheat flour
1 cup coconut, shredded
¼ cup buttermilk
2 tablespoons olive oil
2 garlic cloves, crushed
1 tablespoon fresh lemon
juice
Sea salt and red pepper flakes, to taste
1½ pounds (680 g) shrimp, peeled and deveined

1. Mix the flour, coconut, buttermilk, olive oil, garlic, lemon juice, salt, and red pepper in a mixing bowl.

2. Dip the shrimp in the batter and place them in a well-greased Air Fryer cooking tray.
3. Select Air Fry. Set temperature to 400ºF (205ºC), and set time to 9 minutes, tossing the cooking tray halfway through the cooking time.
4. Bon appétit!

## Authentic Mediterranean Calamari

**Prep time: 10 minutes | Cook time: 5 minutes | Serves 4**

1 pound (454 g) calamari, sliced into rings
2 garlic cloves, minced
1 teaspoon red pepper flakes
2 tablespoons dry white wine
2 tablespoons olive oil
2 tablespoons fresh
lemon juice
1 teaspoon basil, chopped
1 teaspoon dill, chopped
1 teaspoon parsley, chopped
Coarse sea salt and freshly cracked black pepper, to taste

1. Toss all ingredients in a lightly greased Air Fryer cooking tray.
2. Select Air Fry. Set temperature to 400ºF (205ºC), and set time to 5 minutes, tossing the cooking tray halfway through the cooking time.
3. Bon appétit!

## Lobster Tail with Butter and Spring Onions

**Prep time: 5 minutes | Cook time: 8 minutes | Serves 4**

1 pound (454 g) lobster tails
4 tablespoons butter, room temperature
2 garlic cloves, minced
Coarse sea salt and
freshly cracked black pepper, to taste
4 tablespoons springs onions
1 tablespoon fresh lime juice

1. Butterfly the lobster tails by cutting through the shell and place them in a lightly oiled air fryer cooking tray.
2. In a mixing bowl, thoroughly combine the remaining ingredients.
3. Now, spread ½ of the butter mixture over the top of the lobster meat. Select Air Fry. Set temperature to 380ºF (195ºC), and set time to 4 minutes.
4. After that, spread another ½ of the butter mixture on top; continue to cook for a further 4 minutes.
5. Bon appétit!

## Mahi-Mahi Fillets

**Prep time: 10 minutes | Cook time: 14 minutes | Serves 4**

| | |
|---|---|
| 1 pound (454 g) mahi-mahi fillets | ground black pepper, to taste |
| 2 tablespoons butter, at room temperature | 1 teaspoon smoked paprika |
| 2 tablespoons fresh lemon juice | 1 teaspoon garlic, minced |
| | 1 teaspoon dried basil |
| Kosher salt and freshly | 1 teaspoon dried oregano |

1. Toss the fish fillets with the remaining ingredients and place them in a lightly oiled Air Fryer cooking tray.
2. Select Broil. Set temperature to 400ºF (205ºC), and set time to about 14 minutes, turning them over halfway through the cooking time.
3. Bon appétit!

## Codfish Fillet Tacos

**Prep time: 10 minutes | Cook time: 14 minutes | Serves 4**

| | |
|---|---|
| 1 pound (454 g) codfish fillets | mayonnaise |
| 1 tablespoon olive oil | 1 teaspoon mustard |
| 1 avocado, pitted, peeled and mashed | 1 shallot, chopped |
| | 1 habanero pepper, chopped |
| 4 tablespoons | 8 small corn tortillas |

1. Toss the fish fillets with the olive oil; place them in a lightly oiled Air Fryer cooking tray.
2. Select Broil. Set temperature to 400ºF (205ºC), and set time to about 14 minutes, turning them over halfway through the cooking time.
3. Assemble your tacos with the chopped fish and remaining ingredients and serve warm. Bon appétit!

## Cilantro Garlic Swordfish Steak

**Prep time: 10 minutes | Cook time: 10 minutes | Serves 4**

| | |
|---|---|
| 1 pound (454 g) swordfish steaks | 1 tablespoon fresh cilantro, roughly chopped |
| 4 garlic cloves, peeled | 1 teaspoon Spanish paprika |
| 4 tablespoons olive oil | |
| 2 tablespoons fresh lemon juice, more for later | Sea salt and ground black pepper, to taste |

1. Toss the swordfish steaks with the remaining ingredients and place them in a lightly oiled Air Fryer cooking tray.
2. Select Broil. Set temperature to 400ºF (205ºC), and set time to about 10 minutes, turning them over halfway through the cooking time.
3. Bon appétit!

## Chili and Paprika Squid with Capers

**Prep time: 10 minutes | Cook time: 5 minutes | Serves 5**

| | |
|---|---|
| 1½ pounds (680 g) squid, cut into pieces | 1 tablespoon coriander, chopped |
| 1 chili pepper, chopped | 2 tablespoons parsley, chopped |
| 1 small lemon, squeezed | 1 teaspoon sweet paprika |
| 2 tablespoons olive oil | |
| 1 tablespoon capers, drained | Sea salt and ground black pepper, to taste |
| 2 garlic cloves, minced | |

1. Toss all ingredients in a lightly greased Air Fryer cooking tray.
2. Select Air Fry. Set temperature to 400ºF (205ºC), and set time to 5 minutes, tossing the cooking tray halfway through the cooking time.
3. Bon appétit!

## Buttermilk Tilapia Fillet

**Prep time: 10 minutes | Cook time: 10 minutes | Serves 4**

| | |
|---|---|
| ½ cup all-purpose flour | black pepper, to taste |
| 1 large egg | ½ teaspoon cayenne pepper |
| 2 tablespoons buttermilk | |
| ½ cup crackers, crushed | 1 pound (454 g) tilapia fillets, cut into strips |
| 1 teaspoon garlic powder | |
| Sea salt and ground | |

1. In a shallow bowl, place the flour. Whisk the egg and buttermilk in a second bowl, and mix the crushed crackers and spices in a third bowl.
2. Dip the fish strips in the flour mixture, then in the whisked eggs; finally, roll the fish strips over the cracker mixture until they are well coated on all sides.
3. Arrange the fish sticks in the air fryer cooking tray.
4. Select Broil. Set temperature to 400ºF (205ºC), and set time to about 10 minutes, shaking the cooking tray halfway through the cooking time.
5. Bon appétit!

## Jumbo Shrimp with Cilantro

**Prep time: 5 minutes | Cook time: 8 minutes | Serves 4**

| | |
|---|---|
| 1 pound (454 g) jumbo shrimp | 2 tablespoons fresh cilantro, chopped |
| 2 tablespoons butter, at room temperature | 2 tablespoons fresh chives, chopped |
| Coarse sea salt and lemon pepper, to taste | 2 garlic cloves, crushed |

1. Toss all ingredients in a lightly greased Air Fryer cooking tray.
2. Select Air Fry. Set temperature to 400ºF (205ºC), and set time to 8 minutes, tossing the cooking tray halfway through the cooking time.
3. Bon appétit!

## Sea Scallops with Dry White Wine

**Prep time: 5 minutes | Cook time: 7 minutes | Serves 4**

| | |
|---|---|
| 1½ pounds (680 g) sea scallops | Sea salt and ground black pepper, to season |
| 4 tablespoons butter, melted | 2 rosemary sprigs, leaves picked and chopped |
| 1 tablespoon garlic, minced | 4 tablespoons dry white wine |

1. Toss all ingredients in a lightly greased Air Fryer cooking tray.
2. Select Air Fry. Set temperature to 400ºF (205ºC), and set time to 7 minutes, tossing the cooking tray halfway through the cooking time.
3. Bon appétit!

## Salmon Patties

**Prep time: 10 minutes | Cook time: 7 minutes | Serves 4**

| | |
|---|---|
| 1 tablespoon olive oil | 1 egg |
| 1 tablespoon ghee | 1 cup almond flour |
| ¼ teaspoon salt | 1 can wild Alaskan pink salmon |
| ⅛ teaspoon pepper | |

1. Drain can of salmon into a bowl and keep liquid. Discard skin and bones.
2. Add ghee, salt, pepper, and egg to salmon, mixing well with hands to incorporate. Make patties.
3. Dredge in flour and remaining egg. If it seems dry, spoon reserved salmon liquid from the can onto patties.
4. Add patties to air fryer oven and spray with olive oil. Select Broil. Set temperature to 378ºF (190ºC), and set time to 7 minutes, making sure to flip once during cooking process.

## Chili Calamari

**Prep time: 10 minutes | Cook time: 5 minutes | Serves 4**

| | |
|---|---|
| ½ cup milk | ground black pepper, to taste |
| 1 cup all-purpose flour | 1 teaspoon paprika |
| 2 tablespoons olive oil | 1 red chili, minced |
| 1 teaspoon turmeric powder | 1 pound (454 g) calamari, cut into rings |
| Sea salt flakes and | |

1. In a mixing bowl, thoroughly combine the milk, flour, olive oil, turmeric powder, salt, black pepper, paprika, and red chili. Mix to combine well.
2. Now, dip your calamari into the flour mixture to coat.
3. Select Air Fry. Set temperature to 400ºF (205ºC), and set time to 5 minutes, turning them over halfway through the cooking time.
4. Bon appétit!

## Asian Tuna Steak

**Prep time: 10 minutes | Cook time: 9 minutes | Serves 4**

| | |
|---|---|
| 4 small tuna steaks | ginger |
| 2 tablespoons low-sodium soy sauce | ⅛ teaspoon pepper |
| 2 teaspoons sesame oil | 1 stalk lemongrass, bent in half |
| 2 teaspoons rice wine vinegar | 3 tablespoons lemon juice |
| 1 teaspoon grated fresh | |

1. Place the tuna steaks on a plate.
2. In a small bowl, combine the soy sauce, sesame oil, rice wine vinegar, and ginger, and mix well. Pour this mixture over the tuna and marinate for 10 minutes. Rub the soy sauce mixture gently into both sides of the tuna. Sprinkle with the pepper.
3. Place the lemongrass on the air fryer cooking tray and top with the steaks. Put the lemon juice and 1 tablespoon water in the pan below the cooking tray.
4. Select Broil. Set time to 8 to 10 minutes or until the tuna registers at least 145ºF (65ºC). Discard the lemongrass and serve the tuna.

## Mustard Calamari

**Prep time: 5 minutes | Cook time: 5 minutes | Serves 4**

2 cups flour
Sea salt and ground black pepper, to taste
1 teaspoon garlic, minced

1 tablespoon mustard
2 tablespoons olive oil
1 pound (454 g) calamari, sliced into rings

1. In a mixing bowl, thoroughly combine the flour, salt, black pepper, garlic, mustard, and, and olive oil. Mix to combine well.
2. Now, dip your calamari into the flour mixture to coat.
3. Select Air Fry. Set temperature to 400ºF (205ºC), and set time to 5 minutes, turning them over halfway through the cooking time.
4. Bon appétit!

## Calamari with Garlic and Sherry Wine

**Prep time: 10 minutes | Cook time: 5 minutes | Serves 4**

1 pound (454 g) calamari, sliced into rings
2 tablespoons butter, melted
4 garlic cloves, smashed
2 tablespoons sherry wine

2 tablespoons fresh lemon juice
Coarse sea salt and ground black pepper, to taste
1 teaspoon paprika
1 teaspoon dried oregano

1. Toss all ingredients in a lightly greased Air Fryer cooking tray.
2. Select Air Fry. Set temperature to 400ºF (205ºC), and set time to 5 minutes, tossing the cooking tray halfway through the cooking time.
3. Bon appétit!

## Old-Fashioned Fish Salad

**Prep time: 10 minutes | Cook time: 12 minutes | Serves 4**

1 pound (454 g) salmon fillets
Sea salt and ground black pepper, to taste
2 tablespoons olive oil
2 garlic cloves, minced
1 bell pepper, sliced

1 shallot, chopped
½ cup Kalamata olives, pitted and sliced
½ lemon, juiced
1 teaspoon Aleppo pepper, minced

1. Toss the salmon fillets with the salt, black pepper, and olive oil; place them in a lightly oiled Air Fryer cooking tray.
2. Select Broil. Set temperature to 380ºF (195ºC), and set time to about 12 minutes, turning them over halfway through the cooking time.
3. Chop the salmon fillets using two forks and add them to a salad bowl; add in the remaining ingredients and toss to combine.
4. Bon appétit!

## Exotic Fried Prawns

**Prep time: 10 minutes | Cook time: 9 minutes | Serves 4**

1½ pounds (680 g) prawns, peeled and deveined
2 garlic cloves, minced
2 tablespoons fresh chives, chopped
½ cup whole-wheat flour
½ teaspoon sweet

paprika
1 teaspoon hot paprika
Salt and freshly ground black pepper, to taste
2 tablespoons coconut oil
2 tablespoons lemon juice

1. Toss all ingredients in a lightly greased Air Fryer cooking tray.
2. Select Air Fry. Set temperature to 400ºF (205ºC), and set time to 9 minutes, tossing the cooking tray halfway through the cooking time.
3. Bon appétit!

## Greek Monkfish Fillet Pita

**Prep time: 10 minutes | Cook time: 14 minutes | Serves 4**

1 pound (454 g) monkfish fillets
1 tablespoon olive oil
Sea salt and ground black pepper, to taste
1 teaspoon cayenne pepper

4 tablespoons coleslaw
1 avocado, pitted, peeled and diced
1 tablespoon fresh parsley, chopped
4 (6½ inch) Greek pitas, warmed

1. Toss the fish fillets with the olive oil; place them in a lightly oiled Air Fryer cooking tray.
2. Select Broil. Set temperature to 400ºF (205ºC), and set time to about 14 minutes, turning them over halfway through the cooking time.
3. Assemble your pitas with the chopped fish and remaining ingredients and serve warm. Bon appétit!

## Italian-Style Sea Bass

**Prep time: 5 minutes | Cook time: 10 minutes | Serves 4**

1 pound (454 g) sea bass
2 garlic cloves, minced
2 tablespoons olive oil
1 tablespoon Italian
seasoning mix
Sea salt and ground
black pepper, to taste
¼ cup dry white wine

1. Toss the fish with the remaining ingredients; place them in a lightly oiled Air Fryer cooking tray.
2. Select Broil. Set temperature to 400ºF (205ºC), and set time to about 10 minutes, turning them over halfway through the cooking time.
3. Bon appétit!

## Italian Monkfish Fingers

**Prep time: 10 minutes | Cook time: 10 minutes | Serves 4**

½ cup all-purpose flour
Sea salt and ground
black pepper, to taste
1 teaspoon cayenne
pepper
½ teaspoon onion
powder
1 tablespoon Italian
parsley, chopped
1 teaspoon garlic powder
1 egg, whisked
½ cup Pecorino Romano
cheese, grated
1 pound (454 g)
monkfish, sliced into
strips

1. In a shallow bowl, mix the flour, spices, egg, and cheese. Dip the fish strips in the batter until they are well coated on all sides.
2. Arrange the fish strips in the Air Fryer cooking tray.
3. Select Broil. Set temperature to 400ºF (205ºC), and set time to about 10 minutes, shaking the cooking tray halfway through the cooking time.
4. Bon appétit!

## Shrimp Salad Sandwich

**Prep time: 15 minutes | Cook time: 6 minutes | Serves 4**

1 pound (454 g) shrimp,
peeled and chilled
1 teaspoon olive oil
1 stalk celery, sliced
1 English cucumber,
sliced
1 shallot, sliced
1 tablespoon fresh dill,
roughly chopped
1 tablespoon fresh
parsley, roughly chopped
1 tablespoon fresh lime
juice
1 tablespoon apple cider
vinegar
½ cup mayonnaise
1 teaspoon Creole
seasoning mix

1½ teaspoons Dijon
mustard
Coarse sea salt and
lemon pepper, to taste
4 hoagie rolls

1. Toss the shrimp and olive oil in the Air Fryer cooking tray.
2. Select Broil. Set temperature to 400ºF (204ºC), and set time to 6 minutes, tossing the cooking tray halfway through the cooking time.
3. Place the shrimp in a mixing bowl along with the remaining ingredients; toss to combine and serve on the prepared hoagie rolls.
4. Bon appétit!

## Chimichurri Mackerel Fillets

**Prep time: 5 minutes | Cook time: 14 minutes | Serves 4**

1 tablespoon olive oil, or
more to taste
1½ pounds (680 g)
mackerel fillets
Sea salt and ground
black pepper, taste
2 tablespoons parsley
2 garlic cloves, minced
2 tablespoons fresh lime
juice

1. Toss the fish fillets with the remaining ingredients and place them in a lightly oiled Air Fryer cooking tray.
2. Select Broil. Set temperature to 400ºF (205ºC), and set time to about 14 minutes, turning them over halfway through the cooking time.
3. Bon appétit!

## Herb Salmon Fillets

**Prep time: 10 minutes | Cook time: 12 minutes | Serves 4**

1½ pounds (680 g)
salmon fillets
2 sprigs fresh rosemary
1 tablespoon fresh basil
1 tablespoon fresh thyme
1 tablespoon fresh dill
1 small lemon, juiced
2 tablespoons olive oil
Sea salt and ground
black pepper, to taste
1 teaspoon stone-ground
mustard
2 cloves garlic, chopped

1. Toss the salmon with the remaining ingredients; place them in a lightly oiled Air Fryer cooking tray.
2. Select Broil. Set temperature to 380ºF (195ºC), and set time to about 12 minutes, turning them over halfway through the cooking time.
3. Serve immediately and enjoy!

## Tilapia Fish Fillets Burgers

**Prep time: 10 minutes | Cook time: 14 minutes | Serves 4**

| | |
|---|---|
| 1 pound (454 g) tilapia fish fillets, chopped | 2 garlic cloves, minced |
| ½ cup breadcrumbs | 1 tablespoon olive oil |
| 4 tablespoons shallots, chopped | 8 dinner rolls |
| | 8 slices Provolone cheese |

1. Mix all ingredients, except for the dinner rolls and cheese, in a bowl. Shape the mixture into four patties and place them in a lightly oiled Air Fryer cooking tray.
2. Select Broil. Set temperature to 400ºF (205ºC), and set time to about 14 minutes, turning them over halfway through the cooking time.
3. Serve with the cheese and dinner rolls. Enjoy!

## Tiger Prawns with Sherry Wine

**Prep time: 10 minutes | Cook time: 9 minutes | Serves 4**

| | |
|---|---|
| 1½ pounds (680 g) tiger prawns, peeled and deveined | seasoning |
| 1 tablespoon coconut oil | Coarse sea salt and ground black pepper, to taste |
| 1 teaspoon garlic, crushed | ¼ cup sherry wine |
| 1 teaspoon Old Bay | 1 teaspoon Dijon mustard |

1. Toss all ingredients in a lightly greased Air Fryer cooking tray.
2. Select Air Fry. Set temperature to 400ºF (205ºC), and set time to 9 minutes, tossing the cooking tray halfway through the cooking time.
3. Bon appétit!

## Tuna Salad with a Twist

**Prep time: 10 minutes | Cook time: 10 minutes | Serves 4**

| | |
|---|---|
| 1 pound (454 g) fresh tuna steak | 1 small onion, thinly sliced |
| Sea salt and ground black pepper, to taste | 1 carrot, julienned |
| 2 tablespoons fresh lemon juice | 2 cups baby spinach |
| | 2 tablespoons parsley, roughly chopped |

1. Toss the fish with the salt and black pepper; place your tuna in a lightly oiled Air Fryer cooking tray.

2. Select Broil. Set temperature to 400ºF (205ºC), and set time to about 10 minutes, turning it over halfway through the cooking time.
3. Chop your tuna with two forks and add in the remaining ingredients; stir to combine and serve well-chilled.
4. Bon appétit!

## Old Bay Calamari

**Prep time: 10 minutes | Cook time: 15 minutes | Serves 6 to 8**

| | |
|---|---|
| 1-2 pinches of pepper | ½ cup semolina flour |
| ½ teaspoon salt | ½ cup almond flour |
| ½ teaspoon Old Bay seasoning | 5-6 cups olive oil |
| ⅓ cup plain cornmeal | 1½ pounds (680 g) baby squid |

1. Rinse squid in cold water and slice tentacles, keeping just ¼-inch of the hood in one piece.
2. Combine 1-2 pinches of pepper, salt, Old Bay seasoning, cornmeal, and both flours together. Dredge squid pieces into flour mixture and place into the oven. Spray liberally with olive oil.
3. Select Air Fry. Set temperature to 345ºF (175ºC), and set time to 15 minutes, till the coating turns a golden brown.

## Sea Scallop Salad

**Prep time: 10 minutes | Cook time: 7 minutes | Serves 4**

| | |
|---|---|
| 1½ pounds (680 g) sea scallops | 2 garlic cloves, minced |
| Sea salt and ground black pepper, to taste | 2 teaspoons fresh tarragon, minced |
| 2 tablespoons olive oil | 1 teaspoon Dijon mustard |
| 1 tablespoon balsamic vinegar | 1 cup mixed baby greens |
| | 1 small tomato, diced |

1. Toss the scallops, salt, and black pepper in a lightly greased Air Fryer cooking tray.
2. Select Air Fry. Set temperature to 400ºF (205ºC), and set time to 7 minutes, tossing the cooking tray halfway through the cooking time.
3. Toss the scallops with the remaining ingredients and serve at room temperature or well-chilled.
4. Bon appétit!

# Orange Roughy Fillets

**Prep time: 5 minutes | Cook time: 10 minutes | Serves 4**

1 pound (454 g) orange roughy fillets
2 tablespoons butter

2 cloves garlic, minced
Sea salt and red pepper flakes, to taste

1. Toss the fish fillets with the remaining ingredients and place them in a lightly oiled Air Fryer cooking tray.
2. Select Broil. Set temperature to 400ºF (205ºC), and set time to about 10 minutes, turning them over halfway through the cooking time.
3. Bon appétit!

# Tangy Butter Sea Scallops

**Prep time: 5 minutes | Cook time: 7 minutes | Serves 4**

1 pound (454 g) sea scallops
2 tablespoons butter, room temperature
2 tablespoons lemon juice

2 garlic cloves, crushed
Salt and fresh ground black pepper to taste
¼ cup dry white wine

1. Toss all ingredients in a lightly greased Air Fryer cooking tray.
2. Select Air Fry. Set temperature to 400ºF (205ºC), and set time to 7 minutes, tossing the cooking tray halfway through the cooking time.
3. Bon appétit!

# Jumbo Shrimp with Peanut Mix

**Prep time: 10 minutes | Cook time: 10 minutes | Serves 4**

For the Peanut Mix:
1 cup roasted and salted red-skinned Spanish peanuts
8 cloves garlic, smashed and peeled
3 dried red arbol chiles, broken into pieces
1 tablespoon cumin seeds

2 teaspoons vegetable oil
For the Shrimp:
1 pound (454 g) jumbo raw shrimp, peeled and deveined
2 tablespoons vegetable oil
Lime wedges, for serving

Make the Peanut Mix
1. In a 6 × 3-inch round heatproof pan, combine all the ingredients and toss. Place the pan in the air fryer cooking tray. Select Air Fry. Set temperature to 400ºF (205ºC), and set time to 5 minutes, or until all the spices are toasted. Remove the pan from the oven and let the mixture cool.
2. When completely cool, transfer the mixture to a mortar and pestle or clean coffee or spice grinder; crush or pulse to a very coarse texture that won't fall through the grate of the air fryer cooking tray.

Make the Shrimp
3. In a large bowl, combine the shrimp and oil. Toss until well combined. Add the peanut mix and toss again. Place the shrimp and peanut mix in the air fryer cooking tray. Select Air Fry. Set temperature to 350ºF (175ºC), and set time to 5 minutes.
4. Transfer to a serving dish. Cover and allow the shrimp to finish cooking in the residual heat, for about 5 minutes. Serve with lime wedges.

# Chapter 8 Vegetable

## Sesame-Ginger Broccoli Florets

**Prep time: 10 minutes | Cook time: 15 minutes | Serves 4**

3 tablespoons toasted sesame oil
2 teaspoons sesame seeds
1 tablespoon chili-garlic sauce
2 teaspoons minced

fresh ginger
½ teaspoon kosher salt
½ teaspoon black pepper
1 (16 ounce / 454 g) package frozen broccoli florets (do not thaw)

1. In a large bowl, combine the sesame oil, sesame seeds, chili-garlic sauce, ginger, salt, and pepper. Stir until well combined. Add the broccoli and toss until well coated.
2. Arrange the broccoli in the air fryer cooking tray. Select Roast. Set temperature to 325ºF (165ºC), and set time to 15 minutes, or until the broccoli is crisp, tender, and the edges are lightly browned, gently tossing halfway through the cooking time.

## Baby Bella Mushrooms and Bacon

**Prep time: 5 minutes | Cook time: 10 minutes | Serves 4**

16 ounces (454 g) baby bella (cremini) mushrooms, halved
4 slices bacon, each cut into 8 pieces

Kosher salt and black pepper, to taste (optional)
¼ cup chopped fresh parsley, for garnish

1. Place the mushrooms in the air-fryer cooking tray. Sprinkle the bacon over the mushrooms. Select Roast. Set temperature to 10 minutes and cook, very gently shaking the cooking tray halfway through the cooking time—you still want the bacon slices mostly on top. (As the bacon cooks, it drips its luscious fat onto the mushrooms and flavors them with bacon-y goodness.)
2. Taste and season with salt or pepper, if necessary; you may not need any.
3. Sprinkle with the parsley and serve.

## Tart and Spicy Indian Potatoes

**Prep time: 10 minutes | Cook time: 15 minutes | Serves 4**

4 cups quartered baby yellow potatoes
3 tablespoons vegetable oil
1 teaspoon ground turmeric
1 teaspoon amchoor
1 teaspoon kosher salt
¼ teaspoon ground

cumin
¼ teaspoon ground coriander
¼ to ½ teaspoon cayenne pepper
1 tablespoon fresh lime or lemon juice
¼ cup chopped fresh cilantro or parsley

1. In a large bowl, toss together the potatoes, vegetable oil, turmeric, amchoor, salt, cumin, coriander, and cayenne until the potatoes are well coated.
2. Place the seasoned potatoes in the air-fryer cooking tray. Select Roast. Set temperature to 400ºF (205ºC), and set time to 15 minutes, or until they are cooked through and tender when pierced with a fork.
3. Transfer the potatoes to a serving platter or bowl. Drizzle with the lime juice and sprinkle with the cilantro before serving.

## Maple-Roasted Cherry Tomatoes

**Prep time: 10 minutes | Cook time: 20 minutes | Serves 2**

10 ounces (283 g) cherry tomatoes, halved
Kosher salt, to taste
2 tablespoons maple syrup
1 tablespoon vegetable

oil
2 sprigs fresh thyme, stems removed
1 garlic clove, minced
Freshly ground black pepper, to taste

1. Place the tomatoes in a colander and sprinkle liberally with salt. Let them stand for 10 minutes to drain.
2. Transfer the tomatoes cut-side up to a 7-inch round cake pan insert, metal cake pan, or foil pan, then drizzle with the maple syrup, followed by the oil. Sprinkle with the thyme leaves and garlic and season with pepper. Place the pan in the oven and select Roast. Set temperature to 325ºF (165ºC) until the tomatoes are soft, collapsed, and lightly caramelized on top, for about 20 minutes.
3. Serve straight from the pan or transfer the tomatoes to a plate and drizzle with the juices from the pan to serve.

## Cheddar Chile Cornbread with Corn

**Prep time: 10 minutes | Cook time: 15 minutes | Serves 6**

| | |
|---|---|
| 2 large eggs | cheese |
| ¼ cup whole milk | 1 (4-ounce / 113-g) can |
| 1 (8½-ounce / 241-g) | diced mild green chiles, |
| package corn muffin mix | undrained |
| 1 cup corn kernels | Vegetable oil spray |
| ½ cup grated Cheddar | Parchment paper |

1. In a medium bowl, whisk together the eggs and milk. Add the muffin mix and stir until the batter is smooth. Stir in the corn, cheese, and undrained chiles.
2. Spray a 3-cup Bundt pan with vegetable oil spray. Line the pan with parchment paper. (To do this, cut a circle of parchment about 1 inch larger in diameter than the top of the pan. Fold the parchment in half and cut a hole in the middle to accommodate the center of the Bundt pan. Place the parchment in the pan; trim any excess parchment from around the top.)
3. Pour the batter into the prepared pan. Place the pan in the air fryer cooking tray. Select Roast. Set temperature to 350ºF (175ºC), and set time to 15 minutes.
4. Allow the bread to rest in the closed air fryer for 10 minutes before serving.

## Indian Okra

**Prep time: 15 minutes | Cook time: 15 minutes | Serves 4**

| | |
|---|---|
| 1 pound (454 g) okra, | coriander |
| sliced ¼ inch thick | ¼ to ½ teaspoon |
| 1 cup coarsely chopped | cayenne pepper |
| red onion | ¼ teaspoon amchoor |
| 2 tablespoons vegetable | (optional) |
| oil | ½ cup chopped fresh |
| 1 teaspoon ground | tomato |
| turmeric | Juice of 1 lemon |
| 1 teaspoon kosher salt | ¼ cup chopped fresh |
| 1 teaspoon ground cumin | cilantro or parsley |
| 1 teaspoon ground | |

1. In a large bowl, combine the okra and onion. Drizzle with the vegetable oil and sprinkle with the turmeric, salt, cumin, coriander, cayenne, and amchoor (if using).
2. Spread the spiced vegetables over the air-fryer cooking tray, making as even and flat a layer as

possible. Select Roast. Set temperature to 375ºF (190ºC), and set time to 15 minutes, stirring halfway through the cooking time. (Don't panic if you see some stickiness to the okra. This will dissipate once it cooks.) After 10 minutes, add the tomato to the cooking tray. Cook for the remaining 5 minutes, until the tomato is wilted and cooked through.
3. Drizzle the vegetables with the lemon juice and toss to combine. Garnish with the cilantro and serve.

## Yellow Squash

**Prep time: 5 minutes | Cook time: 11 minutes | Serves 4**

| | |
|---|---|
| 1½ cups large yellow | breadcrumbs |
| squash | ¼ cup white cornmeal |
| 2 eggs | ½ teaspoon salt |
| ¼ cup buttermilk | Oil for misting or cooking |
| 1 cup panko | spray |

1. Preheat air fryer oven to 390ºF (200ºC).
2. Cut the squash into ¼-inch slices.
3. In a shallow dish, beat together eggs and buttermilk.
4. In sealable plastic bag or container with lid, combine ¼ cup panko crumbs, white cornmeal, and salt. Shake to mix well.
5. Place the remaining ¾ cup panko crumbs in a separate shallow dish.
6. Dump all the squash slices into the egg/buttermilk mixture. Stir to coat.
7. Remove squash from buttermilk mixture with a slotted spoon, letting excess drip off, and transfer to the panko/cornmeal mixture. Close the bag or the container and shake well to coat.
8. Remove squash from crumb mixture, letting excess fall off. Return squash to egg/buttermilk mixture, stirring gently to coat. If you need more liquid to coat all the squash, add a little more buttermilk.
9. Remove each squash slice from egg wash and dip in a dish of ¾ cup panko crumbs.
10. Mist squash slices with oil or cooking spray and place in air fryer cooking tray. Squash should be in a single layer, but it's okay if the slices crowd together and overlap a little.
11. Select Roast. Set temperature to 390ºF (200ºC), and set time to 5 minutes. Shake cooking tray to break up any that have stuck together. Mist again with oil or spray.
12. Roast for 5 minutes longer and check. If necessary, mist again with oil and cook for an additional minute or two, until squash slices are golden brown and crisp.

## Okra

**Prep time: 5 minutes | Cook time: 12 minutes | Serves 4**

7 to 8 ounces (198 to 227 g) fresh okra
1 egg
1 cup milk
1 cup breadcrumbs
½ teaspoon salt
Oil for misting or cooking spray

1. Remove stem ends from okra and cut in ½-inch slices.
2. In a medium bowl, beat together egg and milk. Add okra slices and stir to coat.
3. In a sealable plastic bag or container with lid, mix together the breadcrumbs and salt.
4. Remove okra from egg mixture, letting excess drip off, and transfer into bag with breadcrumbs.
5. Shake okra in crumbs to coat well.
6. Place all of the coated okra into the air fryer cooking tray and mist with oil or cooking spray. Okra doesn't need to cook in a single layer, nor is it necessary to spray all sides at this point. A good spritz on top will do.
7. Select Roast. Set temperature to 390ºF (200ºC), and set time to 5 minutes. Shake the cooking tray to redistribute and give it another spritz as you shake.
8. Cook for 5 more minutes. Shake and spray again. Cook for 2 to 5 minutes longer or until golden brown and crispy.

## Mashed Potato Tots

**Prep time: 10 minutes | Cook time: 40 minutes | Makes 18–24 tots**

1 medium potato
1 tablespoon real bacon bits
2 tablespoons chopped green onions, tops only
¼ teaspoon onion powder
1 teaspoon dried
chopped chives
Salt, to taste
2 tablespoons flour
1 egg white, beaten
½ cup panko breadcrumbs
Oil for misting or cooking spray

1. Peel potato and cut into ½-inch cubes. (Small pieces cook more quickly.) Place in saucepan, add water to cover, and heat to boil. Lower heat slightly and continue cooking just until tender, for about 10 minutes.
2. Drain potatoes and place in ice-cold water. Allow them to cool for a minute or two, then drain well and mash.
3. Preheat air fryer oven to 390ºF (200ºC).
4. In a large bowl, mix together the potatoes, bacon bits, onions, onion powder, chives, salt to taste, and flour. Add egg white and stir well.
5. Place panko crumbs on a sheet of wax paper.
6. For each tot, use about 2 teaspoons of potato mixture. To shape, drop the measure of potato mixture onto panko crumbs and push crumbs up and around potatoes to coat edges. Then turn tot over to coat other side with crumbs.
7. Mist tots with oil or cooking spray and place in air fryer cooking tray, crowded but not stacked.
8. Select Roast. Set temperature to 390ºF (200ºC), and set time to 10 to 12 minutes, until browned and crispy.
9. Repeat steps 8 and 9 to cook the remaining tots.

## Turkish Leek Fritters

**Prep time: 10 minutes | Cook time: 26 minutes | Serves 4**

2 tablespoons extra-virgin olive oil
3 leeks, white and light green parts only, sliced
Kosher salt and pepper, to taste
1 egg, beaten
3 tablespoons all-
purpose flour
2 tablespoons minced chives
¾ cup panko bread crumbs
Vegetable oil for spraying
Lemon wedges for serving

1. Heat the olive oil in a large, deep skillet over medium heat. Sauté the sliced leeks until softened, for about 10 minutes. Lower the heat as necessary, so the leeks do not brown. Season the leeks well with salt and pepper.
2. Transfer the cooked leeks to a medium bowl. Add the beaten egg, flour, and chives and stir with a fork to combine. The mixture should start to thicken and become a bit pasty. Spread the panko on a plate. Divide the leek mixture into 4 equal quarters and form each quarter into a patty, squeezing as necessary to get the patty to stick together. Dredge the top and bottom of each patty in the panko. Transfer the breaded patties to a plate.
3. Spray the cooking tray of the oven with oil. Carefully transfer the patties to the cooking tray of the oven, working in 2 batches if necessary to avoid overcrowding. Spray the tops of the patties with oil. Select Roast. Set temperature to 375ºF (190ºC) until the tops of the patties are browned, for about 8 minutes. Carefully flip the patties and spray the tops with oil. Cook until the second side is browned, for about 5 minutes.
4. Remove the patties and transfer to a serving platter. Serve the leek patties warm with lemon wedges.

## Honey Butternut Squash

**Prep time: 10 minutes | Cook time: 15 minutes | Serves 2 to 3**

| | |
|---|---|
| 1 butternut squash, peeled | softened |
| Olive oil, in a spray bottle | 2 tablespoons honey |
| Salt and freshly ground black pepper, to taste | Pinch ground cinnamon |
| 2 tablespoons butter, | Pinch ground nutmeg |
| | Chopped fresh sage |

1. Preheat the oven to 370ºF (190ºC).
2. Cut the neck of the butternut squash into disks about ½-inch thick. (Use the base of the butternut squash for another use.) Brush or spray the disks with oil and season with salt and freshly ground black pepper.
3. Transfer the butternut disks to the air fryer in one layer (or just ever so slightly overlapping). Select Roast. Set temperature to 370ºF (190ºC), and set time to 5 minutes.
4. While the butternut squash is cooking, combine the butter, honey, cinnamon and nutmeg in a small bowl. Brush this mixture on the butternut squash, flip the disks over and brush the other side as well. Continue to roast at 370ºF (190ºC), and set time to another 5 minutes. Flip the disks once more, brush with more of the honey butter and roast for another 5 minutes. The butternut should be browning nicely around the edges.
5. Remove the butternut squash from the oven and repeat with additional batches if necessary. Transfer to a serving platter, sprinkle with the fresh sage and serve.

## Latkes with Sour Cream and Applesauce

**Prep time: 10 minutes | Cook time: 12 minutes | Makes 12 latkes**

| | |
|---|---|
| 1 russet potato | pepper, to taste |
| ¼ onion | Canola or vegetable oil, in a spray bottle |
| 2 eggs, lightly beaten | |
| ⅓ cup flour | Chopped chives, for garnish |
| ½ teaspoon baking powder | |
| 1 teaspoon salt | Apple sauce |
| Freshly ground black | Sour cream |

1. Shred the potato and onion with a coarse box grater or a food processor with the shredding blade. Place the shredded vegetables into a colander or mesh strainer and squeeze or press down firmly to remove the excess water.
2. Transfer the onion and potato to a large bowl and add the eggs, flour, baking powder, salt and black pepper. Mix to combine and then shape the mixture into patties, about ¼-cup of mixture each. Brush or spray both sides of the latkes with oil.
3. Preheat the oven to 400ºF (205ºC).
4. Roast the latkes in batches. Transfer one layer of the latkes to the air fryer cooking tray and select Roast. Set temperature to 400ºF (205ºC), and set time to 12 to 13 minutes, flipping them over halfway through the cooking time. Transfer the finished latkes to a platter and cover with aluminum foil, or place them in a warm oven to keep warm.
5. Garnish the latkes with chopped chives and serve with sour cream and applesauce.

## Smashed Fried Baby Red Potatoes

**Prep time: 10 minutes | Cook time: 18 minutes | Serves 3 to 4**

| | |
|---|---|
| 1½ pounds (680 g) baby red or baby Yukon gold potatoes | 1 teaspoon dried parsley |
| | Salt and freshly ground black pepper, to taste |
| ¼ cup butter, melted | 2 scallions, finely chopped |
| 1 teaspoon olive oil | |
| ½ teaspoon paprika | |

1. Bring a large pot of salted water to a boil. Add the potatoes and boil for 18 minutes or until the potatoes are fork-tender.
2. Drain the potatoes and transfer them to a cutting board to cool slightly. Spray or brush the bottom of a drinking glass with a little oil. Smash or flatten the potatoes by pressing the glass down on each potato slowly. Try not to completely flatten the potato or smash it so hard that it breaks apart.
3. Combine the melted butter, olive oil, paprika, and parsley together.
4. Preheat the oven to 400ºF (205ºC).
5. Spray the bottom of the air fryer cooking tray with oil and transfer one layer of the smashed potatoes into the cooking tray. Brush with some of the butter mixture and season generously with salt and freshly ground black pepper.
6. Select Roast. Set temperature to 400ºF (205ºC), and set time to 10 minutes. Carefully flip the potatoes over and roast for an additional 8 minutes until crispy and lightly browned.
7. Keep the potatoes warm in a 170ºF (75ºC) oven or tent with aluminum foil while you cook the second batch. Sprinkle minced scallions over the potatoes and serve warm.

## Mashed Sweet Potato Tots

**Prep time: 10 minutes | Cook time: 24 minutes | Makes 18–24 tots**

1 cup cooked mashed sweet potatoes
1 egg white, beaten
⅛ teaspoon ground cinnamon
1 dash nutmeg
2 tablespoons chopped
pecans
1½ teaspoons honey
Salt, to taste
½ cup panko breadcrumbs
Oil for misting or cooking spray

1. Preheat air fryer oven to 390ºF (200ºC).
2. In a large bowl, mix together the potatoes, egg white, cinnamon, nutmeg, pecans, honey, and salt to taste.
3. Place panko crumbs on a sheet of wax paper.
4. For each tot, use about 2 teaspoons of sweet potato mixture. To shape, drop the measure of potato mixture onto panko crumbs and push crumbs up and around potatoes to coat edges. Then turn tot over to coat other side with crumbs.
5. Mist tots with oil or cooking spray and place in air fryer cooking tray in single layer.
6. Select Roast. Set temperature to 390ºF (200ºC), and set time to 12 to 13 minutes, until browned and crispy.
7. Repeat steps 5 and 6 to cook the remaining tots.

## Bottom Rice with Currants and Pistachios

**Prep time: 10 minutes | Cook time: 20 minutes | Serves 2**

1 tablespoon olive oil
¼ teaspoon ground turmeric
2 cups cooked white basmati, jasmine, or other long-grain rice
¼ cup dried currants
¼ cup roughly chopped pistachios
Kosher salt and freshly ground black pepper, to taste
1 tablespoon thinly sliced fresh cilantro

1. Combine the olive oil and turmeric in the bottom of a 7-inch round cake pan insert, metal cake pan, or foil pan.
2. In a bowl, combine the rice, currants, and pistachios, season with salt and pepper, then spoon the rice over the oil, making sure to not stir the oil up into the rice. Very gently press the rice into an even layer.
3. Place the pan in the oven and select Roast. Set temperature to 300ºF (150ºC) until the rice is warmed through and the bottom is toasted and crispy, 20 to 25 minutes.

4. Remove the pan from the oven and invert onto a serving plate. Break up the crust on the bottom of the rice, sprinkle with the cilantro, and serve warm.

## Green Tomato with Sriracha Mayo

**Prep time: 15 minutes | Cook time: 13 minutes | Serves 4**

3 green tomatoes
Salt and freshly ground black pepper, to taste
⅓ cup all-purpose flour
2 eggs
½ cup buttermilk
1 cup panko breadcrumbs
1 cup cornmeal
Olive oil, in a spray bottle
Fresh thyme sprigs or chopped fresh chives
For the Sriracha Mayo:
½ cup mayonnaise
1 to 2 tablespoons sriracha hot sauce
1 tablespoon milk

1. Cut the tomatoes in ¼-inch slices. Pat them dry with a clean kitchen towel and season generously with salt and pepper.
2. Set up a dredging station using three shallow dishes. Place the flour in the first shallow dish, whisk the eggs and buttermilk together in the second dish, and combine the panko breadcrumbs and cornmeal in the third dish.
3. Preheat the oven to 400ºF (205ºC).
4. Dredge the tomato slices in flour to coat on all sides. Then dip them into the egg mixture and finally press them into the breadcrumbs to coat all sides of the tomato.
5. Spray or brush the air-fryer cooking tray with olive oil. Transfer 3 to 4 tomato slices into the cooking tray and spray the top with olive oil. Select Roast. Set temperature to 400ºF (205ºC), and set time to 8 minutes. Flip them over, spray the other side with oil and roast for an additional 4 minutes until golden brown.
6. While the tomatoes are cooking, make the sriracha mayo. Combine the mayonnaise, 1 tablespoon of the sriracha hot sauce and milk in a small bowl. Stir well until the mixture is smooth. Add more sriracha sauce to taste.
7. When the tomatoes are done, transfer them to a cooling rack or a platter lined with paper towels so the bottom does not get soggy. Before serving, carefully stack the all the tomatoes into the oven and roast at 350ºF (175ºC), and set time to 1 to 2 minutes to heat them back up.
8. Serve the fried green tomatoes hot with the sriracha mayo on the side. Season one last time with salt and freshly ground black pepper and garnish with sprigs of fresh thyme or chopped fresh chives.

## Caribbean Yuca Roots Fries

**Prep time: 5 minutes | Cook time: 25 minutes | Serves 4**

3 yuca roots                 1 teaspoon kosher salt
Vegetable oil for spraying

1. Trim the ends off the yuca roots and cut each one into 2 or 3 pieces depending on the length. Have a bowl of water ready. Peel off the rough outer skin with a paring knife or sharp vegetable peeler. Halve each piece of yuca lengthwise. Place the peeled pieces in a bowl of water to prevent them from oxidizing and turning brown.
2. Fill a large pot with water and bring to a boil over high heat. Season well with salt. Add the yuca pieces to the water and cook until they are tender enough to be pierced with a fork, but not falling apart, approximately 12 to 15 minutes. Drain. Some of the yuca pieces will have fibrous string running down the center. Remove it. Cut the yuca into 2 or 3 pieces to resemble thick-cut french fries.
3. Working in batches, arrange the yuca fries in rotisserie basket. Spray with oil. Select Roast. Set temperature to 400ºF (205ºC), and set time to 10 minutes, until the outside of the fries is crisp and browned and the inside fluffy. Repeat with the remaining fries. Spray the cooked yuca with oil and toss with 1 teaspoon salt.
4. Serve the yuca fries warm with Toum, Chipotle Ketchup, or Mint Chimichurri.

## Blackened Zucchini with Herby Kimchi Sauce

**Prep time: 10 minutes | Cook time: 20 minutes | Serves 2**

2 medium zucchini (6 ounces / 170 g), ends trimmed          plus more for garnish
2 tablespoons olive oil          2 tablespoons rice vinegar
½ cup kimchi, finely chopped          2 teaspoons Asian chili-garlic sauce
¼ cup finely chopped fresh cilantro          1 teaspoon grated fresh ginger
¼ cup finely chopped fresh flat-leaf parsley,          Kosher salt and freshly ground black pepper, to taste

1. Brush the zucchini with half of the olive oil, place in the oven, and select Roast. Set temperature to 400ºF (205ºC), turning halfway through, until lightly charred on the outside and tender, for about 15 minutes.

2. Meanwhile, in a small bowl, combine the remaining 1 tablespoon olive oil, the kimchi, cilantro, parsley, vinegar, chili-garlic sauce, and ginger.
3. Once the zucchini is finished cooking, transfer it to a colander and let it cool for 5 minutes. Using your fingers, pinch and break the zucchini into bite-size pieces, letting them fall back into the colander. Season the zucchini with salt and pepper, toss to combine, then let sit for a further 5 minutes to allow some of its liquid to drain. Pile the zucchini atop the kimchi sauce on a plate and sprinkle with more parsley to serve.

## Hasselback with Sour Cream and Pesto

**Prep time: 10 minutes | Cook time: 40 minutes | Serves 2**

2 medium (8 to 10 ounces / 227 to 283 g) russet potatoes          leaves
5 tablespoons olive oil          1 tablespoon chopped walnuts
Kosher salt and freshly ground black pepper, to taste          1 tablespoon grated Parmesan cheese
¼ cup roughly chopped fresh chives          1 teaspoon fresh lemon juice
2 tablespoons packed fresh flat-leaf parsley          1 small garlic clove, peeled
          ¼ cup sour cream

1. Place the potatoes on a cutting board and lay a chopstick or thin-handled wooden spoon to the side of each potato. Thinly slice the potatoes crosswise, letting the chopstick or spoon handle stop the blade of your knife, and stop ½ inch short of each end of the potato. Rub the potatoes with 1 tablespoon of the olive oil and season with salt and pepper.
2. Place the potatoes in the air fryer and select Roast, cut-side up. Set temperature to 375ºF (190ºC) until golden brown and crisp on the outside and tender inside, for about 40 minutes, drizzling the insides with 1 tablespoon more olive oil and seasoning with more salt and pepper halfway through.
3. Meanwhile, in a small blender or food processor, combine the remaining 3 tablespoons olive oil, the chives, parsley, walnuts, Parmesan, lemon juice, and garlic and puree until smooth. Season the chive pesto with salt and pepper.
4. Remove the potatoes from the air fryer and transfer to plates. Drizzle the potatoes with the pesto, letting it drip down into the grooves, then dollop each with sour cream and serve hot.

## Crispy Fried Shallots

**Prep time: 5 minutes | Cook time: 35 minutes | Makes 2 cups fried shallots**

12 ounces (340 g) shallots

Vegetable oil for spraying
1 teaspoon kosher salt

1. Peel the shallots and slice them as thinly as possible using a sharp knife, a mandoline, or a food processor outfitted with a slicing blade. Place the sliced shallots in the cooking tray of the oven. Select Roast. Set temperature to 250ºF (120ºC), and set time to 5 minutes then open and shake the cooking tray to toss the shallots. Repeat this process, Roasting the shallots at 250ºF (120ºC) and shaking and tossing them every 5 minutes, until they become brown and crispy, approximately 35 to 40 minutes. Halfway through the cooking time, after 15 or 20 minutes, spray the shallots with oil.
2. Once all of the shallots are browned, remove them from the oven. Do not allow the shallots to burn or they will become bitter. (Do not be dismayed if the browned shallots are soft immediately upon removal from the oven; they will crisp as they cool.)
3. Toss the crispy shallots with salt. If not using right away, transfer the shallots to a covered storage container and store at room temperature until needed.

## Feta Bell Pepper Salad

**Prep time: 5 minutes | Cook time: 54 minutes | Serves 4**

4 bell peppers, red, orange, or yellow or a combination thereof
1 tablespoon extra-virgin olive oil plus extra for drizzling
2 tablespoons pine nuts
2 ounces Greek Feta

cheese in brine, crumbled
1 teaspoon red wine vinegar
1 sprig basil, leaves removed and cut into ribbons

1. Simply brush the outside of the peppers with the olive oil and place them in the air fryer cooking tray. You will likely be able to fit 2 or 3 peppers at the most. Select Roast. Set temperature to 400ºF (205ºC), turning several times, until blackened on all sides, for 25 to 30 minutes.
2. Place the cooked peppers in a bowl and cover with a clean towel. Allow the peppers to steam for 10 minutes. While the peppers are steaming, toast the pine nuts. Place the pine nuts in the pizza pan insert for the oven. Place the pan in the air fryer cooking tray. Select Roast. Set temperature to 325ºF (165ºC) until the pine nuts are lightly browned and smell toasty, for 4 to 5 minutes. Check frequently to make sure the pine nuts do not scorch. Remove from the pan and set aside.
3. Once the peppers are cool enough to handle, remove the skin from the peppers and, if necessary, the seeds and core. Tear whole peppers into 3 or 4 pieces.
4. Arrange the peppers on a serving platter. Top with crumbled Feta and toasted pine nuts. Drizzle the peppers with additional olive oil and vinegar. Scatter basil over the peppers. Serve warm or at room temperature.

## Mole-Braised Cauliflower

**Prep time: 15 minutes | Cook time: 18 minutes | Serves 2**

8 ounces (227 g) medium cauliflower florets
1 tablespoon vegetable oil
Kosher salt and freshly ground black pepper, to taste
1½ cups vegetable broth
2 tablespoons New Mexico chile powder (or regular chili powder)
2 tablespoons salted roasted peanuts
1 tablespoon toasted

sesame seeds, plus more for garnish
1 tablespoon finely chopped golden raisins
1 teaspoon kosher salt
1 teaspoon dark brown sugar
½ teaspoon dried oregano
¼ teaspoon cayenne pepper
⅛ teaspoon ground cinnamon

1. In a large bowl, toss the cauliflower with the oil and season with salt and black pepper. Transfer to a 7-inch round cake pan insert, metal cake pan, or foil pan. Place the pan in the oven and select Roast. Set temperature to 375ºF (190ºC) until the cauliflower is tender and lightly browned at the edges, about 10 minutes, stirring halfway through.
2. Meanwhile, in a small blender, combine the broth, chile powder, peanuts, sesame seeds, raisins, salt, brown sugar, oregano, cayenne, and cinnamon and puree until smooth. Pour into a small saucepan or skillet and bring to a simmer over medium heat, then cook until reduced by half, for 3 to 5 minutes.
3. Pour the hot mole sauce over the cauliflower in the pan, stir to coat, then cook until the sauce is thickened and lightly charred on the cauliflower, about 5 minutes or more. Sprinkle with more sesame seeds and serve warm.

Brussels Sprouts, page 107

Roasted Lemony Cauliflower, page 111

White Button Mushrooms, page 113

Maple-Roasted Cherry Tomatoes, page 99

## Brussels Sprouts

**Prep time: 5 minutes | Cook time: 5 minutes | Serves 3**

| | |
|---|---|
| 1 (10 ounce / 283 g) package frozen brussels sprouts, thawed and | halved<br>2 teaspoons olive oil<br>Salt and pepper, to taste |

1. Toss the brussels sprouts and olive oil together.
2. Place them in the air fryer cooking tray and season to taste with salt and pepper.
3. Select Roast. Set temperature to 360ºF (180ºC), and set time to approximately 5 minutes, until the edges begin to brown.

## Broccoli Salad

**Prep time: 5 minutes | Cook time: 7 minutes | Serves**

| | |
|---|---|
| 3 cups fresh broccoli florets<br>2 tablespoons coconut | oil, melted<br>¼ cup sliced spinach<br>½ medium lemon, juiced |

1. Take a 6-inch baking dish and fill with the broccoli florets. Pour the melted coconut oil over the broccoli and add in the sliced spinach. Toss together. Put the dish in the oven.
2. Select Roast. Set temperature to 380ºF (195ºC), and set time to 7 minutes, stirring at the halfway point.
3. Place the broccoli in a bowl and drizzle the lemon juice over it.

## Fingerling Potatoes with Dried Parsley

**Prep time: 5 minutes | Cook time: 15 minutes | Serves 4**

| | |
|---|---|
| 1 pound (454 g) fingerling potatoes<br>1 tablespoon light olive oil | ½ teaspoon dried parsley<br>½ teaspoon lemon juice<br>Coarsely ground sea salt |

1. Cut potatoes in half lengthwise.
2. In a large bowl, combine potatoes, oil, parsley, and lemon juice. Stir well to coat potatoes.
3. Place potatoes in air fryer cooking tray and select Roast. Set temperature to 360ºF (180ºC), and set time to 15 to 20 minutes or until lightly browned and tender inside.
4. Sprinkle with sea salt before serving.

## Green Peas with Fresh Mint

**Prep time: 5 minutes | Cook time: 5 minutes | Serves 4**

| | |
|---|---|
| 1 cup shredded lettuce<br>1 (10 ounce / 283 g) package frozen green peas, thawed | 1 tablespoon fresh mint, shredded<br>1 teaspoon melted butter |

1. Lay the shredded lettuce in the air fryer cooking tray.
2. Toss together the peas, mint, and melted butter and spoon over the lettuce.
3. Select Roast. Set temperature to 360ºF (180ºC), and set time to 5 minutes, until peas are warm and lettuce wilts.

## Shawarma Green Beans

**Prep time: 5 minutes | Cook time: 10 minutes | Serves 2**

| | |
|---|---|
| 2 cups halved fresh green beans<br>2 tablespoons vegetable oil | 1 tablespoon Lebanese Shawarma Spice Mix<br>½ teaspoon kosher salt |

1. In a medium bowl, toss together the green beans, vegetable oil, spice mix, and salt until well coated.
2. Place the seasoned green beans in the air-fryer cooking tray. Select Roast. Set temperature to 375ºF (190ºC), and set time to 10 minutes, shaking the cooking tray halfway through the cooking time.

## Parmesan Zucchini Gratin

**Prep time: 5 minutes | Cook time: 13 minutes | Serves 2**

| | |
|---|---|
| 5 ounces (142 g) Parmesan cheese, shredded<br>1 tablespoon coconut flour | 1 tablespoon dried parsley<br>2 zucchinis<br>1 teaspoon butter, melted |

1. Mix the Parmesan and coconut flour together in a bowl, seasoning with parsley to taste.
2. Cut the zucchini in half lengthwise and chop the halves into four slices.
3. Preheat the oven at 400ºF (205ºC).
4. Pour the melted butter over the zucchini and then dip the zucchini into the Parmesan-flour mixture, coating it all over. Select Roast. Set temperature to 400ºF (205ºC), and set time to 13 minutes.

## Green Beans and Bacon

**Prep time: 5 minutes | Cook time: 20 minutes | Serves 4**

| | |
|---|---|
| 3 cups frozen cut green beans (do not thaw) | 3 slices bacon, chopped |
| 1 medium onion, chopped | ¼ cup water |
| | Kosher salt and black pepper, to taste |

1. In a 6 × 3-inch round heatproof pan, combine the frozen green beans, onion, bacon, and water. Toss to combine. Place the pan in the air fryer cooking tray. Select Roast. Set temperature to 375ºF (190ºC), and set time to 15 minutes.
2. Raise the oven temperature to 400ºF (205ºC), and set time to 5 minutes. Season the beans with salt and pepper to taste and toss well.
3. Remove the pan from the air fryer cooking tray and cover with foil. Let the beans rest for 5 minutes before serving.

## Parmesan Coated Artichokes

**Prep time: 5 minutes | Cook time: 10 minutes | Serves 4**

| | |
|---|---|
| 2 medium artichokes, trimmed and quartered, with the centers removed | 1 egg, beaten |
| 2 tablespoons coconut oil, melted | ½ cup Parmesan cheese, grated |
| | ¼ cup blanched, finely ground flour |

1. Place the artichokes in a bowl with the coconut oil and toss to coat, then dip the artichokes into a bowl of beaten egg.
2. In a separate bowl, mix together the Parmesan cheese and the flour. Combine with the pieces of artichoke, making sure to coat each piece well. Transfer the artichoke to the oven.
3. Select Roast. Set temperature to 400ºF (205ºC), and set time to 10 minutes, shaking occasionally throughout the cooking time. Serve hot.

## Gobi Manchurian

**Prep time: 15 minutes | Cook time: 20 minutes | Serves 4**

| | |
|---|---|
| For the Cauliflower: | turmeric |
| 4 cups chopped cauliflower | For the Sauce: |
| 1 cup chopped yellow onion | 3 tablespoons ketchup |
| 1 large bell pepper, chopped | 2 tablespoons soy sauce |
| 2 tablespoons vegetable oil | 1 tablespoon rice vinegar |
| 2 teaspoons kosher salt | 1 teaspoon minced garlic |
| 1 teaspoon ground | 1 teaspoon minced fresh ginger |
| | 1 teaspoon sriracha or other hot sauce |

Make the Cauliflower
1. In a large bowl, combine the cauliflower, onion, and bell pepper. Drizzle with the vegetable oil and sprinkle with the salt and turmeric. Stir until the cauliflower is well coated.
2. Place the cauliflower in the air-fryer cooking tray. Select Roast. Set temperature to 400ºF (205ºC), and set time to 20 minutes, stirring the cauliflower halfway through the cooking time.
Make the Sauce
3. In a small bowl, combine the ketchup, soy sauce, vinegar, garlic, ginger, and sriracha.
4. Transfer the cauliflower to a large bowl. Pour the sauce over and toss well to combine. Serve immediately.

## Cauliflower with Tahini Sauce

**Prep time: 10 minutes | Cook time: 20 minutes | Serves 4**

| | |
|---|---|
| For the Cauliflower: | ½ teaspoon kosher salt |
| 5 cups cauliflower florets | For the Sauce: |
| 6 garlic cloves, smashed and cut into thirds | 2 tablespoons tahini (sesame paste) |
| 3 tablespoons vegetable oil | 2 tablespoons hot water |
| ½ teaspoon ground cumin | 1 tablespoon fresh lemon juice |
| ½ teaspoon ground coriander | 1 teaspoon minced garlic |
| | ½ teaspoon kosher salt |

Make the Cauliflower
1. In a large bowl, combine the cauliflower florets and garlic. Drizzle with the vegetable oil. Sprinkle with the cumin, coriander, and salt. Toss until well coated.
2. Place the cauliflower in the air-fryer cooking tray. Select Roast. Set temperature to 400ºF (205ºC), and set time to 20 minutes, turning the cauliflower halfway through the cooking time.
Make the Sauce
1. In a small bowl, combine the tahini, water, lemon juice, garlic, and salt. (The sauce will appear curdled at first, but keep stirring until you have a thick, creamy, smooth mixture.)
2. Transfer the cauliflower to a large serving bowl. Pour the sauce over and toss gently to coat. Serve immediately.

## Chiles Rellenos with Red Chile Sauce

**Prep time: 20 minutes | Cook time: 30 minutes | Serves 2**

For the Peppers:
2 poblano peppers, rinsed and dried
⅔ cup thawed frozen or drained canned corn kernels
1 scallion, sliced
2 tablespoons chopped fresh cilantro
½ teaspoon kosher salt
¼ teaspoon black pepper
⅔ cup grated Monterey Jack cheese
For the Sauce:
3 tablespoons extra-virgin olive oil

½ cup finely chopped yellow onion
2 teaspoons minced garlic
1 (6-ounce / 170-g) can tomato paste
2 tablespoons ancho chile powder
1 teaspoon dried oregano
1 teaspoon ground cumin
½ teaspoon kosher salt
2 cups chicken broth
2 tablespoons fresh lemon juice
Mexican crema or sour cream, for serving

Make the Peppers
1. Place the peppers in the air-fryer cooking tray. Select Roast. Set temperature to 400ºF (205ºC), and set time to 10 minutes, turning the peppers halfway through the cooking time, until their skins are charred. Transfer the peppers to a resealable plastic bag, seal, and set aside to steam for 5 minutes. Peel the peppers and discard the skins. Cut a slit down the center of each pepper, start at the stem and continue to the tip. Remove the seeds, being careful not to tear the chile.
2. In a medium bowl, combine the corn, scallion, cilantro, salt, black pepper, and cheese; set aside.
Make the Sauce
3. In a large skillet, heat the olive oil over medium-high heat. Add the onion, cook, and stir until tender, for about 5 minutes. Add the garlic and cook, stirring, for 30 seconds. Stir in the tomato paste, chile powder, oregano, and cumin, and salt. Cook and stir for 1 minute. Whisk in the broth and lemon juice. Bring to a simmer and cook, stirring occasionally, while the stuffed peppers finish cooking.
4. Cut a slit down the center of each poblano pepper, starting at the stem and continuing to the tip. Remove the seeds, being careful not to tear the chile.
5. Carefully stuff each pepper with half the corn mixture. Place the stuffed peppers in a 7-inch round baking pan with 4-inch sides. Place the pan in the air-fryer cooking tray. Select Roast. Set temperature to 400ºF (205ºC), and set time to 10 minutes, or until the cheese has melted.
6. Transfer the stuffed peppers to a serving platter and drizzle with the sauce and some crema.

## Vegetable with Grated Eggs

**Prep time: 5 minutes | Cook time: 12 minutes | Serves 4**

2 teaspoons melted butter
1 cup chopped mushrooms
1 cup cooked rice
1 cup peas
1 carrot, chopped

1 red onion, chopped
1 garlic clove, minced
Salt and black pepper, to taste
2 hard-boiled eggs, grated
1 tablespoon soy sauce

1. Coat a baking dish with melted butter.
2. Stir together the mushrooms, carrot, peas, onion, garlic, cooked rice, salt, and pepper in a large bowl until well mixed.
3. Pour the mixture into the prepared baking dish and transfer to the oven.
4. Select Roast. Set temperature to 380ºF (195ºC), and set time to 12 minutes until the vegetables are tender.
5. Divide the mixture among four plates. Serve warm with a sprinkle of grated eggs and a drizzle of soy sauce.

## Spiced Glazed Carrot

**Prep time: 10 minutes | Cook time: 30 minutes | Serves 4**

Vegetable oil spray
4 cups frozen sliced carrots (do not thaw)
2 tablespoons brown sugar
2 tablespoons water
½ teaspoon ground

cumin
½ teaspoon ground cinnamon
¼ teaspoon kosher salt
2 tablespoons coconut oil
Chopped fresh parsley, for garnish

1. Spray a 6 × 4-inch round heatproof pan with vegetable oil spray.
2. In a medium bowl, combine the carrots, brown sugar, water, cumin, cinnamon, and salt. Toss to coat. Transfer to the prepared pan. Dot the carrots with the coconut oil, distributing it evenly across the pan. Cover the pan with foil.
3. Place the pan in the air fryer cooking tray. Select Roast. Set temperature to 400ºF (205ºC), and set time to 10 minutes. Remove the foil and stir well. Place the uncovered pan back in the oven. Select Roast. Set temperature to 400ºF (205ºC), and set time to 20 minutes, or until the glaze is bubbling and the carrots are cooked through.
4. Garnish with parsley and serve.

## Jerk Rubbed Corn on the Cob

**Prep time: 10 minutes | Cook time: 6 minutes | Serves 4**

| | |
|---|---|
| 1 teaspoon ground allspice | nutmeg |
| 1 teaspoon dried thyme | ⅛ teaspoon ground cayenne pepper |
| ½ teaspoon ground ginger | 1 teaspoon salt |
| ½ teaspoon ground cinnamon | 2 tablespoons butter, melted |
| ¼ teaspoon ground | 4 ears of corn, husked |

1. Preheat the oven to 380ºF (195ºC).
2. Combine all the spices in a bowl. Brush the corn with the melted butter and then sprinkle the spices generously on all sides of each ear of corn.
3. Transfer the ears of corn to the air fryer cooking tray. It's ok if they are crisscrossed on top of each other. Select Roast. Set temperature to 380ºF (195ºC), and set time to 6 minutes, rotating the ears as they cook.
4. Brush more butter on at the end and sprinkle with any remaining spice mixture.

## Asparagus with Tarragon

**Prep time: 5 minutes | Cook time: 5 minutes | Serves 4**

| | |
|---|---|
| 1 (1-pound / 454-g) bunch asparagus, washed and trimmed | tarragon, crushed |
| ⅛ teaspoon dried | Salt and pepper, to taste |
| | 1 to 2 teaspoons extra-light olive oil |

1. Spread asparagus spears on cookie sheet or cutting board.
2. Sprinkle with tarragon, salt, and pepper.
3. Drizzle with 1 teaspoon of oil and roll the spears or mix by hand. If needed, add up to 1 more teaspoon of oil and mix again until all spears are lightly coated.
4. Place spears in air fryer cooking tray. If necessary, bend the longer spears to make them fit. It doesn't matter if they don't lie flat.
5. Select Broil. Set temperature to 390ºF (200ºC), and set time to 5 minutes. Shake air fryer cooking tray or stir spears with a spoon.
6. Cook for an additional 4 to 5 minutes or just until crisp-tender.

## Cheddar Potato Pot

**Prep time: 10 minutes | Cook time: 15 minutes | Serves 4**

| | |
|---|---|
| 3 cups cubed red potatoes (unpeeled, cut into ½-inch cubes) | garnish (optional) |
| | For the Sauce: |
| ½ teaspoon garlic powder | 2 tablespoons milk |
| | 1 tablespoon butter |
| Salt and pepper, to taste | 2 ounces (57 g) sharp Cheddar cheese, grated |
| 1 tablespoon oil | 1 tablespoon sour cream |
| Chopped chives for | |

1. Place potato cubes in large bowl and sprinkle with garlic, salt, and pepper. Add oil and stir to coat well.
2. Select Roast. Set temperature to 390ºF (200ºC), and set time to 13 to 15 minutes or until potatoes are tender. Stir every 4 or 5 minutes during cooking time.
3. While potatoes are cooking, combine milk and butter in a small saucepan. Warm over medium-low heat to melt butter. Add cheese and stir until it melts. The melted cheese will remain separated from the milk mixture. Remove from heat until potatoes are done.
4. When ready to serve, add sour cream to cheese mixture and stir over medium-low heat just until warmed. Place cooked potatoes in a serving bowl. Pour sauce over potatoes and stir to combine.
5. Garnish with chives if desired.

## Creole Potato Wedges

**Prep time: 10 minutes | Cook time: 10 minutes | Serves 3 to 4**

| | |
|---|---|
| 1 pound (454 g) medium Yukon gold potatoes | ½ teaspoon salt |
| ½ teaspoon cayenne pepper | ½ teaspoon smoked paprika |
| ½ teaspoon thyme | 1 cup dry breadcrumbs |
| ½ teaspoon garlic powder | Oil for misting or cooking spray |

1. Wash potatoes, cut into thick wedges, and drop wedges into a bowl of water to prevent browning.
2. Mix together the cayenne pepper, thyme, garlic powder, salt, paprika, and breadcrumbs and spread on a sheet of wax paper.
3. Remove potatoes from water and, without drying them, roll in the breadcrumb mixture.
4. Spray air fryer cooking tray with oil or cooking spray and pile potato wedges into cooking tray It's okay if they form more than a single layer.
5. Select Air Fry. Set temperature to 390ºF (200ºC), and set time to 8 minutes. Shake cooking tray, then continue cooking for 2 to 7 minutes longer, until the coating is crisp and potato centers are soft. Total cooking time will vary, depending on thickness of potato wedges.

# Balsamic Pearl Onions

**Prep time: 10 minutes | Cook time: 18 minutes | Serves 3**

1 package(14½ ounces / 411.1 g) frozen pearl onions (do not thaw)
2 tablespoons extra-virgin olive oil
2 tablespoons balsamic vinegar
2 teaspoons finely chopped fresh rosemary
½ teaspoon kosher salt
¼ teaspoon black pepper

1. In a medium bowl, combine the onions, olive oil, vinegar, rosemary, salt, and pepper until well coated.
2. Transfer the onions to the air fryer cooking tray. Select Roast. Set temperature to 400ºF (205ºC), and set time to 18 minutes, or until the onions are tender and lightly charred, stirring once or twice during the cooking time.

# Chinese Five-Spiced Butternut Squash

**Prep time: 5 minutes | Cook time: 15 minutes | Serves 4**

4 cups 1-inch-cubed butternut squash
2 tablespoons vegetable oil
1 to 2 tablespoons brown sugar
1 teaspoon Chinese five-spice powder

1. In a medium bowl, combine the squash, oil, sugar, and five-spice powder. Toss to coat.
2. Place the squash in the air fryer cooking tray. Select Roast. Set temperature to 400ºF (205ºC), and set time to 15 minutes or until tender.

# Roasted Lemony Cauliflower

**Prep time: 5 minutes | Cook time: 15 minutes | Serves 2**

1 medium head cauliflower
2 tablespoons salted butter, melted
1 medium lemon
1 teaspoon dried parsley
½ teaspoon garlic powder

1. Having removed the leaves from the cauliflower head, brush it with the melted butter. Grate the rind of the lemon over it and then drizzle some juice. Finally add the parsley and garlic powder on top.
2. Transfer the cauliflower to the cooking tray of the oven.

3. Select Roast. Set temperature to 350ºF (175ºC), and set time to 15 minutes, checking regularly to ensure it doesn't overcook. The cauliflower is ready when it is hot and fork-tender.
4. Take care when removing it from the oven, cut up and serve.

# Cheddar Mushroom Loaf

**Prep time: 5 minutes | Cook time: 15 minutes | Serves 2**

2 cups mushrooms, chopped
½ cups Cheddar cheese, shredded
¾ cup flour
2 tablespoons butter, melted
2 eggs
salt and pepper (optional)

1. In a food processor, pulse together the mushrooms, cheese, flour, melted butter, and eggs, along with some salt and pepper if desired, until a uniform consistency is achieved.
2. Transfer into a silicone loaf pan, spreading and leveling with a palette knife.
3. Preheat the oven at 375ºF (190ºC) and put the rack inside.
4. Select Roast. Set temperature to 375ºF (190ºC), and set time to 15 minutes.
5. Take care when removing the pan from the fryer and leave it to cool. Then slice and serve.

# Stuffed Eggplant Shell

**Prep time: 5 minutes | Cook time: 28 minutes | Serves 2**

Large eggplant
¼ medium yellow onion, diced
2 tablespoons red bell
pepper, diced
1 cup spinach
¼ cup artichoke hearts, chopped

1. Cut the eggplant lengthwise into slices and spoon out the flesh, leaving a shell about a half-inch thick. Chop it up and set aside.
2. Set a skillet over a medium heat and spritz with cooking spray. Cook the onions for about 3 to 5 minutes to soften. Then add the pepper, spinach, artichokes, and the flesh of eggplant. Cook for a further 5 minutes, then remove from the heat.
3. Scoop this mixture in equal parts into the eggplant shells and place each one in the oven.
4. Select Roast. Set temperature to 320ºF (160ºC), and set time to 20 minutes until the eggplant shells are soft. Serve warm.

## Super Vegetable Rolls

**Prep time: 20 minutes | Cook time: 10 minutes | Serves 6**

| | |
|---|---|
| 2 potatoes, mashed | 1 small onion, chopped |
| ¼ cup peas | ½ cup bread crumbs |
| ¼ cup mashed carrots | 1 packet spring roll |
| 1 small cabbage, sliced | sheets |
| ¼ cups beans | ½ cup cornstarch slurry |
| 2 tablespoons sweetcorn | |

1. Boil all the vegetables in water over a low heat. Rinse and allow to dry.
2. Unroll the spring roll sheets and spoon equal amounts of vegetables onto the center of each one. Fold into spring rolls and coat each one with the slurry and bread crumbs.
3. Select Roast. Set temperature to 390ºF (200ºC), and set time to 10 minutes.
4. Serve warm.

## Garlicky Carrot with Sesame Seeds

**Prep time: 5 minutes | Cook time: 16 minutes | Serves 4 to 6**

| | |
|---|---|
| 1 pound (454 g) baby carrots | Freshly ground black pepper, to taste |
| 1 tablespoon sesame oil | 6 cloves garlic, peeled |
| ½ teaspoon dried dill | 3 tablespoons sesame seeds |
| Pinch salt | |

1. In a medium bowl, drizzle the baby carrots with the sesame oil. Sprinkle with the dill, salt, and pepper and toss to coat well.
2. Place the baby carrots in the air fryer cooking tray and select Roast. Set temperature to 380ºF (195ºC), and set time to 8 minutes.
3. Remove the cooking tray and stir in the garlic. Return the cooking tray to the oven and roast for another 8 minutes, or until the carrots are lightly browned.
4. Serve sprinkled with the sesame seeds.

## Heirloom Carrots with Thyme

**Prep time: 5 minutes | Cook time: 12 minutes | Serves 2**

| | |
|---|---|
| 10 to 12 heirloom(1 pound / 454 g) or rainbow carrots, scrubbed but not peeled | Salt and freshly ground black pepper, to taste |
| 1 teaspoon olive oil | 1 tablespoon butter |
| | 1 teaspoon fresh orange zest |
| 1 teaspoon chopped | fresh thyme |

1. Preheat the oven to 400ºF (205ºC).
2. Scrub the carrots and halve them lengthwise. Toss them in the olive oil, season with salt and freshly ground black pepper and transfer to the oven.
3. Select Roast. Set temperature to 400ºF (205ºC), and set time to 12 minutes, shaking the cooking tray every once in a while to rotate the carrots as they cook.
4. As soon as the carrots have finished cooking, add the butter, orange zest and thyme and toss all the ingredients together in the air fryer cooking tray to melt the butter and coat evenly. Serve warm.

## Caesar Whole Cauliflower

**Prep time: 10 minutes | Cook time: 30 minutes | Serves 2 to 4**

| | |
|---|---|
| 3 tablespoons olive oil | minced |
| 2 tablespoons red wine vinegar | Kosher salt and freshly ground black pepper, to taste |
| 2 tablespoons Worcestershire sauce | 1 small head (1 pound / 454 g) cauliflower, green leaves trimmed and stem trimmed flush with the bottom of the head |
| 2 tablespoons grated Parmesan cheese | |
| 1 tablespoon Dijon mustard | |
| 4 garlic cloves, minced | 1 tablespoon roughly chopped fresh flat-leaf parsley (optional) |
| 4 oil-packed anchovy fillets, drained and finely | |

1. In a liquid measuring cup, whisk together the olive oil, vinegar, Worcestershire, Parmesan, mustard, garlic, anchovies, and salt and pepper to taste. Place the cauliflower head upside down on a cutting board and use a paring knife to make an "x" through the full length of the core. Transfer the cauliflower head to a large bowl and pour half the dressing over it. Turn the cauliflower head to coat it in the dressing, then let it rest in the dressing for at least 10 minutes and up to 30 minutes, stem-side up, to allow the dressing to seep into all its nooks and crannies.
2. Transfer the cauliflower head, stem-side down, to the oven and select Roast. Set temperature to 340ºF (170ºC), and set time to 25 minutes. Drizzle the remaining dressing over the cauliflower and roast at 400ºF (205ºC) until the top of the cauliflower is golden brown and the core is tender, for about 5 minutes or more.
3. Remove the cooking tray from the oven and transfer the cauliflower to a large plate. Sprinkle with the parsley, if you like, and serve hot.

# Mexican Corn in a Cup

**Prep time: 10 minutes | Cook time: 10 minutes | Serves 4**

4 cups frozen corn kernels (do not thaw)
Vegetable oil spray
2 tablespoons butter
¼ cup sour cream
¼ cup mayonnaise
¼ cup grated Parmesan cheese (or Feta, cotija, or

queso fresco)
2 tablespoons fresh lemon or lime juice
1 teaspoon chili powder
Chopped fresh green onion (optional)
Chopped fresh cilantro (optional)

1. Place the corn in the bottom of the air fryer cooking tray and spray with vegetable oil spray. Select Roast. Set temperature to 350ºF (175ºC), and set time to 10 minutes.
2. Transfer the corn to a serving bowl. Add the butter and stir until melted. Add the sour cream, mayonnaise, cheese, lemon juice, and chili powder; stir until well combined. Serve immediately with green onion and cilantro (if using).

# Parmesan Broccoli Crust

**Prep time: 5 minutes | Cook time: 28 minutes | Serves 1**

3 cups broccoli rice, steamed
½ cup Parmesan cheese, grated
1 egg

3 tablespoons low-carb Alfredo sauce
½ cup Mozzarella cheese, grated

1. Drain the broccoli rice and combine with the Parmesan cheese and egg in a bowl, mixing well.
2. Cut a piece of parchment paper roughly the size of the base of the fryer's cooking tray. Spoon four equal-sized amounts of the broccoli mixture onto the paper and press each portion into the shape of a pizza crust. You may have to complete this part in two batches. Transfer the parchment to the fryer.
3. Select Roast. Set temperature to 370ºF (190ºC), and set time to 5 minutes. When the crust is firm, flip it over and roast for an additional 2 minutes.
4. Add the Alfredo sauce and Mozzarella cheese on top of the crusts and select Broil for an additional 7 minutes. The crusts are ready when the sauce and cheese have melted. Serve hot.

# White Button Mushrooms

**Prep time: 10 minutes | Cook time: 10 minutes | Serves 4**

8 ounces (227 g)whole white button mushrooms
½ teaspoon salt
⅛ teaspoon pepper
¼ teaspoon garlic powder
¼ teaspoon onion powder

5 tablespoons potato starch
1 egg, beaten
¾ cup panko breadcrumbs
Oil for misting or cooking spray

1. Place mushrooms in a large bowl. Add the salt, pepper, garlic and onion powders, and stir well to distribute seasonings.
2. Add potato starch to mushrooms and toss in bowl until well coated.
3. Dip mushrooms in beaten egg, roll in panko crumbs, and mist with oil or cooking spray.
4. Place mushrooms in air fryer cooking tray. You can cook them all at once, and it's okay if a few are stacked.
5. Select Roast. Set temperature to 390ºF (200ºC), and set time to 5 minutes. Shake air fryer cooking tray, then continue cooking for 5 to 7 minutes, until golden brown and crispy.

# Chapter 9 Bread, Sandwiches and Pizza

## Tuscan Toast

**Prep time: 5 minutes | Cook time: 5 minutes | Serves 4**

¼ cup butter
½ teaspoon lemon juice
½ clove garlic
½ teaspoon dried parsley
flakes
4 slices Italian bread,
1-inch thick

1. Place butter, lemon juice, garlic, and parsley in a food processor. Process for about 1 minute, or until garlic is pulverized and ingredients are well blended.
2. Spread garlic butter on both sides of bread slices.
3. Place bread slices upright in air fryer cooking tray, then put it into the air fryer oven.
4. Select Bake, set the temperature to 390ºF (200ºC), and set the time to 5 minutes or until toasty brown.

## Vegan Crushed Tomato Pizza

**Prep time: 10 minutes | Cook time: 8 minutes | Makes 1 pizza**

1 tablespoon walnut halves
1½ teaspoons nutritional yeast
½ teaspoon garlic powder
4 ounces (113 g) pizza dough
2 teaspoons olive oil
2 canned whole peeled tomatoes, crushed by hand and drained
Kosher salt and freshly ground black pepper, to taste
1 tablespoon thinly sliced fresh flat-leaf parsley

1. Set a Microplane grater over a small bowl and grate the walnuts into the bowl. Stir in the nutritional yeast and garlic powder. Roll and stretch the pizza dough into a 6-inch round.
2. Lay the dough round in the air fryer cooking tray, then brush with 1 teaspoon of the olive oil. Arrange the crushed tomatoes over the dough and sprinkle with the walnut "Parmesan" mixture. Season with salt and pepper, drizzle with the remaining 1 teaspoon olive oil, and select Pizza, set the temperature to 350ºF (177ºC), and set the time to 8 minutes or until the dough is cooked through, the tomatoes are dried out, and the "Parmesan" is browned.
3. Transfer the pizza to a plate, sprinkle with the parsley, and serve hot.

## Mushroom and Tomato Pita Pizza

**Prep time: 10 minutes | Cook time: 3 minutes | Serves 4**

4 (3-inch) pitas
1 tablespoon olive oil
¾ cup pizza sauce
1 jar (4 ounces /113g) sliced mushrooms, drained
½ teaspoon dried basil
2 green onions, minced
1 cup grated Mozzarella or provolone cheese
1 cup sliced grape tomatoes

1. Brush each piece of pita with oil and top with the pizza sauce.
2. Add the mushrooms and sprinkle with basil and green onions. Top with the grated cheese.
3. Select Pizza, and set the time to 3 to 6 minutes or until the cheese is melted and starts to brown. Top with the grape tomatoes and serve immediately.

## Chocolate Bread

**Prep time: 15 minutes | Cook time: 15 minutes | Serves 12**

1 tablespoon flax egg (1 tablespoon flax meal + 3 tablespoons water)
1 cup zucchini, shredded and squeezed
½ cup sunflower oil
½ cup maple syrup
1 teaspoon vanilla extract
1 teaspoon apple cider
vinegar
½ cup milk
1 cup flour
1 teaspoon baking soda
½ cup unsweetened cocoa powder
¼ teaspoon salt
⅓ cup chocolate chips

1. Preheat your Air Fryer oven to 350ºF (175ºC).
2. Take a baking dish small enough to fit inside the fryer and line it with parchment paper.
3. Mix together the flax egg, zucchini, sunflower oil, maple, vanilla, apple cider vinegar and milk in a bowl.
4. Incorporate the flour, cocoa powder, salt and baking soda, stirring all the time to combine everything well.
5. Finally, throw in the chocolate chips.
6. Transfer the batter to the baking dish and select Bake, set the temperature to 350ºF (175ºC), and set the time to 15 minutes. Make sure to test with a toothpick before serving by sticking it in the center. The bread is ready when the toothpick comes out clean.

## Banana Bread

**Prep time: 10 minutes | Cook time: 20 minutes | Makes 1 loaf**

Cooking spray
1 cup white wheat flour
½ teaspoon baking powder
¼ teaspoon salt
¼ teaspoon baking soda
1 egg

½ cup mashed ripe banana
¼ cup plain yogurt
¼ cup pure maple syrup
2 tablespoons coconut oil
½ teaspoon pure vanilla extract

1. Preheat air fryer oven to 330ºF (165ºC).
2. Lightly spray 6 x 6-inch baking dish with cooking spray.
3. In a medium bowl, mix together the flour, baking powder, salt, and soda.
4. In a separate bowl, beat the egg and add the mashed banana, yogurt, syrup, oil, and vanilla. Mix until well combined.
5. Pour liquid mixture into dry ingredients and stir gently to blend. Do not beat. Batter may be slightly lumpy.
6. Pour batter into baking dish and select Bake, set the temperature to 330ºF (165ºC), and set the time to 20 minutes or until toothpick inserted in center of loaf comes out clean.

## Homemade Pizza Dough

**Prep time: 5 minutes | Cook time: 0 minutes | Makes 3 (6- to 8-ounce) dough balls**

4 cups bread flour, pizza flour or all-purpose flour
1 teaspoon active dry yeast

2 teaspoons sugar
2 teaspoons salt
1½ cups water
1 tablespoon olive oil

1. Combine the flour, yeast, sugar and salt in the bowl of a stand mixer. Add the olive oil to the flour mixture and start to mix using the dough hook attachment. As you're mixing, add 1¼ cups of the water, mixing until the dough comes together. Continue to knead the dough with the dough hook for another 10 minutes, adding enough water to the dough to get it to the right consistency.
2. Transfer the dough to a floured counter and divide it into 3 equal portions. Roll each portion into a ball. Lightly coat each dough ball with oil and transfer to the refrigerator, covered with plastic wrap. You can place them all on a baking sheet, or place each dough ball into its own oiled zipper sealable plastic

bag or container. (You can freeze the dough balls at this stage, removing as much air as possible from the oiled bag.) Keep in the refrigerator for at least one day, or as long as five days.
3. When you're ready to use the dough, remove your dough from the refrigerator at least 1 hour prior to baking and let it sit on the counter, covered gently with plastic wrap.

## Parmesan Bread Ring

**Prep time: 10 minutes | Cook time: 30 minutes | Serves 6 to 8**

½ cup unsalted butter, melted
¼ teaspoon salt (omit if using salted butter)
¾ cup grated Parmesan cheese
3 to 4 cloves garlic,

minced
1 tablespoon chopped fresh parsley
1 pound (454 g) frozen bread dough, defrosted
Olive oil
1 egg, beaten

1. Combine the melted butter, salt, Parmesan cheese, garlic and chopped parsley in a small bowl.
2. Roll the dough out into a rectangle that measures 8 inches by 17 inches. Spread the butter mixture over the dough, leaving a half-inch border un-buttered along one of the long edges. Roll the dough from one long edge to the other, ending with the un-buttered border. Pinch the seam shut tightly. Shape the log into a circle sealing the ends together by pushing one end into the other and stretching the dough around it.
3. Cut out a circle of aluminum foil that is the same size as the air fryer cooking tray. Brush the foil circle with oil and place an oven-safe ramekin or glass in the center. Transfer the dough ring to the aluminum foil circle, around the ramekin. This will help you make sure the dough will fit in the cooking tray and maintain its ring shape. Use kitchen shears to cut 8 slits around the outer edge of the dough ring halfway to the center. Brush the dough ring with egg wash.
4. Preheat the oven to 400ºF (205ºC) for 4 minutes. Brush the sides of the cooking tray with oil and transfer the dough ring, foil circle and ramekin into the cooking tray. Slide the drawer back into the oven, but do not turn the oven on. Let the dough rise inside the warm air fryer oven for 30 minutes.
5. After the bread has proofed in the air fryer oven for 30 minutes, select Air Fry, set the temperature to 340ºF (170ºC), and set the time to 15 minutes. Flip the bread over by inverting it onto a plate or cutting board and sliding it back into the air fryer cooking tray. Air fry for another 15 minutes.

## Whole-Grain Corn Bread

**Prep time: 15 minutes | Cook time: 25 minutes | Serves 6**

2 tablespoons ground flaxseed
3 tablespoons water
½ cup cornmeal
½ cup whole-wheat pastry flour
⅓ cup coconut sugar
½ tablespoon baking powder
¼ teaspoon sea salt
¼ teaspoon baking soda
½ tablespoon apple cider vinegar
½ cup plus 1 tablespoon non-dairy milk (unsweetened)
¼ cup neutral-flavored oil (such as sunflower, safflower, or melted refined coconut)
Cooking oil spray (sunflower, safflower, or refined coconut)

1. In a small bowl, combine the flaxseed and water. Set aside for 5 minutes, or until thick and gooey.
2. In a medium bowl, add the cornmeal, flour, sugar, baking powder, salt, and baking soda. Combine thoroughly, stirring with a whisk. Set aside.
3. Add the vinegar, milk, and oil to the flaxseed mixture and stir well.
4. Add the wet mixture to the dry mixture and stir gently, just until thoroughly combined.
5. Spray (or coat) a 6-inch round, 2-inch deep baking pan with oil. Pour the batter into it and select Bake, set the time to 25 minutes or until golden-browned and a knife inserted in the center comes out clean. Cut into wedges, top with a little vegan margarine if desired.

## Sherry Cheesy Pull-Apart Bread

**Prep time: 10 minutes | Cook time: 20 minutes | Serves 2 to 4**

1 small sourdough boule
2 tablespoons olive oil
1 tablespoon sherry vinegar
2 teaspoons Worcestershire sauce
1 teaspoon minced anchovies or anchovy paste (optional)
2 garlic cloves, minced
Kosher salt and freshly ground black pepper, to taste
⅔ cup grated smoked Mozzarella cheese
2 tablespoons grated pecorino cheese

1. Place the sourdough boule on a cutting board and, if necessary, trim its edges so it fits snugly within your air fryer's cooking tray. Cut through the top of the bread in a crisscross pattern, spacing the cuts every ½ inch and making sure to not cut all the way through so the bread stays together.

2. In a bowl, whisk together the olive oil, vinegar, Worcestershire, anchovies (if using), and garlic. Season liberally with salt and pepper and whisk again to combine. Working on a cutting board, drizzle the dressing evenly into all the grooves of the bread. Sprinkle the bread evenly with the Mozzarella and then the pecorino.
3. Place the bread in the air fryer, tent with a round of foil, and select Bake, set the temperature to 310ºF (155ºC), and set the time to 12 minutes. Uncover the bread and bake until the bread is toasted at the edges and the cheese is golden brown, about 8 minutes more. Remove the bread from the air fryer and serve hot.

## Cheesy Olive and Roasted Pepper Bread

**Prep time: 10 minutes | Cook time: 14 minutes | Serves 8**

7-inch round bread boule
Olive oil
½ cup mayonnaise
2 tablespoons butter, melted
1 cup grated Mozzarella or Fontina cheese
¼ cup grated Parmesan cheese
½ teaspoon dried oregano
½ cup black olives, sliced
½ cup green olives, sliced
½ cup coarsely chopped roasted red peppers
2 tablespoons minced red onion
Freshly ground black pepper, to taste

1. Preheat the air fryer oven to 370ºF (188ºC).
2. Cut the bread boule in half horizontally. If your bread boule has a rounded top, trim the top of the boule so that the top half will lie flat with the cut side facing up. Lightly brush both sides of the boule halves with olive oil.
3. Place one-half of the boule into the air fryer cooking tray with the center cut side facing down. Select Air Fry, set the temperature to 370ºF (190ºC), and set the time to 2 minutes to lightly toast the bread. Repeat with the other half of the bread boule.
4. Combine the mayonnaise, butter, Mozzarella cheese, Parmesan cheese and dried oregano in a small bowl. Fold in the black and green olives, roasted red peppers and red onion and season with freshly ground black pepper. Spread the cheese mixture over the untoasted side of the bread, covering the entire surface.
5. Select Air Fry, set the temperature to 350ºF (175ºC), and set time to 5 minutes until the cheese is melted and browned. Repeat with the other half. Cut into slices and serve warm.

# Cheddar and Mango Chutney Puff Pie

**Prep time: 5 minutes | Cook time: 20 minutes | Serves 1 to 2**

1 sheet puff pastry
3 ounces (85 g) extra-sharp Cheddar cheese, cut into thin slices
¼ cup chunky mango chutney
Kosher salt and freshly ground black pepper, to taste
Egg wash
Crackers and crudités, for serving

1. With a rolling pin, roll the puff pastry sheet into a 14-inch square. Cut out two 7-inch rounds and discard the scraps (or save for another use). Arrange the Cheddar in the middle of one round, then top with the chutney and season with salt and pepper. Brush the edge of the round with egg wash and top with the second pastry round. Use a fork to press and crimp the edges together.
2. Transfer the pastry round to the air fryer oven and select Bake, set the temperature to 325ºF (165ºC), and set the time to 20 minutes or until the pastry is puffed and golden brown and the cheese is melted inside.
3. Transfer the puff pie to a cutting board and let it cool for 5 minutes. Cut the pie into 4 wedges and serve warm with crackers and crudités.

# XL Chimichurri Beef Empanadas

**Prep time: 10 minutes | Cook time: 24 minutes | Serves 2**

½ pound (227 g) trimmed beef sirloin, cut into ½-inch pieces, at room temperature
1 tablespoon chopped fresh flat-leaf parsley leaves
1 tablespoon chopped fresh cilantro leaves
1 tablespoon chopped fresh mint leaves
1 tablespoon olive oil
2 teaspoons red wine vinegar
½ teaspoon kosher salt
¼ teaspoon ground cumin
2 garlic cloves, minced
Freshly ground black pepper, to taste
12 ounces (340 g) pizza dough

1. In a bowl, toss together the beef, parsley, cilantro, mint, olive oil, vinegar, salt, cumin, garlic, and pepper.
2. Divide the dough in half and flatten each portion into a 10-inch round. Divide the beef mixture between the 2 dough rounds, then fold them in half to create 2 half-moons. Use a fork or your fingers to crimp and twist the edges of the dough in on itself to seal the empanadas completely.
3. Place one empanada in the air fryer cooking tray, cut a hole in the top with a paring knife to vent, and select Bake, set the temperature to 350ºF (175ºC), and set the time to 12 minutes or until the dough is golden brown and the beef is cooked through. Transfer the empanada to a plate and let it cool for 2 minutes before serving. Repeat for the second empanada.

# Sweet Rosemary Knots

**Prep time: 15 minutes | Cook time: 14 minutes | Makes 8 garlic knots**

¼ cup milk, heated to 115ºF (46ºC) in the microwave
½ teaspoon active dry yeast
1 tablespoon honey or agave syrup
⅔ cup all-purpose flour, plus more for dusting
½ teaspoon kosher salt
2 tablespoons unsalted
butter, at room temperature, plus more for greasing and brushing
2 tablespoons olive oil
1 tablespoon finely chopped fresh rosemary
1 teaspoon garlic powder
2 garlic cloves, minced
¼ teaspoon freshly ground black pepper
Flaky sea salt

1. In a large bowl, whisk together the milk, yeast, and honey and let them stand until foamy, about 10 minutes. Stir in the flour and kosher salt until just combined. Stir in the butter until completely absorbed. Scrape the dough onto a lightly floured work surface and knead until smooth, for about 6 minutes. Transfer the dough to a bowl lightly greased with more butter, cover loosely with a sheet of plastic wrap or a kitchen towel, and let sit until nearly doubled in size, for about 1 hour.
2. Uncover the dough, lightly press it down to expel the bubbles, then portion it into 8 equal pieces. Roll each piece into a 6-inch rope, then tie it into a simple knot, tucking the loose ends into each side of the "hoop" made by the knot. Return the knots to the bowl they proofed in, then add the olive oil, rosemary, garlic powder, fresh garlic, and pepper. Toss the knots until coated in the oil and spices, then nestle them side by side in the air fryer cooking tray. Cover the knots loosely with plastic wrap and let sit until lightly risen and puffed, for 20 to 30 minutes.
3. Uncover the knots and select Bake, set the temperature to 280ºF (138ºC), and set the time to 14 minutes or until the knots are golden brown outside and tender and fluffy inside. Remove the garlic knots from the air fryer and brush with a little more butter, if you like, and sprinkle with a pinch of sea salt. Serve warm.

## BLT Sandwich

**Prep time: 10 minutes | Cook time: 10 minutes | Serves 3**

6 ounces (170 g) bacon, thick-cut
2 tablespoons brown sugar
2 teaspoons chipotle chile powder
1 teaspoon cayenne pepper

1 tablespoon Dijon mustard
1 heads lettuce, torn into leaves
2 medium tomatoes, sliced
6 (½-inch) slices white bread

1. Toss the bacon with the sugar, chipotle chile powder, cayenne pepper, and mustard.
2. Place the bacon in the Air Fryer cooking tray. Then select Bake, set the temperature to 400ºF (205ºC), and set the time to 10 minutes, tossing the cooking tray halfway through the cooking time.
3. Assemble your sandwiches with the bacon, lettuce, tomato and bread.
4. Bon appétit!

## Samosa Veggie Pot Pie

**Prep time: 15 minutes | Cook time: 51 minutes | Serves 2**

3 tablespoons vegetable oil
1 teaspoon brown mustard seeds
1 medium yellow onion, roughly chopped
½ to 1 serrano chile, seeded and minced
1 teaspoon garam masala
1 teaspoon ground coriander
½ teaspoon ground cumin
½ teaspoon ground turmeric
½ teaspoon sweet

paprika
3 garlic cloves, minced
1 pound (454 g) russet potatoes, peeled, boiled, and cut into 1-inch chunks
½ cup thawed frozen peas
2 teaspoons fresh lemon juice
Kosher salt and freshly ground black pepper, to taste
All-purpose flour, for rolling/dusting
2 sheets puff pastry, thawed if frozen

1. In a medium saucepan, heat the oil over medium-high heat. Add the mustard seeds and cook until they begin popping, for 1 to 1½ minutes. Add the onion and chile and cook, stirring, until soft and caramelized at the edges, for about 10 minutes.
2. Add the garam masala, coriander, cumin, turmeric, paprika, and garlic and cook until fragrant, about

1 minute. Stir in the potatoes, peas, and lemon juice, breaking the potatoes up slightly and stirring until everything is coated in the yellow stain of the turmeric. Remove the pan from the heat, season the filling with salt and pepper, and let it cool completely. The filling can be made and stored in a bowl in the refrigerator for up to 3 days before you plan to cook the pie.
3. Working on a lightly floured surface, roll 1 pastry sheet into a 10-inch square, then cut out a 10-inch round, discarding the scraps. Mound the cooled potato filling in the center of the dough round, then press and mold it with your hands into a 7-inch disk. Cut a 7-inch round out of the second pastry sheet (no need to roll) and place it over the filling disk. Brush the edge of the bottom dough round with water just to moisten, then lift it up to meet the top dough round. Pinch and fold the edges together all around the filling to form and enclose the pie.
4. Transfer the pie to the air fryer, and cut a slit in the top of the pie with a paring knife to vent. Cover the top of the pie loosely with a round of foil, and select Bake, set the temperature to 310ºF (155ºC), and set the time to 20 minutes. Remove the foil and bake at 330ºF (165ºC) until the pastry is golden brown and the filling is piping hot, about 20 minutes or more.

## Cumin Lamb, Green Olive, and Cheese Pizza

**Prep time: 10 minutes | Cook time: 8 minutes | Makes 1 pizza**

4 ounces (113 g) pizza dough
2 teaspoons olive oil
1½ ounces ground lamb, crumbled into small bits
¼ teaspoon ground cumin
¼ teaspoon smoked

paprika
6 pitted green olives, roughly chopped
1 ounce (28 g) Feta cheese, crumbled
Kosher salt and freshly ground black pepper, to taste

1. Roll and stretch the pizza dough into a 6-inch round.
2. Lay the dough round in the air fryer, then brush with 1 teaspoon of the olive oil. Arrange the lamb crumbles over the dough and sprinkle with the cumin and paprika, followed by the olives and Feta. Season with salt and pepper, drizzle with the remaining 1 teaspoon of olive oil, and select Pizza, set the temperature to 350ºF (180ºC), and set the time to 8 minutes or until the dough is cooked through and the meat is browned and crisp on top.
3. Transfer the pizza to a plate and serve hot.

## Egg Salad Sandwich

**Prep time: 10 minutes | Cook time: 22 minutes | Serves 3**

6 eggs
2 tablespoons scallions, chopped
2 garlic cloves, minced
¼ cup sour cream
¼ cup mayonnaise
1 teaspoon yellow

mustard
Sea salt and ground black pepper, to taste
1 garlic clove, minced
6 slices whole-grain bread

1. Place the eggs in the Air Fryer cooking tray.
2. Select Air Fry, set the temperature to 270ºF (130ºC), and set the time to 15 minutes.
3. Peel and chop the eggs; place them in a salad bowl and add in the remaining ingredients. Gently toss to combine.
4. Next, for the bread slices, select Air Fry, set the temperature to 330ºF (165ºC), and set the time to 4 minutes. Turn them over and air fry for a further 3 to 4 minutes.
5. Lastly, assemble your sandwiches with the egg salad and toasted bread.
6. Bon appétit!

## Double Cheese Salami and Kale Pizza

**Prep time: 10 minutes | Cook time: 8 minutes | Makes 1 pizza**

4 ounces (113 g) pizza dough
2 teaspoons olive oil
¼ cup packed torn kale leaves
5 slices (1½ to 2 inch diameters) salami
3 tablespoons grated

Asiago cheese
2 tablespoons shredded low-moisture Mozzarella cheese
Kosher salt and freshly ground black pepper, to taste

1. Roll and stretch the pizza dough into a 6-inch round.
2. Lay the dough round in the air fryer, then brush with 1 teaspoon of the olive oil. Arrange the kale leaves over the dough, followed by the salami slices. Sprinkle with the Asiago and Mozzarella. Season with salt and pepper, drizzle with the remaining 1 teaspoon olive oil, and select Pizza, set the temperature to 350ºF (177ºC), and set the time to 8 minutes or until the dough is cooked through and the cheese is melted and golden brown.
3. Transfer the pizza to a plate and serve hot.

## Strawberry Soda Bread

**Prep time: 10 minutes | Cook time: 28 minutes | Makes 1 loaf**

½ cup frozen strawberries in juice, completely thawed (do not drain)
1 cup flour
½ cup sugar

1 teaspoon cinnamon
½ teaspoon baking soda
⅛ teaspoon salt
1 egg, beaten
⅓ cup oil
Cooking spray

1. Cut any large berries into smaller pieces no larger than ½ inch.
2. Preheat air fryer oven to 330ºF (165ºC).
3. In a large bowl, stir together the flour, sugar, cinnamon, soda, and salt.
4. In a small bowl, mix together the egg, oil, and strawberries. Add to dry ingredients and stir together gently.
5. Spray 6 × 6-inch baking pan with cooking spray.
6. Pour batter into prepared pan and select Bake, set the temperature to 330ºF (165ºC), and set the time to 28 minutes.
7. When bread is done, let cool for 10 minutes before removing from pan.

## Pumpkin Cinnamon Loaf

**Prep time: 15 minutes | Cook time: 20 minutes | Makes 1 loaf**

Cooking spray
1 large egg
½ cup granulated sugar
⅓ cup oil
½ cup canned pumpkin (not pie filling)
½ teaspoon vanilla
⅔ cup flour plus 1

tablespoon
½ teaspoon baking powder
½ teaspoon baking soda
½ teaspoon salt
1 teaspoon pumpkin pie spice
¼ teaspoon cinnamon

1. Spray 6 × 6-inch baking dish lightly with cooking spray.
2. Place baking dish in air fryer cooking tray and preheat air fryer oven to 330ºF (165ºC).
3. In a large bowl, beat eggs and sugar together with a hand mixer.
4. Add oil, pumpkin, and vanilla and mix well.
5. Sift together all dry ingredients. Add to pumpkin mixture and beat well, about 1 minute.
6. Pour batter in baking dish and select Bake, set the temperature to 330ºF (165ºC), and set the time to 20 minutes or until toothpick inserted in center of loaf comes out clean.

## Peanut Butter Bread

**Prep time: 5 minutes | Cook time: 5 minutes | Serves 3**

1 tablespoon oil
2 tablespoons peanut butter
4 slices bread
1 banana, sliced

1. Spread the peanut butter on top of each slice of bread, then arrange the banana slices on top. Sandwich two slices together, then the other two.
2. Bursh oil the inside of the Air Fryer cooking tray and select Bake, set the temperature to 300ºF (149ºC), and set the time to 5 minutes.
3. Serve.

## Mini Pita Breads

**Prep time: 25 minutes | Cook time: 6 minutes | Makes 8 mini pitas**

2 teaspoons active dry yeast
1 tablespoon sugar
1¼ to 1½ cups warm water, 100ºF (38ºC)
3¼ cups all-purpose flour
2 teaspoons salt
1 tablespoon olive oil, plus more for brushing
Kosher salt (optional)

1. Dissolve the yeast, sugar and water in the bowl of a stand mixer. Let the mixture sit for 5 minutes to make sure the yeast is active – it should foam a little. (If there's no foaming, discard and start again with new yeast.)
2. Combine the flour and salt in a bowl, and add it to the water, along with the olive oil. Mix with the dough hook until combined. Add a little more flour if needed to get the dough to pull away from the sides of the mixing bowl, or add a little more water if the dough seems too dry.
3. Knead the dough until it is smooth and elastic (about 8 minutes in the mixer or 15 minutes by hand). Transfer the dough to a lightly oiled bowl, cover and let it rise in a warm place until doubled in bulk.
4. Divide the dough into 8 portions and roll each portion into a circle about 4-inches in diameter. Don't roll the balls too thin, or you won't get the pocket inside the pita.
5. Preheat the oven to 400ºF (205ºC).
6. Brush both sides of the dough with olive oil, and sprinkle with kosher salt if desired. Select Air Fry, set the temperature to 400ºF (205ºC), and set the time to 6 minutes, flipping it over when there are 2 minutes left in the cooking time.

## Chicken Breast English Muffin Sandwiches

**Prep time: 5 minutes | Cook time: 12 minutes | Serves 4**

1 pound (454 g) chicken breasts
1 tablespoon olive oil
Sea salt and black pepper, to taste
4 slices Cheddar cheese
4 teaspoons yellow mustard
4 English muffins, lightly toasted

1. Pat the chicken dry with kitchen towels. Toss the chicken breasts with the olive oil, salt, and pepper.
2. Select Bake, set the temperature to 380ºF (193ºC), and set the time to 12 minutes, turning them over halfway through the cooking time.
3. Shred the chicken using two forks and serve with cheese, mustard, and English muffins. Bon appétit!

## Maple Banana Chia Bread

**Prep time: 15 minutes | Cook time: 27 minutes | Serves 6**

2 large bananas, very ripe, peeled
2 tablespoons neutral-flavored oil (sunflower or safflower)
2 tablespoons maple syrup
½ teaspoon vanilla
½ tablespoon chia seeds
½ tablespoon ground flaxseed
1 cup whole-wheat pastry
flour
¼ cup coconut sugar
½ teaspoon cinnamon
¼ teaspoon salt
¼ teaspoon nutmeg
¼ teaspoon baking powder
¼ teaspoon baking soda
Cooking oil spray (sunflower, safflower, or refined coconut)

1. In a medium bowl, mash the peeled bananas with a fork until very mushy. Add the oil, maple syrup, vanilla, chia, and flaxseeds and stir well.
2. Add the flour, sugar, cinnamon, salt, nutmeg, baking powder, and baking soda, and stir just until thoroughly combined.
3. Preheat a 6-inch round, 2-inch deep baking pan in the oven for 2 minutes.
4. Open the oven to spray the baking pan with oil, and pour the batter into it. Smooth out the top with a rubber spatula and select Bake, set the temperature to 350ºF (175ºC) and set the time to 25 minutes or until a knife inserted in the center comes out clean.
5. Remove and cool for a minute or two, then cut into wedges and serve.

## Reuben Sandwich

**Prep time: 5 minutes | Cook time: 10 minutes | Serves 2**

4 slices sourdough bread
2 tablespoons butter, room temperature
4 slices Cheddar cheese
½ pound (227 g) corned beef

1. Butter one side of each slice of bread.
2. Assemble your sandwiches with cheese and corned beef.
3. Select Air Fry, set the temperature to 380ºF (193ºC), and set the time to 10 minutes.
4. Bon appétit!

## Italian Sausage Sandwich

**Prep time: 5 minutes | Cook time: 15 minutes | Serves 3**

1 pound (454 g) sweet Italian sausage
6 white bread slices
2 teaspoons mustard

1. Place the sausage in a lightly greased Air fryer cooking tray.
2. Select Air Fry, set the temperature to 370ºF (190ºC), and set the time to 15 minutes, tossing the cooking tray halfway through the cooking time.
3. Assemble the sandwiches with the bread, mustard, and sausage, and serve immediately.
4. Bon appétit!

## Broccoli Cheese Cornbread

**Prep time: 10 minutes | Cook time: 18 minutes | Makes 1 loaf**

1 cup frozen chopped broccoli, thawed and drained
¼ cup cottage cheese
1 egg, beaten
2 tablespoons minced onion
2 tablespoons melted butter
½ cup flour
½ cup yellow cornmeal
1 teaspoon baking powder
½ teaspoon salt
¼ cup milk, plus 2 tablespoons
Cooking spray

1. Place thawed broccoli in colander and press with a spoon to squeeze out excess moisture.
2. Stir together all ingredients in a large bowl.
3. Spray 6 × 6-inch baking pan with cooking spray.
4. Spread batter in pan and select Bake, set the temperature to 330ºF (165ºC), and set the time to

18 minutes or until cornbread is lightly browned and loaf starts to pull away from sides of pan.

## Southern Sweet Cornbread

**Prep time: 10 minutes | Cook time: 17 minutes | Serves 6 to 8**

Cooking spray
½ cup white cornmeal
½ cup flour
2 teaspoons baking powder
½ teaspoon salt
4 teaspoons sugar
1 egg
2 tablespoons oil
½ cup milk

1. Preheat air fryer oven to 360ºF (180ºC).
2. Spray air fryer cooking tray with nonstick cooking spray.
3. In a medium bowl, stir together the cornmeal, flour, baking powder, salt, and sugar.
4. In a small bowl, beat together the egg, oil, and milk. Stir into dry ingredients until well combined.
5. Pour batter into prepared cooking tray.
6. Select Bake, set the temperature to 360ºF (180ºC), and set the time to 17 minutes or until toothpick inserted in center comes out clean or with crumbs clinging.

## Smoked Mozzarella, Mushroom, and Thyme Pizza

**Prep time: 10 minutes | Cook time: 8 minutes | Makes 1 pizza**

4 ounces (113 g) pizza dough
2 teaspoons olive oil
½ cup oyster mushrooms, torn into small pieces
1 teaspoon fresh thyme leaves
¼ cup shredded smoked Mozzarella cheese
⅛ teaspoon crushed red chile flakes
Kosher salt and freshly ground black pepper, to taste

1. Roll and stretch the pizza dough into a 6-inch round.
2. Lay the dough round in the air fryer, then brush with 1 teaspoon of the olive oil. Arrange the mushrooms over the dough, followed by the thyme leaves. Sprinkle with the smoked Mozzarella and chile flakes. Season with salt and black pepper, drizzle with the remaining 1 teaspoon of olive oil, and select Pizza, set the temperature to 350ºF (180ºC), and set the time to 8 minutes or until the dough is cooked through and the cheese is melted and golden brown.
3. Transfer the pizza to a plate and serve hot.

## Bacon Cheese Pizza

**Prep time: 10 minutes | Cook time: 20 minutes | Serves 4**

Flour, for dusting
Nonstick baking spray with flour
4 frozen large whole-wheat dinner rolls, thawed
5 cloves garlic, minced
¾ cup pizza sauce

½ teaspoon dried oregano
½ teaspoon garlic salt
8 slices precooked bacon, cut into 1-inch pieces
1¼ cups shredded Cheddar cheese

1. On a lightly floured surface, press out each dinner roll to a 5-by-3-inch oval.
2. Spray four 6-by-4-inch pieces of heavy-duty foil with nonstick spray and place one crust on each piece.
3. Select Bake, cook for 2 minutes or until the crusts are set, but not browned.
4. Meanwhile, in a small bowl, combine the garlic, pizza sauce, oregano, and garlic salt. When the pizza crusts are set, spread each with some of the sauce. Top with the bacon pieces and Cheddar cheese.
5. Select Pizza, cook for 18 minutes or until the crust is browned and the cheese is melted and starting to brown.

Banana Bread, page 116

Broccoli Cheese Cornbread, page 122

Sweet Rosemary Knots, page 118

Mushroom and Tomato Pita Pizza, page 115

# Chapter 10 Snacks and Appetizers

## Curried Chickpeas

**Prep time: 5 minutes | Cook time: 15 minutes | Makes 1 cup**

1 can (15 ounces / 425g) chickpeas, drained
2 teaspoons curry powder
¼ teaspoon salt
1 tablespoon olive oil

1. Drain chickpeas thoroughly and spread in a single layer on paper towels. Cover with another paper towel and press gently to remove extra moisture. Don't press too hard or you'll crush the chickpeas.
2. Mix curry powder and salt together.
3. Place chickpeas in a medium bowl and sprinkle with seasonings. Stir well to coat.
4. Add olive oil and stir again to distribute oil.
5. Select Air Fry. Set temperature to 390ºF (200ºC), and set time to 15 minutes, stopping to shake cooking tray about halfway through cooking time.
6. Cool completely and store in an airtight container.

## Sweet and Spicy Chicken Wings

**Prep time: 10 minutes | Cook time: 25 minutes | Makes 16 wings**

8 chicken wings
1 tablespoon olive oil
⅓ cup brown sugar
2 tablespoons honey
⅓ cup apple cider vinegar
2 cloves garlic, minced
½ teaspoon dried red pepper flakes
¼ teaspoon salt

1. Cut each chicken wing into three pieces. You'll have one large piece, one medium piece, and one small end. Discard the small end or save it for stock.
2. In a medium bowl, toss the wings with the oil. Transfer to the air fryer cooking tray and select Air Fry set the temperature to 350 ºF and set time to 20 minutes, shaking the cooking tray twice while cooking.
3. Meanwhile, in a small bowl, combine the sugar, honey, vinegar, red pepper flakes, and salt, and whisk until combined.
4. Remove the wings from the air fryer cooking tray and put into a 6-by-6-by-2-inch pan. Pour the sauce over the wings and toss.
5. Return to the air fryer and cook for 5 minutes or until the wings are glazed.

## Potato Chips

**Prep time: 5 minutes | Cook time: 15 minutes | Serves 2 to 3**

2 medium potatoes
2 teaspoons extra-light olive oil
Oil for misting or cooking spray
Salt and pepper, to taste

1. Peel the potatoes.
2. Using a mandoline or paring knife, shave potatoes into thin slices, dropping them into a bowl of water as you cut them.
3. Dry potatoes as thoroughly as possible with paper towels or a clean dish towel. Toss potato slices with the oil to coat completely.
4. Spray air fryer cooking tray with cooking spray and add potato slices.
5. Stir and separate with a fork.
6. Select Air Fry 390ºF (200ºC), and set time to 5 minutes. Stir and separate potato slices. Cook for 5 more minutes. Stir and separate potatoes again. Cook for another 5 minutes.
7. Season with salt and pepper.

## Vegan Avocado Fries

**Prep time: 10 minutes | Cook time: 10 minutes | Serves 4**

¼ cup almond or coconut milk
1 tablespoon lime juice
⅛ teaspoon hot sauce
2 tablespoons flour
¾ cup panko
breadcrumbs
¼ cup cornmeal
¼ teaspoon salt
1 large avocado
Oil for misting or cooking spray

1. In a small bowl, whisk together the almond or coconut milk, lime juice, and hot sauce.
2. Place flour on a sheet of wax paper.
3. Mix panko, cornmeal, and salt and place on another sheet of wax paper.
4. Split avocado in half and remove pit. Peel or use a spoon to lift avocado halves out of the skin.
5. Cut avocado lengthwise into ½-inch slices. Dip each in flour, then milk mixture, then roll in panko mixture.
6. Mist with oil or cooking spray and select Roast. Set temperature to 390ºF (200ºC), and set time to 10 minutes, until the crust is brown and crispy.

## Fried Peaches

**Prep time: 10 minutes | Cook time: 6 minutes | Serves 4**

2 egg whites
1 tablespoon water
¼ cup sliced almonds
2 tablespoons brown sugar
½ teaspoon almond extract

1 cup crisp rice cereal
2 medium, very firm peaches, peeled and pitted
¼ cup cornstarch
Oil for misting or cooking spray

1. Preheat air fryer oven to 390ºF (200ºC).
2. Beat together egg whites and water in a shallow dish.
3. In a food processor, combine the almonds, brown sugar, and almond extract. Process until ingredients combine well and the nuts are finely chopped.
4. Add cereal and pulse just until cereal crushes. Pour crumb mixture into a shallow dish or onto a plate.
5. Cut each peach into eighths and place in a plastic bag or container with lid. Add cornstarch, seal, and shake to coat.
6. Remove peach slices from bag or container, tapping them hard to shake off the excess cornstarch. Dip in egg wash and roll in crumbs. Spray with oil.
7. Place in air fryer cooking tray and select Air Fry for 5 minutes. Shake cooking tray, separate any that have stuck together, and spritz a little oil on any spots that aren't browning.
8. Cook for 1 to 3 minutes or longer, until golden brown and crispy.

## Chile-Brined Fried Calamari

**Prep time: 10 minutes | Cook time: 8 minutes | Serves 2**

1 jar (8 ounces) sweet or hot pickled cherry peppers
½ pound calamari bodies and tentacles, bodies cut into ½-inch-wide rings
1 zested lemon and zest
2 cups all-purpose flour
Kosher salt and freshly

ground black pepper, to taste
3 large eggs, lightly beaten
Cooking spray
½ cup mayonnaise
1 teaspoon finely chopped rosemary
1 garlic clove, minced

1. Drain the pickled pepper brine into a large bowl and tear the peppers into bite-size strips. Add the pepper strips and calamari to the brine and let stand in the refrigerator for 20 minutes or up to 2 hours.
2. Grate the lemon zest into a large bowl then whisk in the flour and season with salt and pepper. Dip

the calamari and pepper strips in the egg, then toss them in the flour mixture until fully coated. Spray the calamari and peppers liberally with cooking spray, then transfer half to the air fryer. Select Air Fry. Set temperature to 400ºF (204ºC), shaking the cooking tray halfway into cooking, until the calamari is cooked through and golden brown, about 8 minutes. Transfer to a plate and repeat with the remaining pieces.

3. In a small bowl, whisk together the mayonnaise, rosemary, and garlic. Squeeze half the zested lemon to get 1 tablespoon of juice and stir it into the sauce. Season with salt and pepper. Cut the remaining zested lemon half into 4 small wedges and serve alongside the calamari, peppers, and sauce.

## Soft Chocolate Cannoli Cookies

**Prep time: 5 minutes | Cook time: 10 minutes | Serves 6**

4 ounces (113 g) cream cheese (½ cup) (Kite Hill brand cream cheese style spread if dairy-free), softened
½ cup (1 stick) unsalted butter (or coconut oil if dairy-free), softened
¾ cup Swerve confectioners' style sweetener or equivalent amount of liquid or powdered sweetener
1 tablespoon almond

extract or other extract of choice, such as orange, lemon, or vanilla
1 large egg
½ tablespoon fine sea salt
2 cups blanched almond flour
¼ cup unsweetened cocoa powder
¼ cup coconut flour
¼ tablespoon baking powder
Pinch of fine sea salt

1. Preheat the oven to 300°F (149°C). Use parchment paper to line a baking sheet and grease the parchment.
2. Add the cream cheese and softened butter to a large bowl, use a hand mixer to cream for 1 minute. Add the sweetener and continue mixing until creamy. Add the extract, egg, and salt and mix again. Add the cocoa powder, flours, baking powder, and pinch of salt and combine well.
3. Scoop up a heaping tablespoon of the dough and use your hands to roll it into a ball, then place it on the greased parchment. Repeat with the rest of the dough, placing the balls about 2 inches apart.
4. Select COOKIES, cook at 300°F (149°C) about 12 to 15 minutes. Allow the cookies to cool completely on the pan.
5. Serve immediately and place extras in an airtight container, and store in the refrigerator for up to 3 days, or freeze for up to 1 month.

## Buffalo Meatballs

**Prep time: 5 minutes | Cook time: 22 minutes | Makes 16 meatballs**

| | |
|---|---|
| 1 pound (454 g) ground chicken | 2 ounces (57 g) Gruyère cheese, cut into 16 cubes |
| 8 tablespoons buffalo wing sauce | 1 tablespoon maple syrup |

1. Mix 4 tablespoons of buffalo wing sauce into all the ground chicken.
2. Shape chicken into a log and divide into 16 equal portions.
3. With slightly damp hands, mold each chicken portion around a cube of cheese and shape into a firm ball. When you have shaped 8 meatballs, place them in air fryer cooking tray.
4. Select Roast. Set temperature to 390ºF (200ºC), and set time to approximately 5 minutes. Shake cooking tray, reduce temperature to 360ºF (180ºC), and roast for 5 to 6 minutes or longer.
5. While the first batch is cooking, shape remaining chicken and cheese into 8 more meatballs.
6. Repeat step 4 to cook the second batch of meatballs.
7. In a medium bowl, mix the remaining 4 tablespoons of buffalo wing sauce with the maple syrup. Add all the cooked meatballs and toss to coat.
8. Place meatballs back into air fryer cooking tray and roast at 390ºF (200ºC), and set time to 2 to 3 minutes to set the glaze. Skewer each with a toothpick and serve.

## Mozzarella Cheese Sticks

**Prep time: 5 minutes | Cook time: 8 minutes | Serves 36**

| | |
|---|---|
| 1 package Mozzarella sticks | butter, melted |
| 1 package (8 ounces / 227g) crescent roll dough | ¼ cup panko bread crumbs |
| 3 tablespoons unsalted | Marinara sauce, for dipping (optional) |

1. Spray the air fryer cooking tray with olive oil.
2. Cut each cheese stick into thirds.
3. Unroll the crescent roll dough. Using a pizza cutter or sharp knife, cut the dough into 36 even pieces.
4. Wrap each small cheese stick in a piece of dough. Make sure that the dough is wrapped tightly around the cheese. Pinch the dough together at both ends, and pinch along the seam to ensure that the dough is completely sealed.
5. Using tongs, dip the wrapped cheese sticks in the melted butter, then dip the cheese sticks in the panko bread crumbs.
6. Place the cheese sticks in the greased air fryer cooking tray in a single layer. (You may have to cook the cheese sticks in more than one batch.)
7. Select Bake. Set temperature to 370ºF (190ºC), and set time to 5 minutes. After 5 minutes, the tops should be golden brown.
8. Using tongs, flip the cheese sticks and bake for another 3 minutes, or until golden brown on all sides.
9. Repeat until you use all of the dough.
10. Plate, serve with the marinara sauce (if you like), and enjoy!

## Asian Rice Logs

**Prep time: 15 minutes | Cook time: 5 minutes | Makes 8 rice logs**

| | |
|---|---|
| 1½ cups cooked jasmine or sushi rice | ⅓ cup plain breadcrumbs |
| ¼ teaspoon salt | ¾ cup panko breadcrumbs |
| 2 teaspoons five-spice powder | 2 tablespoons sesame seeds |
| 2 teaspoons diced shallots | For the Orange Marmalade Dipping Sauce: |
| 1 tablespoon tamari sauce | ½ cup all-natural orange marmalade |
| 1 egg, beaten | 1 tablespoon soy sauce |
| 1 teaspoon sesame oil | |
| 2 teaspoons water | |

1. Make the rice according to package instructions. While the rice is cooking, make the dipping sauce by combining the marmalade and soy sauce and set aside.
2. Stir together the cooked rice, salt, five-spice powder, shallots, and tamari sauce.
3. Divide rice into 8 equal pieces. With slightly damp hands, mold each piece into a log shape. Chill in freezer for 10 to 15 minutes.
4. Mix the egg, sesame oil, and water together in a shallow bowl.
5. Place the plain breadcrumbs on a sheet of wax paper.
6. Mix the panko breadcrumbs with the sesame seeds and place on another sheet of wax paper.
7. Roll the rice logs in plain breadcrumbs, then dip in egg wash, and then dip in the panko and sesame seeds.
8. Select Air Fry. Set temperature to 390ºF (200ºC), and set time to approximately 5 minutes, until golden brown.
9. Cool slightly before serving with orange marmalade dipping sauce.

## Eggplant Fries

**Prep time: 10 minutes | Cook time: 15 minutes | Serves 4**

1 medium eggplant
1 teaspoon ground coriander
1 teaspoon cumin
1 teaspoon garlic powder
½ teaspoon salt
1 cup crushed panko breadcrumbs
1 large egg
2 tablespoons water
Oil for misting or cooking spray

1. Peel and cut the eggplant into fat fries, ⅜- to ½-inch thick.
2. Preheat air fryer oven to 390ºF (200ºC).
3. In a small cup, mix together the coriander, cumin, garlic, and salt.
4. Combine 1 teaspoon of the seasoning mix and panko crumbs in a shallow dish.
5. Place eggplant fries in a large bowl, sprinkle with remaining seasoning, and stir well to combine.
6. Beat eggs and water together and pour over eggplant fries. Stir to coat.
7. Remove eggplant from egg wash, shake off excess, and roll in panko crumbs.
8. Spray with oil.
9. Place half of the eggplant fries in air fryer rotisserie basket.
10. Select Roast for 5 minutes. Shake basket, mist lightly with oil, and cook 2 to 3 minutes longer, until browned and crispy.
11. Repeat step 9 and 10 to cook remaining eggplant fries.

## Everything Seasoned Sausage Rolls

**Prep time: 10 minutes | Cook time: 10 minutes | Serves 6**

For the Seasoning:
2 tablespoons sesame seeds
1½ teaspoons poppy seeds
1½ teaspoons dried minced onion
1 teaspoon salt
1 teaspoon dried minced
garlic
For the Sausages:
1 package (8 ounces / 227g) crescent roll dough
1 package (12 ounces / 340g) mini smoked sausages (cocktail franks)

Make the Seasoning
1. In a small bowl, combine the sesame seeds, poppy seeds, onion, salt, and garlic and set aside.
Make the Sausages
2. Spray the air fryer cooking tray with olive oil.

3. Remove the crescent dough from the package and lay it out on a cutting board. Separate the dough at the perforations. Using a pizza cutter or sharp knife, cut each triangle of dough into fourths.
4. Drain the sausages and pat them dry with a paper towel.
5. Roll each sausage in a piece of dough.
6. Sprinkle seasoning on top of each roll.
7. Place the seasoned sausage rolls into the greased air fryer cooking tray in a single layer. (You will have to bake these in at least 2 batches.)
8. Select Roast. Set temperature to 330ºF (165ºC), and set time to 5 minutes.
9. Using tongs, remove the sausages from the air fryer and place them on a platter.
10. Repeat steps 6 through 8 with the second batch.

## Shrimp Pirogues

**Prep time: 10 minutes | Cook time: 5 minutes | Serves 8**

12 ounces (340 g) small, peeled, and deveined raw shrimp
3 ounces (85 g) cream cheese, room temperature
2 tablespoons plain yogurt
1 teaspoon lemon juice
1 teaspoon dried dill weed, crushed
Salt, to taste
4 small hothouse cucumbers, each approximately 6 inches long

1. Pour 4 tablespoons of water in bottom of air fryer drawer.
2. Place shrimp in air fryer cooking tray in single layer and select Air Fry. Set temperature to 390ºF (200ºC), and set time to 4 to 5 minutes, just until done. Watch carefully because shrimp cooks quickly, and overcooking makes it tough.
3. Chop shrimp into small pieces, no larger than ½ inch. Refrigerate while mixing the remaining ingredients.
4. With a fork, mash and whip the cream cheese until smooth.
5. Stir in the yogurt and beat until smooth. Stir in lemon juice, dill weed, and chopped shrimp.
6. Taste for seasoning. If needed, add ¼ to ½ teaspoon salt to suit your taste.
7. Store in refrigerator until serving time.
8. When ready to serve, wash and dry cucumbers and split them lengthwise. Scoop out the seeds and turn cucumbers upside down on paper towels to drain for 10 minutes.
9. Just before filling, wipe centers of cucumbers dry. Spoon the shrimp mixture into the pirogues and cut in half crosswise. Serve immediately.

## Strawberry Thumbprint Cookies

**Prep time: 15 minutes | Cook time: 15 minutes | Serves 12 cookies**

½ cup strawberry jam, divided
3 tablespoons coconut oil
1½ cups sunflower seeds
¼ cup maple syrup

1. Preheat the oven to 350°F(180°C).
2. Use parchment paper to line a baking sheet.
3. Add the sunflower seed into a blender, food processor, or spice grinder, process into a fine meal. Transfer to a large bowl.
4. Add the coconut oil, use a spoon to mash it into the sunflower meal as if you are crumbling butter into flour. Stir in the maple syrup. Mix well.
5. Scoop the dough onto the prepared sheet with a tablespoon measure, making 12 cookies. Use a wet spoon to gently press down on the cookies to flatten them.
6. Make imprints in the center of each cookie with your thumb. Fill each depression with 2 teaspoons of strawberry jam.
7. Put the sheet in the preheated oven, select COOKIE, bake at 350°F (180°C) for 12 to 14 minutes.
8. Remove from the oven and let it cool before eating.

## Cheddar Cheese Wafers

**Prep time: 5 minutes | Cook time: 5 minutes | Makes 4 dozen**

4 ounces (113 g) sharp Cheddar cheese, grated
¼ cup butter
½ cup flour
¼ teaspoon salt
½ cup crisp rice cereal
Oil for misting or cooking spray

1. Cream the butter and grated cheese together. You can do it by hand, but using a stand mixer is faster and easier.
2. Sift flour and salt together. Add it to the cheese mixture and mix until well blended.
3. Stir in cereal.
4. Place dough on wax paper and shape into a long roll about 1 inch in diameter. Wrap well with the wax paper and chill for at least 4 hours.
5. When ready to cook, preheat air fryer oven to 360ºF (180ºC).
6. Cut cheese roll into ¼-inch slices.
7. Spray air fryer cooking tray with oil or cooking spray and place slices in a single layer, close but not touching.
8. Select Bake for 5 to 6 minutes or until golden brown.

When done, place them on paper towels to cool.

9. Repeat previous step to cook the remaining cheese bites.

## Masala Onion Rings with Mint-Mayo Dip

**Prep time: 15 minutes | Cook time: 10 minutes | Serves 2 to 4**

1 (14 to 16 ounces / 397 to 454 g) large red onion
¼ cup garam masala
2 tablespoons sweet paprika
2 tablespoons curry powder
2 tablespoons kosher salt, plus more as needed
2 cups all-purpose flour
6 large eggs, lightly
beaten
2 cups panko breadcrumbs
½ cup mayonnaise
2 tablespoons finely chopped fresh mint
2 teaspoons fresh lemon juice
1 scallion, finely chopped
Cooking spray
Ketchup, for serving

1. Trim the ends from the onion and peel away the papery outer skin. Cut the onion crosswise into slices of ¾ to 1 inch thick, then separate the slices into rings, discarding the feathery skin between the rings.
2. In a small bowl, whisk together the garam masala, paprika, curry powder, and salt. Place the flour, eggs, and breadcrumbs in three separate shallow bowls and season each with one-third (2 tablespoons plus 2½ teaspoons) of the spice mixture. Dip 1 onion ring in the spiced egg, dredge in the flour, then repeat with the egg and flour once more. Dip the ring back into the egg again, then coat in the spiced breadcrumbs. Repeat to coat all the onion rings and arrange them on a wire rack set over a baking sheet. Place the onion rings in the freezer and chill until firm, at least 30 minutes or up to 1 week.
3. Meanwhile, whisk together the mayonnaise, mint, lemon juice, and scallion in a bowl and season with salt. Refrigerate to marry the flavors in the sauce while the onion rings freeze.
4. When ready to fry, spray 5 or 6 of the onion rings liberally with cooking spray and arrange them loosely in the air fryer cooking tray, laying some flat and leaning some against the side of the cooking tray. Select Air Fry. Set temperature to 375ºF (190ºC) until the onion rings are tender and the breading is golden brown and crisp, about 10 minutes. Season with more salt once they come out of the fryer and continue frying as many onion rings as you like. Serve hot with the mint-mayo sauce and ketchup on the side.

## Apple Wedges

**Prep time: 10 minutes | Cook time: 8 minutes | Serves 4**

| | |
|---|---|
| ¼ cup panko breadcrumbs | ¼ cup cornstarch |
| ¼ cup pecans | 1 egg white |
| 1½ teaspoons cinnamon | 2 teaspoons water |
| 1½ teaspoons brown sugar | 1 medium apple |
| | Oil for misting or cooking spray |

1. In a food processor, combine panko, pecans, cinnamon, and brown sugar. Process to make small crumbs.
2. Place cornstarch in a plastic bag or bowl with lid. In a shallow dish, beat together the egg white and water until slightly foamy.
3. Preheat air fryer oven to 390ºF (200ºC).
4. Cut apple into small wedges. The thickest edge should be no more than ⅜ to ½ inch thick. Cut away the core, but do not peel.
5. Place apple wedges in cornstarch, reseal bag or bowl, and shake to coat.
6. Dip wedges in egg wash, shake off excess, and roll in crumb mixture. Spray with oil.
7. Place apples in air fryer cooking tray in single layer and select Air Fry for 5 minutes. Shake cooking tray and break apart any apples that have stuck together. Mist lightly with oil and cook for 3 to 4 minutes or longer, until crispy.

## Potato with Spicy Tomato Ketchup

**Prep time: 10 minutes | Cook time: 18 minutes | Serves 2**

| | |
|---|---|
| 1 (12 ounces/ 340g)large russet potato | ½ cup canned crushed tomatoes |
| 2 tablespoons vegetable oil | 2 tablespoons apple cider vinegar |
| 1 tablespoon hot smoked paprika | 1 tablespoon dark brown sugar |
| ½ teaspoon garlic powder | 1 tablespoon Worcestershire sauce |
| Kosher salt and freshly ground black pepper, to taste | 1 teaspoon mild hot sauce, such as Cholula or Frank's |

1. Spiralize the potato, and then place in a large colander. (If you don't have a spiralizer, cut the potato into thin ⅛-inch-thick matchsticks.) Rinse the potatoes under cold running water until the water runs clear. Spread the potatoes out on a double-thick layer of paper towels and pat completely dry.
2. In a large bowl, combine the potatoes, oil, paprika, and garlic powder. Season with salt and pepper and toss to combine. Transfer the potatoes to the air fryer and select Roast. Set temperature to 400ºF (204ºC) until the potatoes are browned and crisp, for 15 minutes, shaking the cooking tray halfway through.
3. Meanwhile, in a small blender, puree the tomatoes, vinegar, brown sugar, Worcestershire, and hot sauce until smooth. Pour into a small saucepan or skillet and simmer over medium heat until reduced by half, for 3 to 5 minutes. Pour the homemade ketchup into a bowl and let it cool.
4. Remove the spiralized potato nest from the air fryer and serve hot with the ketchup.

## Stuffed Onion with Herby-Lemon Breadcrumb

**Prep time: 10 minutes | Cook time: 15 minutes | Serves 2**

| | |
|---|---|
| 1 large yellow onion | 3 tablespoons mayonnaise |
| 1 tablespoon olive oil | 1 tablespoon fresh lemon juice |
| Kosher salt and freshly ground black pepper, to taste | 1 tablespoon chopped fresh flat-leaf parsley |
| ¼ cup plus 2 tablespoons panko breadcrumbs | 2 teaspoons whole-grain Dijon mustard |
| ¼ cup grated Parmesan cheese | 1 garlic clove, minced |

1. Place the onion on a cutting board and trim the top off and peel off the outer skin. Turn the onion upside down and use a paring knife, cut vertical slits halfway through the onion at ½-inch intervals around the onion, keeping the root intact. When you turn the onion right side up, it should open up like the petals of a flower. Drizzle the cut sides of the onion with the olive oil and season with salt and pepper. Place petal-side up in the air fryer and select Air Fry. Set temperature to 350ºF (177ºC), and set time to 10 minutes.
2. Meanwhile, in a bowl, stir together the panko, Parmesan, mayonnaise, lemon juice, parsley, mustard, and garlic until incorporated into a smooth paste.
3. Remove the onion from the fryer and stuff the paste all over and in between the onion "petals." Return the onion to the air fryer and cook at 375ºF (190ºC) until the onion is tender in the center and the breadcrumb mixture is golden brown, about 5 minutes. Remove the onion from the air fryer, transfer to a plate, and serve hot.

Asian Five-Spice Chicken Wings, page 135

Vegan Avocado Fries, page 125

Potato Chips, page 125

String Bean Fries, page 132

## Turkey and Pineapple Burger Sliders

**Prep time: 10 minutes | Cook time: 5 minutes | Makes 8 sliders**

1 pound (454 g) ground turkey
¼ teaspoon curry powder
1 teaspoon hoisin sauce
½ teaspoon salt
8 slider buns
½ cup slivered red onions
½ cup slivered green or

red bell pepper
½ cup fresh chopped pineapple (or pineapple tidbits from kids' fruit cups, drained)
Light cream cheese, softened

1. Combine turkey, curry powder, Hoisin sauce, and salt and mix together well.
2. Shape turkey mixture into 8 small patties.
3. Place patties in air fryer cooking tray and select Roast. Set temperature to 360ºF (180ºC), and set time to 5 to 7 minutes, until patties are well done and juices run clear.
4. Place each patty on the bottom half of a slider bun and top with onions, peppers, and pineapple. Spread the remaining bun halves with cream cheese to taste, place on top, and serve.

## Stuffed Button Mushrooms

**Prep time: 5 minutes | Cook time: 10 minutes | Serves 4**

12 medium button mushrooms
½ cup bread crumbs
1 teaspoon salt

½ teaspoon freshly ground black pepper
5 to 6 tablespoons olive oil

1. Spray the air fryer cooking tray with olive oil.
2. Separate the cap from the stem of each mushroom. Discard the stems.
3. In a small mixing bowl, combine the bread crumbs, salt, pepper, and olive oil until you have a wet mixture.
4. Rub the mushrooms with olive oil on all sides.
5. Using a spoon, fill each mushroom with the bread crumb stuffing.
6. Place the mushrooms in the greased air fryer cooking tray in a single layer.
7. Select Roast. Set temperature to 360ºF (180ºC), and set time to 10 minutes.
8. Using tongs, remove the mushrooms from the air fryer, place them on a platter, and serve.

## String Bean Fries

**Prep time: 10 minutes | Cook time: 5 minutes | Serves 4**

½ pound (227 g) fresh string beans
2 eggs
4 teaspoons water
½ cup white flour
½ cup breadcrumbs
¼ teaspoon salt

¼ teaspoon ground black pepper
¼ teaspoon dry mustard (optional)
Oil for misting or cooking spray

1. Preheat air fryer oven to 360ºF (180ºC).
2. Trim stem ends from string beans, wash, and pat dry.
3. In a shallow dish, beat eggs and water together until well blended.
4. Place flour in a second shallow dish.
5. In a third shallow dish, stir together the breadcrumbs, salt, pepper, and dry mustard if using.
6. Dip each string bean in egg mixture, flour, egg mixture again, then breadcrumbs.
7. When you finish coating all the string beans, open air fryer and place them in cooking tray.
8. Select Air Fry, and set time to 3 minutes.
9. Stop and mist string beans with oil or cooking spray.
10. Cook for 2 to 3 more minutes or until string beans are crispy and nicely browned.

## Glazed Chicken Wings

**Prep time: 10 minutes | Cook time: 24 minutes | Serves 4**

8 chicken wings
3 tablespoons honey
1 tablespoon lemon juice
1 tablespoon low sodium chicken stock
2 cloves garlic, minced

¼ cup thinly sliced green onion
¾ cup low sodium barbecue sauce
4 stalks celery, cut into pieces

1. Pat the chicken wings dry. Cut off the small end piece and discard or freeze it to make chicken stock later.
2. Put the wings into the air fryer cooking tray. Select Air Fry, Set temperature to 350ºF and set time to 20 minutes, shaking the cooking tray twice while cooking.
3. Meanwhile, combine the honey, lemon juice, chicken stock, and garlic, and whisk until combined.
4. Remove the wings from the air fryer and put into a 6 × 2 inch pan. Pour the sauce over the wings and toss gently to coat.
5. Return the pan to the oven and air fry for another 4 to 5 minutes or until the wings are glazed and a food thermometer registers 165ºF (75ºC). Sprinkle with the green onion and serve the wings with the barbecue sauce and celery.

## Yellow Potato Chips

**Prep time: 5 minutes | Cook time: 15 minutes | Serves 4**

4 yellow potatoes
1 tablespoon olive oil
1 tablespoon salt (plus more for topping)

1. Using a mandoline or sharp knife, slice the potatoes into ⅛-inch-thick slices.
2. In a medium mixing bowl, toss the potato slices with the olive oil and salt until the potatoes are thoroughly coated with oil.
3. Place the potatoes in the air fryer cooking tray in a single layer. (You may have to fry the potato chips in more than one batch.)
4. Select Air Fry. Set temperature to 375ºF (190ºC), and set time to 15 minutes.
5. Shake the cooking tray several times during cooking, so the chips crisp evenly and don't burn.
6. Check to see if they are fork-tender; if not, add another 5 to 10 minutes, checking frequently. They will crisp up after they are removed from the air fryer.
7. Season with additional salt, if desired.

## Buffalo Chicken Tender

**Prep time: 10 minutes | Cook time: 7 minutes | Serves 4**

⅔ cup sour cream
¼ cup creamy blue cheese salad dressing
¼ cup crumbled blue cheese
1 celery stalk, finely chopped
1 pound (454 g) chicken
tenders, cut into thirds crosswise
3 tablespoons Buffalo chicken wing sauce
1 cup panko bread crumbs
2 tablespoons olive oil

1. In a small bowl, combine the sour cream, salad dressing, blue cheese, and celery, and set aside.
2. In a medium bowl, combine the chicken pieces and Buffalo wing sauce and stir to coat. Let them sit while you get the bread crumbs ready.
3. Combine the bread crumbs and olive oil on a plate and mix.
4. Coat the chicken pieces in the bread crumb mixture, patting each piece so the crumbs adhere.
5. Select Air Fry, set the temperature to 350 ºF and set time to 8minutes, shaking the cooking tray once, until the chicken is cooked to 165ºF (75ºC) and is golden brown. Serve with the blue cheese sauce on the side.

## Ranch Lemony Chickpeas

**Prep time: 5 minutes | Cook time: 10 minutes | Serves 4**

1 can (15 ounces / 425g) chickpeas, drained and rinsed
1 tablespoon olive oil
3 tablespoons ranch
seasoning mix
1 teaspoon and additional salt
2 tablespoons freshly squeezed lemon juice

1. Spray the air fryer cooking tray with olive oil.
2. Using paper towels, pat the chickpeas dry.
3. In a medium mixing bowl, mix together the chickpeas, oil, seasoning mix, salt, and lemon juice.
4. Put the chickpeas in the air fryer cooking tray and spread them out in a single layer. (You may need to cook the chickpeas in more than one batch.)
5. Set the temperature to 350ºF (180ºC). Select Roast, and set time to 4 minutes. Remove the drawer and shake vigorously to redistribute the chickpeas so they cook evenly. Reset the timer and roast for 6 minutes or more.
6. When the time is up, release the air fryer cooking tray from the drawer and pour the chickpeas into a bowl. Season with additional salt, if desired. Enjoy!

## Air Fried Pita Chips

**Prep time: 5 minutes | Cook time: 6 minutes | Serves 4**

2 pieces whole-wheat pita bread
3 tablespoons olive oil
1 teaspoon freshly
squeezed lemon juice
1 teaspoon salt
1 teaspoon dried basil
1 teaspoon garlic powder

1. Spray the air fryer cooking tray with olive oil.
2. Using a pair of kitchen shears or a pizza cutter, cut the pita bread into small wedges.
3. Place the wedges in a small mixing bowl and add the olive oil, lemon juice, salt, dried basil, and garlic powder.
4. Mix well, coating each wedge.
5. Place the seasoned pita wedges in the greased air fryer cooking tray in a single layer, being careful not to overcrowd them. (You may have to bake the pita chips in more than one batch.)
6. Select Air Fry. Set temperature to 350ºF (180ºC), and set time to 6 minutes. Every 2 minutes or so, remove the drawer and shake the pita chips so they redistribute in the cooking tray for even cooking.
7. Serve with your choice of dip or alone as a tasty snack.

## Mozzarella Buttered Eggplant Chips

**Prep time: 10 minutes | Cook time: 15 minutes | Serves 4**

1 pound (454 g) eggplant, cut into slices
2 tablespoons butter, melted
½ teaspoon smoked paprika
1 teaspoon Italian seasoning
Sea salt and ground black pepper, to taste
1 cup Mozzarella cheese, shredded

1. Toss the eggplant with the rest ingredients. Arrange the eggplant slices in the Air Fryer cooking tray.
2. Select Air Fry. Set temperature to 400ºF (204ºC), and set time to 15 minutes, shaking the cooking tray halfway through the cooking time.
3. Bon appétit!

## Parmesan Dill Pickles

**Prep time: 5 minutes | Cook time: 8 minutes | Serves 4**

1 jar (16 ounces / 454g) sliced dill pickles
⅔ cup panko bread crumbs
⅓ cup grated Parmesan cheese
¼ teaspoon dried dill
2 large eggs

1. Line a platter with a double thickness of paper towels. Spread the pickles out in a single layer on the paper towels. Let the pickles drain on the towels for 20 minutes. After 20 minutes have passed, pat the pickles again with a clean paper towel to get them as dry as possible before breading.
2. Spray the air fryer cooking tray with olive oil.
3. In a small mixing bowl, combine the panko bread crumbs, Parmesan cheese, and dried dill. Mix well.
4. In a separate small bowl, crack the eggs and beat until frothy.
5. Dip each pickle into the egg mixture, then into the bread crumb mixture. Make sure the pickle is fully coated in breading.
6. Place the breaded pickle slices in the greased air fryer cooking tray in a single layer. (You may have to fry your pickles in more than one batch.)
7. Spray the pickles with a generous amount of olive oil.
8. Select Air Fry. Set temperature to 390ºF (200ºC), and set time to 4 minutes.
9. Open the air fryer drawer and use tongs to flip the pickles. Spray them again with olive oil. Reset the timer and air fry for another 4 minutes.
10. Using tongs, remove the pickles from the drawer. Plate, serve, and enjoy!

## Sweet Bagel Chips

**Prep time: 5 minutes | Cook time: 3 minutes | Makes 2½ cups**

1 large plain bagel
2 teaspoons sugar
1 teaspoon ground
cinnamon
Butter-flavored cooking spray

1. Preheat air fryer oven to 390ºF (200ºC).
2. Cut bagel into ¼-inch slices or thinner.
3. Mix the seasonings together.
4. Spread out the slices, mist with oil or cooking spray, and sprinkle with half of the seasonings.
5. Turnover and repeat to coat the other side with oil or cooking spray and seasonings.
6. Place in air fryer cooking tray and select Bagel. Set temperature to 390ºF (200ºC), and set time to 2 minutes. Shake cooking tray or stir a little and continue cooking for 1 to 2 minutes or until toasty brown and crispy.

## Spinach Dip with Bread Knots

**Prep time: 10 minutes | Cook time: 10 minutes | Serves 6**

Nonstick cooking spray
1 package (8 ounces / 227g) cream cheese, cut into cubes
¼ cup sour cream
½ cup frozen chopped spinach, thawed and drained
½ cup grated Swiss
cheese
2 green onions, chopped
½ (11-ounce / 311.8g) can refrigerated breadstick dough
2 tablespoons melted butter
3 tablespoons grated Parmesan cheese

1. Spray a 6-by-6-by-2-inch pan with nonstick cooking spray.
2. In a medium bowl, combine the cream cheese, sour cream, spinach, Swiss cheese, and green onions, and mix well. Spread into the prepared pan and bake for 8 minutes or until hot.
3. While the dip is baking, unroll six of the breadsticks and cut them in half crosswise to make 12 pieces.
4. Gently stretch each piece of dough and tie into a loose knot; tuck in the ends.
5. When the dip is hot, remove from the air fryer and carefully place each bread knot on top of the dip, covering the surface of the dip. Brush each knot with melted butter and sprinkle Parmesan cheese on top.
6. Select Bake, set the temperature to 350 ºF and set time to 10 minutes or until the bread knots are golden brown and cooked through.

## Asian Five-Spice Chicken Wings

**Prep time: 5 minutes | Cook time: 13 minutes | Serves 4**

2 pounds (907 g) chicken wings
½ cup Asian-style salad dressing
2 tablespoons Chinese five-spice powder

1. Cut off wing tips and discard or freeze for stock. Cut remaining wing pieces in two at the joint.
2. Place wing pieces in a large sealable plastic bag. Pour in the Asian dressing, seal bag, and massage the marinade into the wings until well coated. Refrigerate for at least an hour.
3. Remove wings from bag, drain off excess marinade, and place wings in air fryer cooking tray.
4. Select Air Fry. Set temperature to 360ºF (180ºC), and set time to 13 to 15 minutes or until juices run clear. About halfway through cooking time, shake the cooking tray or stir wings for more even cooking.
5. Transfer cooked wings to plate in a single layer. Sprinkle half of the Chinese five-spice powder on the wings, turn, and sprinkle other side with remaining seasoning.

## Hot Fried Pickles

**Prep time: 5 minutes | Cook time: 11 minutes | Makes 2 cups**

1 egg
1 tablespoon milk
¼ teaspoon hot sauce
2 cups sliced dill pickles,
well drained
¾ cup breadcrumbs
Oil for misting or cooking spray

1. Preheat air fryer oven to 390ºF (200ºC).
2. Beat together egg, milk, and hot sauce in a bowl large enough to hold all the pickles.
3. Add pickles to the egg wash and stir well to coat.
4. Place breadcrumbs in a large plastic bag or container with lid.
5. Drain egg wash from pickles and place them in bag with breadcrumbs. Shake to coat.
6. Pile pickles into air fryer cooking tray and spray with oil.
7. Select Air Fry for 5 minutes. Shake cooking tray and spray with oil.
8. Cook for 5 more minutes. Shake and spray again. Separate any pickles that have stuck together and mist any spots you've missed.
9. Cook for 1 to 5 minutes longer or until dark golden brown and crispy.

## Hot Paprika Zucchini Fries

**Prep time: 110 minutes | Cook time: 20 minutes | Serves 4**

1 pound (454 g) zucchini, cut into sticks
½ cup Parmesan cheese
½ cup almond flour
1 egg, whisked
2 tablespoons olive oil
1 teaspoon hot paprika
Sea salt and ground black pepper, to taste

1. Preheat your Air Fryer oven to 390ºF (200ºC).
2. Toss the zucchini sticks with the remaining ingredients and arrange them in a single layer in the rotisserie basket.
3. Select Roast for about 10 minutes at 390ºF (200ºC), shaking the basket halfway through the cooking time. Work in batches.
4. Bon appétit!

## Beef Steak Sliders

**Prep time: 10 minutes | Cook time: 16 minutes | Makes 8 sliders**

1 pound (454 g) top sirloin steaks, about ¾-inch thick
Salt and pepper, to taste
2 large onions, thinly sliced
1 tablespoon extra-light olive oil
8 slider buns
For the Horseradish Mayonnaise:
1 cup light mayonnaise
4 teaspoons prepared horseradish
2 teaspoons Worcestershire sauce
1 teaspoon coarse brown mustard

1. Place steak in air fryer cooking tray and select Roast. Set temperature to 390ºF (200ºC), and set time to 6 minutes. Turn and cook 5 to 6 more minutes for medium rare. If you prefer your steak medium, continue cooking for 2 to 3 minutes.
2. While the steak is cooking, prepare the Horseradish Mayonnaise by mixing all ingredients together.
3. When steak is cooked, remove from air fryer, sprinkle with salt and pepper to taste, and set aside to rest.
4. Toss the onion slices with the oil and place in air fryer cooking tray. Cook at 390ºF (200ºC), and set time to 5 to 7 minutes, until onion rings are soft and browned.
5. Slice steak into very thin slices.
6. Spread slider buns with the horseradish mayo and pile on the meat and onions. Serve with remaining horseradish dressing for dipping.

## Greek Street Feta Tacos

**Prep time: 5 minutes | Cook time: 3 minutes | Makes 8 small tacos**

8 (4-inch diameter) small flour tortillas
8 tablespoons hummus
4 tablespoons crumbled Feta cheese
4 tablespoons chopped kalamata or other olives (optional)
Olive oil for misting

1. Place 1 tablespoon of hummus in the center of each tortilla. Top with 1 teaspoon of Feta crumbles and 1 teaspoon of chopped olives, if using.
2. Using your finger or a small spoon, moisten the edges of the tortilla all around with water.
3. Fold tortilla over to make a half-moon shape. Press center gently. Then press the edges firmly to seal in the filling.
4. Mist both sides with olive oil.
5. Place in air fryer cooking tray very close but try not to overlap.
6. Select Broil. Set temperature to 390ºF (200ºC), and set time to 3 minutes, just until lightly browned and crispy.

## Loaded Potato Skins

**Prep time: 10 minutes | Cook time: 12 minutes | Serves 4**

4 medium russet potatoes, baked
Olive oil
Salt, to taste
Freshly ground black pepper, to taste
2 cups shredded Cheddar cheese
4 slices cooked bacon, chopped
Finely chopped scallions, for topping
Sour cream, for topping
Finely chopped olives, for topping

1. Spray the air fryer cooking tray with oil.
2. Cut each baked potato in half.
3. Using a large spoon, scoop out the center of each potato half, leaving about 1 inch of the potato flesh around the edges and the bottom.
4. Rub olive oil over the inside of each baked potato half and season with salt and pepper, then place the potato skins in the greased air fryer cooking tray.
5. Select Bake. Set temperature to 400ºF (205ºC), and set time to 10 minutes.
6. After 10 minutes, remove the potato skins, fill them with the shredded Cheddar cheese and bacon, and then bake in the air fryer for another 2 minutes, just until the cheese is melted.

7. Garnish the potato skins with the scallions, sour cream, and olives.

## Red Beets Chips

**Prep time: 5 minutes | Cook time: 30 minutes | Serves 4**

1 pound (454 g) red beets, peeled and cut into ⅛-inch slices
1 tablespoon olive oil
1 teaspoon cayenne pepper
Sea salt and ground black pepper, to taste

1. Preheat your Air Fryer oven to 330ºF (166ºC).
2. Toss the beets with the remaining ingredients and place them in the Air Fryer cooking tray.
3. Select Air Fry, cook for 30 minutes at 330ºF (166ºC), shaking the cooking tray occasionally and working in batches.
4. Enjoy!

## Fresh Potatoes Wedges

**Prep time: 5 minutes | Cook time: 20 minutes | Serves 4**

4 russet potatoes
2 teaspoons salt, divided
1 teaspoon freshly ground black pepper
1 teaspoon paprika
1 to 3 tablespoons olive oil, divided

1. Cut the potatoes into ½-inch-thick wedges. Try to make the wedges uniform in size, so they cook at an even rate.
2. In a medium mixing bowl, combine the potato wedges with 1 teaspoon of salt, pepper, paprika, and 1 tablespoon of olive oil. Toss until all the potatoes are thoroughly coated with oil. Add additional oil, if needed.
3. Place the potato wedges in the rotisserie basket. (You may have to roast them in batches.)
4. Select Roast. Set temperature to 400ºF (205ºC), and set time to 5 minutes.
5. After 5 minutes, shake the potatoes to keep them from sticking. Reset the timer and roast the potatoes for another 5 minutes, then shake again. Repeat this process until the potatoes have cooked for a total of 20 minutes.
6. Check and see if the potatoes are cooked. If they are not fork-tender, roast for 5 minutes or more.
7. Using tongs, remove the potato wedges from the rotisserie basket and transfer them to a bowl. Toss with the remaining salt.

# Healthy Carrot Chips

**Prep time: 5 minutes | Cook time: 6 minutes | Serves 6**

1 pound (454 g) carrots, peeled and sliced ⅛ inch thick

2 tablespoons olive oil
1 teaspoon sea salt

1. In a large mixing bowl, combine the carrots, olive oil, and salt. Toss them together until the carrot slices are thoroughly coated with oil.
2. Place the carrot chips in the air fryer cooking tray in a single layer. (You may have to bake the carrot chips in more than one batch.)
3. Select Air Fry. Set temperature to 360ºF (180ºC), and set time to 3 minutes. Remove the air fryer drawer and shake to redistribute the chips for even cooking. Reset the timer and cook for 3 minutes or more.
4. Check the carrot chips for doneness. If you like them extra crispy, give the cooking tray another shake and cook them for another 1 to 2 minutes.
5. When the chips are done, release the air fryer cooking tray from the drawer, pour the chips into a bowl, and serve.

# Bacon-Wrapped Jalapeño Peppers

**Prep time: 10 minutes | Cook time: 12 minutes | Serves 12**

12 jalapeño peppers
1 package (8 ounces / 227g) cream cheese, at room temperature
1 cup shredded Cheddar cheese

1 teaspoon onion powder
1 teaspoon salt
½ teaspoon freshly ground black pepper
12 slices bacon, cut in half

1. Spray the air fryer cooking tray with olive oil.
2. Cut each pepper in half, then use a spoon to scrape out the veins and seeds.
3. In a small mixing bowl, mix together the cream cheese, Cheddar cheese, onion powder, salt, and pepper.
4. Using a small spoon, fill each pepper half with the cheese mixture.
5. Wrap each stuffed pepper half with a half slice of bacon.
6. Place the bacon-wrapped peppers into the greased air fryer cooking tray in a single layer. (You may have to cook the peppers in more than one batch.)
7. Select Roast. Set temperature to 320ºF (160ºC), and set time to 12 minutes.
8. Using tongs, remove the peppers from the air fryer, place them on a platter, and serve.

# Allergen Friendly Breakfast Cookies

**Prep time: 10 minutes | Cook time: 12 minutes | Serves 10**

3 very ripe bananas
2 tablespoons. raw honey
½ cup almond butter
2 tablespoons. vanilla extract
1 tbsp. coconut oil, melted

1 tsp. ground cinnamon
1 tsp. baking powder
½ tsp. salt
2½ cups rolled oats
chocolate chips (optional)

1. Preheat the oven to 350°F(180°C).
2. Use parchment paper to line a large baking sheet.
3. Use a potato masher or a fork to mash the bananas in a large bowl.
4. Add the honey, almond butter, vanilla and coconut oil, stir until well mixed.
5. Sprinkle the banana mixture with the cinnamon, baking powder, and salt. Add the oats and chocolate chips (if using) in batches, stirring after each addition until all ingredients are incorporated.
6. On the prepared sheet, add heaping tablespoons of dough, leaving at least 1 inch between dough balls.
7. Select COOKIES, cook at 350°F(180°C) for 10 to 12 minutes.
8. Allow the cookies to rest in the pan for 5 minutes, and then transfer to a cooling rack. Place the cookies in a sealed container, and store in the refrigerator for several days.

# Chapter 11 Desserts

## Old-Fashioned Pumpkin Cake

**Prep time: 5 minutes | Cook time: 12 minutes | Serves 2**

⅓ cup pumpkin puree
½ cup peanut butter
2 eggs, beaten
1 teaspoon vanilla extract

½ teaspoon pumpkin pie spice
½ teaspoon baking powder

1. Mix all the ingredients to make the batter. Pour the batter into a lightly oiled baking pan.
2. Place the pan in the Air Fryer cooking tray.
3. Select Bake. Set temperature to 350ºF (180ºC), and set time to about 12 minutes or until it is golden brown around the edges.
4. Bon appétit!

## Honey and Balsamic Strawberry Tart

**Prep time: 5 minutes | Cook time: 25 minutes | Serves 2**

1 pound (454 g) strawberries, hulled and thinly sliced
1 tablespoon balsamic vinegar
1 tablespoon honey

1 sprig basil
1 sheet frozen puff pastry, thawed according to package instructions
1 egg beaten with 1 tablespoon water

1. Place the strawberries in a 7-inch round pizza pan insert for the oven and mound them slightly in the center. In a small bowl, whisk together the balsamic vinegar and honey. Drizzle the mixture over the strawberries. Slice the leaves from the sprig of basil into ribbons and sprinkle them over the strawberries.
2. Cut out an 8-inch square from the sheet of puff pastry. Drape the pastry over the strawberries in the pan. Poke holes in the puff pastry with the tines of a fork. Brush the top of the pastry with the egg wash. Place the pan in the air fryer cooking tray.
3. Select Bake. Set temperature to 325ºF (165ºC), and set time to 25 minutes until the top of the pastry is golden brown and glossy and the underside of the pastry is cooked. Remove the pan from the cooking tray of the air fryer. If desired, cut the pastry in half and divide the dessert among 2 plates. Alternatively, for less mess, two people can enjoy this tart right out of the pan.

## Favorite Fudge Cake

**Prep time: 10 minutes | Cook time: 20 minutes | Serves 5**

½ cup butter, melted
1 cup turbinado sugar
3 eggs
1 teaspoon vanilla extract
¼ teaspoon salt
¼ teaspoon ground cloves

½ teaspoon ground cinnamon
½ cup all-purpose flour
¼ cup almond flour
5 ounces (142 g) chocolate chips

1. Preheat your Air Fryer oven to 340ºF (170ºC). Now, spritz the sides and bottom of a baking pan with a nonstick cooking spray.
2. In a mixing bowl, beat the butter and sugar until fluffy. Next, fold in the eggs and beat again until well combined.
3. After that, add in the remaining ingredients. Mix until everything is well combined.
4. Select Bake. Set temperature to 340ºF (170ºC), and set time to 20 minutes. Enjoy!

## Brown Sugar-Coconut Chocolate Cake

**Prep time: 10 minutes | Cook time: 20 minutes | Serves 6**

½ cup coconut oil, room temperature
1 cup brown sugar
2 chia eggs (2 tablespoons ground chia seeds + 4 tablespoons water)
¼ cup all-purpose flour

¼ cup coconut flour
½ cup cocoa powder
½ cup dark chocolate chips
A pinch of grated nutmeg
A pinch of sea salt
2 tablespoons coconut milk

1. Preheat your Air Fryer oven to 340ºF (170ºC). Now, spritz the sides and bottom of a baking pan with a nonstick cooking spray.
2. In a mixing bowl, beat the coconut oil and brown sugar until fluffy. Next, fold in the chia eggs and beat again until well combined.
3. After that, add in the remaining ingredients. Mix until everything is well incorporated.
4. Select Bake. Set temperature to 340ºF (170ºC), and set time to 20 minutes. Enjoy!

## Spoon Brownies

**Prep time: 10 minutes | Cook time: 30 minutes | Serves 4 to 6**

1 cup granulated sugar
⅓ cup Dutch-process cocoa powder
½ teaspoon kosher salt
8 tablespoons unsalted butter, melted
1 teaspoon vanilla extract
2 large eggs, lightly beaten
¼ cup all-purpose flour
½ cup roughly chopped bittersweet chocolate
Vanilla ice cream and flaky sea salt (optional), for serving

1. In a bowl, whisk together the sugar, cocoa powder, and salt. Then add the melted butter, vanilla, and eggs and whisk until smooth. Stir in the flour and chocolate and pour the batter into a 7-inch round cake or pizza pan insert, metal cake pan, or foil pan. Place the pan in the oven and select Bake. Set temperature to 310ºF (155ºC) until the brownie "pudding" is set at the edges but still jiggly in the middle (it may form a "skin" in the middle, but it doesn't affect the taste), for about 30 minutes.
2. Let the brownie pan cool in the air fryer for 5 minutes, enough time to grab some bowls and allow the ice cream to soften to the perfect scooping consistency. Divide the gooey brownies among serving bowls and top with a scoop of ice cream and, if you like, a decent pinch of flaky sea salt.

## Strawberry Scone Shortcake

**Prep time: 10 minutes | Cook time: 20 minutes | Serves 4 to 6**

1⅓ cups all-purpose flour
3 tablespoons granulated sugar
1½ teaspoons baking powder
1 teaspoon kosher salt
8 tablespoons unsalted butter, cubed and chilled
1⅓ cups heavy cream, chilled
Turbinado sugar, such as Sugar In The Raw, for sprinkling
2 tablespoons powdered sugar, plus more for dusting
½ teaspoon vanilla extract
1 cup quartered fresh strawberries

1. In a large bowl, whisk together the flour, granulated sugar, baking powder, and salt. Add the butter and use your fingers to break apart the butter pieces while working them into the flour mixture, until pea-size pieces form. Pour ⅔ cup of the cream over the flour mixture and, using a rubber spatula, mix the ingredients together until just combined.

2. Transfer the dough to a work surface and form into a 7-inch-wide disk. Brush the top with water, then sprinkle with some turbinado sugar. Using a large metal spatula, transfer the dough to the oven and select Bake. Set temperature to 350ºF (180ºC) until golden brown and fluffy, for about 20 minutes. Let it cool in the air fryer cooking tray for 5 minutes, then turn out onto a wire rack, right-side up, to cool completely.
3. Meanwhile, in a bowl, beat the remaining cream, the powdered sugar, and vanilla until stiff peaks form. Split the scone like a hamburger bun and spread the strawberries over the bottom. Top with the whipped cream and cover with the top of the scone. Dust with powdered sugar and cut into wedges to serve.

## Spiced Apple Cake

**Prep time: 15 minutes | Cook time: 30 minutes | Serves 6**

Vegetable oil
2 cups diced peeled Gala apples
1 tablespoon fresh lemon juice
¼ cup unsalted butter, softened
⅓ cup granulated sugar
2 large eggs
1¼ cups unbleached all-purpose flour
1½ teaspoons baking powder
1 tablespoon apple pie spice
½ teaspoon ground ginger
¼ teaspoon ground cardamom
¼ teaspoon ground nutmeg
½ teaspoon kosher salt
¼ cup whole milk
Confectioners' sugar, for dusting

1. Grease a 3-cup Bundt pan with oil; set aside.
2. In a medium bowl, toss the apples with the lemon juice until well coated; set aside.
3. In a large bowl, combine the butter and sugar. Beat with an electric hand mixer on medium speed until the sugar has dissolved. Add the eggs and beat until fluffy. Add the flour, baking powder, apple pie spice, ginger, cardamom, nutmeg, salt, and milk. Mix until the batter is thick but pourable.
4. Pour the batter into the prepared pan. Top batter evenly with the apple mixture. Place the pan in the air fryer cooking tray. Select Bake. Set temperature to 350ºF (180ºC), and set time to 30 minutes, or until a toothpick inserted in the center of the cake comes out clean. Close the oven and let the cake rest for 10 minutes. Turn the cake out onto a wire rack and cool completely.
5. Right before serving, dust the cake with confectioners' sugar.

## Almond Coconut-Chocolate Cake

**Prep time: 15 minutes | Cook time: 20 minutes | Serves 6**

1 stick butter, melted
½ cups brown sugar
2 eggs, at room temperature
5 ounces (142 g) chocolate chips
½ teaspoon pure vanilla extract
½ teaspoon pure almond extract
¼ cup cocoa powder
¼ cup all-purpose flour
½ cup almond flour
½ teaspoon baking powder
2 ounces (57 g) almonds, slivered
4 tablespoons coconut milk

1. Preheat your Air Fryer oven to 340ºF (170ºC). Then, brush the sides and bottom of a baking pan with a nonstick cooking spray.
2. In a mixing bowl, beat the butter and sugar until fluffy. Next, fold in the eggs and beat again until well combined.
3. After that, add in the remaining ingredients. Mix until everything is well combined.
4. Select Bake. Set temperature to 340ºF (170ºC), and set time to 20 minutes. Enjoy!

## Pumpkin-Spice Bread Pudding

**Prep time: 15 minutes | Cook time: 50 minutes | Serves 6**

For the Bread Pudding:
¾ cup heavy whipping cream
½ cup canned pumpkin
⅓ cup whole milk
⅓ cup sugar
1 large egg plus 1 yolk
½ teaspoon pumpkin pie spice
⅛ teaspoon kosher salt
4 cups 1-inch cubed day-old baguette or crusty
country bread
4 tablespoons unsalted butter, melted
For the Sauce:
⅓ cup pure maple syrup
1 tablespoon unsalted butter
½ cup heavy whipping cream
½ teaspoon pure vanilla extract

Make the Bread Pudding
1. In a medium bowl, combine the cream, pumpkin, milk, sugar, egg and yolk, pumpkin pie spice, and salt. Whisk until well combined.
2. In a large bowl, toss the bread cubes with the melted butter. Add the pumpkin mixture and gently toss until the ingredients are well combined.
3. Transfer the mixture to an ungreased 6 × 3 inch heatproof pan. Place the pan in the air fryer cooking

tray. Select Bake. Set temperature to 350ºF (180ºC), and set time to 35 minutes, or until custard is set in the middle.

Make the Sauce
4. In a small saucepan, combine the syrup and butter. Heat over medium heat, stirring, until the butter melts. Stir in the cream and simmer, stirring often, until the sauce has thickened, for about 15 minutes. Stir in the vanilla. Remove the pudding from the air fryer.
5. Let the pudding stand for 10 minutes before serving with the warm sauce.

## Apple Turnovers

**Prep time: 10 minutes | Cook time: 45 minutes | Serves 4**

3½ ounces (99.2 g) dried apples
¼ cup golden raisins
1 tablespoon granulated sugar
1 tablespoon freshly squeezed lemon juice
½ teaspoon cinnamon
1 pound (454 g) frozen puff pastry, defrosted according to package instructions
1 egg beaten with 1 tablespoon water
Turbinado or demerara sugar for sprinkling

1. Place the dried apples in a medium saucepan and cover with about 2 cups of water. Bring the mixture to a boil over medium-high heat, then reduce the heat to low, cover, and simmer until the apples have absorbed most of the liquid, for about 20 minutes. Remove the apples from the heat and allow to cool. Add the raisins, sugar, lemon juice, and cinnamon to the dried apples and set aside.
2. On a well-floured board, roll the puff pastry out to a 12-inch square. Cut the square into 4 equal quarters. Divide the filling equally among the 4 squares, mounding it in the middle of each square. Brush the edges of each square with water and fold the pastry diagonally over the apple mixture, creating a triangle. Seal the edges by pressing them with the tines of a fork. Transfer the turnovers to a sheet pan lined with parchment paper.
3. Brush the top of 2 turnovers with egg wash and sprinkle with turbinado sugar. Make 2 small slits in the top of the turnovers for venting and select Bake. Set temperature to 325ºF (165ºC), and set time to 25 minutes, until the top is browned and puffed and the pastry is cooked through. Remove the cooked turnovers to a cooling rack and cook the remaining 2 turnovers in the same manner. Serve warm or at room temperature.

## Lemon-Lavender Doughnuts

**Prep time: 10 minutes | Cook time: 10 minutes | Makes 6 to 8 doughnuts**

½ cup milk, warmed to between 100°F and 110°F (38°C to 43°C)
1 teaspoon yeast
¼ cup granulated sugar, divided
2 cups all-purpose flour
½ teaspoon kosher salt
Zest and juice of 1 lemon
4 tablespoons unsalted butter, melted
1 egg
Vegetable oil for spraying
1½ cups powdered sugar, sifted
Dried lavender for culinary use (optional)

1. Combine the warm milk, yeast, and a pinch of the sugar in a small bowl and whisk to combine. Allow them to sit until the yeast blooms and looks bubbly, for about 5 to 10 minutes. Meanwhile, whisk together the remaining sugar, flour, and salt. Add the zest of the lemon to the dry ingredients.
2. When the yeast has bloomed, add the milk mixture to the dry ingredients and stir to combine. Add the melted butter and the egg and stir to form a thick dough. Turn the dough out onto a well-floured board and knead until smooth, for 1 to 2 minutes. Place the dough in an oiled bowl, cover, and allow to rise in the refrigerator overnight.
3. The following day, remove the dough from the refrigerator and allow it to come to room temperature. Turn the risen dough out onto a well-floured board. Roll the dough out until it is approximately ¼ inch thick. Using a 3- or 4-inch circular cookie cutter, cut out as many doughnuts as possible. Use a 1-inch round cookie cutter to cut out holes from the center of each doughnut. With the dough scraps, you can either cut out additional doughnut holes using the 1-inch cutter or, if desired, gather the scraps and roll them out again to cut out more doughnuts. (The doughnuts from the rerolled scraps will not rise as well as the other doughnuts.)
4. Transfer the doughnuts and doughnut holes to a lined baking sheet. Cover with a clean kitchen towel and allow to proof in a warm place until puffy and, when pressed with a finger, the dough slowly springs back, for 30 minutes to 1 hour.
5. While the dough is proofing, prepare the glaze. In a medium bowl, whisk together the sifted powdered sugar and the juice from the lemon. Set aside.
6. When the doughnuts have proofed, spray the air fryer cooking tray with oil. Transfer no more than 3 or 4 of the doughnuts and 2 or 3 of the holes to the cooking tray. Spray the doughnuts lightly with oil. Select Bake. Set temperature to 360ºF (180ºC), and set time to 5 minutes, flipping once halfway through,

until browned and cooked through. Transfer the cooked doughnuts and holes to a cooling rack and repeat with the remaining doughnuts and holes.

7. Once the doughnuts are cool enough to handle, dip the tops into the glaze. Return the dipped doughnuts to the rack to allow the excess glaze to drip off. Once the glaze has hardened, dip each doughnut again to create a nice opaque finish. While the second glaze is still wet, if desired, sprinkle a few buds of lavender on top of each doughnut.

## Fast French Dessert

**Prep time: 10 minutes | Cook time: 7 minutes | Serves 2**

2 eggs
2 tablespoons coconut oil, melted
¼ cup milk
½ teaspoon vanilla extract
¼ teaspoon ground cinnamon
⅛ teaspoon ground nutmeg
4 thick slices baguette

1. In a mixing bowl, thoroughly combine the eggs, coconut oil, milk, vanilla, cinnamon, and nutmeg.
2. Then, dip each piece of bread into the egg mixture; place the bread slices in a lightly greased baking pan.
3. Select Bake. Set temperature to 330ºF (165ºC), and set time to 4 minutes, turn them over and cook for a further 3 to 4 minutes. Enjoy!

## Spanish Churros

**Prep time: 10 minutes | Cook time: 10 minutes | Serves 4**

¾ cup all-purpose flour
½ teaspoon baking powder
¾ cup water
4 tablespoons butter
1 tablespoon granulated
sugar
½ teaspoon vanilla extract
½ teaspoon sea salt
1 large egg

1. In a mixing bowl, thoroughly combine all ingredients. Place the batter in a piping bag fitted with a large open star tip.
2. Pipe the churros into 6-inch long ropes and lower them onto the greased Air Fryer pan.
3. Select Bake. Set temperature to 360ºF (180ºC), and set time to 10 minutes, flipping them halfway through the cooking time.
4. Repeat with the remaining batter and serve warm. Enjoy!

## Caramelized Peach Shortcakes with Whipped Cream

**Prep time: 15 minutes | Cook time: 23 minutes | Serves 4**

For the Shortcakes:
1 cup self-rising flour
½ cup plus 1 tablespoon heavy cream
Vegetable oil for spraying
For the Caramelized Peaches:
2 peaches, preferably freestone
1 tablespoon unsalted

butter, melted
2 teaspoons brown sugar
1 teaspoon cinnamon
For the Whipped Cream:
1 cup cold heavy cream
1 tablespoon granulated sugar
½ teaspoon vanilla extract
Zest of 1 lime

Make the Shortcakes

1. Place the flour in a medium bowl and whisk to remove any lumps. Make a well in the center of the flour. While stirring with a fork, slowly pour in ½ cup plus 1 tablespoon of the heavy cream. Continue to stir until the dough has mostly come together. With your hands, gather the dough, incorporating any dry flour, and form into a ball.
2. Place the dough on a lightly floured board and pat into a rectangle that is ½ to ¾ inch thick. Fold in half. Turn and repeat. Pat the dough into a ¾-inch-thick square. Cut dough into 4 equally sized square biscuits.
3. Preheat the air fryer oven to 325ºF (163ºC). Spray the air fryer cooking tray with oil to prevent sticking. Place the biscuits in the cooking tray. Select Bake for 15 minutes until the tops are browned and the insides fully cooked. (May be done ahead.)

Make the Peaches

4. Cut the peaches in half and remove the pit. Brush the peach halves with the melted butter and sprinkle ½ teaspoon of the brown sugar and ¼ teaspoon of the cinnamon on each peach half. Arrange the peaches in a single layer in the air fryer cooking tray. Select Bake. Set temperature to 375ºF (190°C) for 8 minutes until the peaches are soft and the tops caramelized.
5. While the peaches are cooking, whip the cream. Pour the cold heavy cream, sugar, and vanilla (if using) into the bowl of a stand mixer or a metal mixing bowl. Beat with the whisk attachment for your stand mixer or a handheld electric mixer on high speed until stiff peaks form, about 1 minute. (If not using the cream right away, cover with plastic wrap and refrigerate until needed.)
6. To assemble the shortcakes, cut each biscuit in half horizontally. Place a peach on the bottom half of each biscuit and place the top half on top of the peach. Top each shortcake with whipped cream and

a sprinkle of lime zest. Serve immediately.

## Persian Doughnuts with Saffron and Rose Water

**Prep time: 10 minutes | Cook time: 27 minutes | Makes 18 to 20 doughnuts**

For the Doughnuts:
3 tablespoons unsalted butter
1 tablespoon granulated sugar
1 cup water
1 cup all-purpose flour
2 eggs

Vegetable oil for spraying
For the Syrup:
1 cup granulated sugar
¾ cup water
1 teaspoon rose water
Pinch saffron threads dissolved in ¼ cup boiling water

1. Combine the butter, sugar, and water in a medium saucepan and melt the butter over low heat. Add the flour and stir to form a cohesive dough. Cook over medium-low heat for 2 minutes to get rid of the raw flour taste. Remove from the heat and allow it to cool to room temperature. Beat the eggs in one at a time, making sure the first egg is fully incorporated before the adding the second. The dough will look curdled at first, but keep beating vigorously until the dough becomes smooth. Once the eggs are fully incorporated, let the dough rest for 30 minutes.
2. While the dough is resting, prepare the rose water syrup. Combine the sugar and water in a small saucepan and bring to a boil, stirring to dissolve the sugar. Turn down the heat and simmer for 5 minutes until thickened. Remove from the heat and add the rose water and 1 tablespoon of the saffron water, reserving the remaining saffron water for another use, such as rice pilaf. Keep warm.
3. Once the dough has rested, place the dough in a piping bag outfitted with a large, star-shaped tip. Lightly oil the cooking tray of the air fryer. Pipe the dough directly onto the air fryer cooking tray, forming doughnuts approximately 3 inches long and 1 inch wide. Use a knife or scissors to cut the dough when you have achieved the desired length. Work in batches so as not to overcrowd the cooking tray. Spray lightly with oil. Select Bake. Set temperature to 360ºF (180ºC), shaking the cooking tray once or twice, for 10 minutes until the outside of the doughnuts is golden brown and the inside is fully cooked.
4. Pour the warm syrup in a shallow bowl and place the first batch of doughnuts in the syrup. Allow them to soak for 5 minutes then remove to a plate or platter. Repeat the process with the remaining dough and syrup. Serve warm or at room temperature.

## Rum Banana Fritters

**Prep time: 10 minutes | Cook time: 10 minutes | Serves 4**

¾ cup all-purpose flour
¾ cup water
1 tablespoon rum
4 tablespoons butter
1 banana, mashed
1 tablespoon caster sugar
¼ teaspoon salt
¼ teaspoon grated nutmeg

1. In a mixing bowl, thoroughly combine all the ingredients.
2. Drop a spoonful of batter onto the greased Air Fryer pan. Select Bake. Set temperature to 360ºF (180ºC), and set time to 10 minutes, flipping them halfway through the cooking time.
3. Repeat with the remaining batter and serve warm. Enjoy!

## Coconut Vanilla Pancake Cups

**Prep time: 10 minutes | Cook time: 5 minutes | Serves 4**

½ cup flour
2 eggs
⅓ cup coconut milk
1 tablespoon coconut oil, melted
1 teaspoon vanilla paste
¼ teaspoon ground cinnamon
A pinch of ground cardamom

1. Mix all the ingredients until well combined.
2. Let the batter stand for 20 minutes. Spoon the batter into a greased muffin tin.
3. Select Bake. Set temperature to 330ºF (165ºC), and set time to 5 minutes or until golden brown. Serve with toppings of choice.
4. Bon appétit!

## Old-Fashioned Stuffed Apples

**Prep time: 10 minutes | Cook time: 17 minutes | Serves 2**

2 medium apples
4 tablespoons pecans, chopped
4 tablespoons Sultanas
2 tablespoons butter, at
room temperature
½ teaspoon cinnamon
¼ teaspoon grated nutmeg

1. Cut the apples in halves and spoon out some of the flesh.
2. In a mixing bowl, thoroughly combine the remaining ingredients. Stuff the apple halves and transfer them

to the Air Fryer cooking tray.
3. Pour ¼ cup of water into an Air Fryer safe dish. Place the apples in the dish.
4. Select Bake. Set temperature to 340ºF (170ºC), and set time to 17 minutes. Serve at room temperature. Bon appétit!

## Apple Pie

**Prep time: 10 minutes | Cook time: 35 minutes | Serves 4**

12 ounces (340 g) refrigerated 2 pie crusts
3 cups apples, peeled and thinly sliced
¼ cup brown sugar
1 tablespoon lemon juice
1 teaspoon pure vanilla extract
½ teaspoon cinnamon
A pinch of ground cardamom
A pinch of kosher salt

1. Place the first pie crust on a lightly greased pie plate.
2. In a mixing bowl, thoroughly combine the remaining ingredients to make the filling. Spoon the filling into the prepared pie crust.
3. Unroll the second pie crust and place it on top of the filling.
4. Select Bake. Set temperature to 350ºF (180ºC), and set time to 35 minutes or until the top is golden brown. Bon appétit!

## Raisin Chocolate Cupcakes

**Prep time: 15 minutes | Cook time: 15 minutes | Serves 4**

¾ cup all-purpose flour
½ teaspoon baking powder
½ cup unsweetened cocoa powder
A pinch of kosher salt
¼ teaspoon grated nutmeg
½ teaspoon ground
cinnamon
4 tablespoons coconut oil
¾ cup brown sugar
2 eggs, whisked
½ teaspoon vanilla extract
¾ cup yogurt
2 tablespoons raisins

1. Preheat your Air Fryer oven to 330ºF (165ºC).
2. Mix all the ingredients in a bowl. Scrape the batter into silicone baking molds; place them in the Air Fryer cooking tray.
3. Select Bake. Set temperature to 330ºF (165ºC), and set time to 15 minutes or until a tester comes out dry and clean.
4. Allow the cupcakes to cool before unmolding and serving. Bon appétit!

Spanish Churros, page 142

Simple Chocolate Cupcakes, page 149

Southern-Style Baked Peaches, page 146

Cinnamon Donuts, page 150

## Fried Plums

**Prep time: 5 minutes | Cook time: 17 minutes | Serves 4**

| | |
|---|---|
| 1 pound (454 g) plums, halved and pitted | sugar |
| | 4 whole cloves |
| 2 tablespoons coconut oil | 1 cinnamon stick |
| 4 tablespoons brown | 4 whole star anise |

1. Toss the plums with the remaining ingredients.
2. Pour ¼ cup of water into an Air Fryer safe dish. Place the plums in the dish.
3. Select Bake. Set temperature to 340ºF (170ºC), and set time to 17 minutes. Serve at room temperature. Bon appétit!

## Banana Slices

**Prep time: 5 minutes | Cook time: 13 minutes | Serves 1**

| | |
|---|---|
| 1 banana, peeled and sliced | sugar |
| | ½ teaspoon ground |
| 1 tablespoon coconut oil | cinnamon |
| 2 tablespoons granulated | |

1. Preheat your Air Fryer oven to 390ºF (199ºC).
2. Toss banana slices with the remaining ingredients.
3. Select Bake. Set temperature to 390ºF (200ºC), and set time to 13 minutes, flipping them halfway through the cooking time.
4. Bon appétit!

## Southern-Style Baked Peaches

**Prep time: 10 minutes | Cook time: 15 minutes | Serves 3**

| | |
|---|---|
| 3 peaches, halved | ½ teaspoon grated |
| 1 tablespoon fresh lime juice | nutmeg |
| | ½ cup brown sugar |
| ½ teaspoon ground cinnamon | 4 tablespoons coconut oil |

1. Toss the peaches with the remaining ingredients.
2. Pour ¼ cup of water into an Air Fryer safe dish. Place the peaches in the dish.
3. Select Bake. Set temperature to 340ºF (170ºC), and set time to 15 minutes. Serve at room temperature. Bon appétit!

## Indian-Style Unnakai Malabar

**Prep time: 5 minutes | Cook time: 13 minutes | Serves 1**

| | |
|---|---|
| 1 plantain, peeled | powder |
| ¼ cup coconut flakes | 1 tablespoon ghee |
| ¼ teaspoon cinnamon powder | 2 tablespoons brown sugar |
| ¼ teaspoon cardamom | |

1. Preheat your Air Fryer oven to 390ºF (200ºC).
2. Toss the plantain with the remaining ingredients.
3. Select Bake. Set temperature to 390ºF (200ºC), and set time to 13 minutes, flipping it halfway through the cooking time.
4. Bon appétit!

## Homemade Beignets

**Prep time: 10 minutes | Cook time: 10 minutes | Serves 4**

| | |
|---|---|
| ¾ cup all-purpose flour | 2 eggs, beaten |
| 1 teaspoon baking powder | ¼ cup granulated sugar |
| | 2 tablespoons coconut |
| ¼ teaspoon kosher salt | oil, melted |
| ¼ cup yogurt | |

1. In a mixing bowl, thoroughly combine all the ingredients.
2. Drop a spoonful of batter onto the greased Air Fryer pan. Select Bake. Set temperature to 360ºF (180ºC), and set time to 10 minutes, flipping them halfway through the cooking time.
3. Repeat with the remaining batter and serve warm. Enjoy!

## Colorful Fruit Skewers

**Prep time: 10 minutes | Cook time: 10 minutes | Serves 4**

| | |
|---|---|
| 1 cup melon, cut into 1-inch chunks | 1 peach, cut into 1-inch chunks |
| 1 cup pineapple, cut into 1-inch chunks | 2 tablespoons coconut oil, melted |
| 1 banana, cut into 1-inch chunks | 2 tablespoons honey |

1. Toss your fruits with the coconut oil and honey.
2. Thread the fruits onto skewers and place them in the Air Fryer cooking tray.
3. Then, select Roast. Set temperature to 400ºF (205ºC), and set time to approximately 10 minutes, turning them over halfway through the cooking time.
4. Bon appétit!

## Vanilla-Cinnamon Pears in Red Wine

**Prep time: 5 minutes | Cook time: 17 minutes | Serves 3**

3 pears, peeled and cored
1 vanilla pod
1 cinnamon stick
2 to 3 cloves
1 cup caster sugar
1 cup red wine

1. Place the pears, vanilla, cinnamon, cloves, sugar, and wine in an Air Fryer safe dish.
2. Select Bake. Set temperature to 340ºF (170ºC), and set time to 17 minutes.
3. Serve at room temperature. Bon appétit!

## Roasted Bourbon Cherry

**Prep time: 5 minutes | Cook time: 20 minutes | Serves 4**

2 cups cherries, pitted
4 tablespoons brown sugar
1 tablespoon coconut oil
2 tablespoons bourbon
¼ teaspoon ground cinnamon

1. Toss the cherries with the remaining ingredients; place your cherries in a lightly greased baking dish.
2. Select Roast. Set temperature to 370ºF (190ºC), and set time to 20 minutes.
3. Serve at room temperature. Bon appétit!

## Banana Fritters

**Prep time: 5 minutes | Cook time: 10 minutes | Serves 1**

1 banana, mashed
1 egg, beaten
1 tablespoon coconut oil
¼ teaspoons ground
cinnamon
1 tablespoon brown sugar

1. In a mixing bowl, thoroughly combine all the ingredients.
2. Ladle the batter into a lightly greased Air Fryer pan.
3. Select Bake. Set temperature to 360ºF (180ºC), and set time to 10 minutes, flipping it halfway through the cooking time.
4. Enjoy!

## Buttery Pears

**Prep time: 5 minutes | Cook time: 17 minutes | Serves 2**

2 pears, peeled, cored, and cut into sticks
2 tablespoons butter
A pinch of grated nutmeg
A pinch of sea salt
½ teaspoon ground cinnamon
1 teaspoon fresh ginger, grated

1. Toss the pears with the remaining ingredients.
2. Pour ¼ cup of water into an Air Fryer safe dish. Place the pears in the dish.
3. Select Bake. Set temperature to 340ºF (170ºC), and set time to 17 minutes. Serve at room temperature. Bon appétit!

## Fluffy Blueberry Fritters

**Prep time: 10 minutes | Cook time: 10 minutes | Serves 4**

¾ cup all-purpose flour
1 teaspoon baking powder
½ cup coconut milk
2 tablespoons coconut sugar
A pinch of sea salt
1 egg
2 tablespoons melted butter
2 ounces (57 g) fresh blueberries

1. In a mixing bowl, thoroughly combine all the ingredients.
2. Drop a spoonful of batter onto the greased Air Fryer pan. Select Bake. Set temperature to 360ºF (180ºC), and set time to 10 minutes, flipping them halfway through the cooking time.
3. Repeat with the remaining batter and serve warm. Enjoy!

## American-Style Crullers

**Prep time: 10 minutes | Cook time: 20 minutes | Serves 4**

¾ cup all-purpose flour
¼ cup butter
¼ cup water
½ cup full-fat milk
¼ teaspoon kosher salt
A pinch of grated nutmeg
3 eggs, beaten

1. In a mixing bowl, thoroughly combine all ingredients. Place the batter in a piping bag fitted with a large open star tip.
2. Pipe your crullers into circles and lower them onto the greased Air Fryer pan.
3. Select Bake. Set temperature to 360ºF (180ºC), and set time to 10 minutes, flipping them halfway through the cooking time.
4. Repeat with the remaining batter and serve immediately. Enjoy!

## Cinnamon Vanilla French Toast

**Prep time: 10 minutes | Cook time: 7 minutes | Serves 3**

1 egg, whisked
¼ cup coconut milk
2 tablespoons butter, melted
1 teaspoon vanilla paste
½ teaspoon ground cinnamon
A pinch of grated nutmeg
3 slices bread

1. In a mixing bowl, thoroughly combine the eggs, milk, butter, vanilla, cinnamon, and nutmeg.
2. Then dip each piece of bread into the egg mixture; place the bread slices in a lightly greased baking pan.
3. Select Bake. Set temperature to 330ºF (165ºC), and set time to about 4 minutes; turn them over and cook for a further 3 to 4 minutes. Enjoy!

## Autumn Pumpkin Pie

**Prep time: 10 minutes | Cook time: 32 minutes | Serves 4**

12 ounces (340 g) refrigerated pie crusts
½ cup pumpkin puree, canned
1 ounce (28 g) walnuts, coarsely chopped
½ cup granulated sugar
1 teaspoon pumpkin pie spice mix
1 teaspoon fresh ginger, peeled and grated

1. Place the first pie crust in a lightly greased pie plate.
2. In a mixing bowl, thoroughly combine the remaining ingredients to make the filling. Spoon the filling into the prepared pie crust.
3. Unroll the second pie crust and place it on top of the filling.
4. Select Bake. Set temperature to 350ºF (180ºC), and set time to 32 minutes or until the top is golden brown. Bon appétit!

## Danish Cinnamon Rolls Baked

**Prep time: 5 minutes | Cook time: 10 minutes | Serves 4**

9 ounces (255 g) refrigerated crescent rolls
1 tablespoon coconut oil
4 tablespoons caster
sugar
1 teaspoon ground cinnamon

1. Separate the dough into rectangles. Mix the remaining ingredients until well combined.
2. Spread each rectangle with the cinnamon mixture;

roll them up tightly.
3. Place the rolls in the Air Fryer cooking tray.
4. Select Bake. Set temperature to 300ºF (150ºC), and set time to 5 minutes, turn them over and bake for a further 5 minutes.
5. Bon appétit!

## Brownies with a Twist

**Prep time: 10 minutes | Cook time: 20 minutes | Serves 6**

1 stick butter, melted
1 cup brown sugar
2 eggs
¾ cup all-purpose flour
½ teaspoon baking powder
¼ cup cocoa powder
2 tablespoons coconut oil
1 teaspoon coconut extract
A pinch of sea salt

1. Preheat your Air Fryer oven to 340ºF (170ºC). Now, spritz the sides and bottom of a baking pan with a nonstick cooking spray.
2. In a mixing bowl, beat the melted butter and sugar until fluffy. Next, fold in the eggs and beat again until well combined.
3. After that, add in the remaining ingredients. Mix until everything is well incorporated.
4. Select Bake. Set temperature to 340ºF (170ºC), and set time to 20 minutes. Enjoy!

## Greek Yogurt and Walnut Stuffed Pears

**Prep time: 10 minutes | Cook time: 17 minutes | Serves 2**

2 pears
¼ teaspoon cloves
⅛ teaspoon grated nutmeg
¼ teaspoon ground cinnamon
2 tablespoons honey
2 tablespoons walnuts, chopped
2 ounces (57 g) Greek-style yogurt

1. Cut the pears in half and spoon out some of the flesh.
2. In a mixing bowl, thoroughly combine the remaining ingredients. Stuff the pear halves and transfer them to the Air Fryer cooking tray.
3. Pour ¼ cup of water into an Air Fryer safe dish. Place the pears in the dish.
4. Select Bake. Set temperature to 340ºF (170ºC), and set time to 17 minutes. Serve at room temperature. Bon appétit!

## Brown Sugar Apple Wedges

**Prep time: 5 minutes | Cook time: 17 minutes | Serves 2**

2 apples, peeled, cored, and cut into wedges
2 teaspoons coconut oil
2 tablespoons brown sugar

1 teaspoon pure vanilla extract
1 teaspoon ground cinnamon
¼ cup water

1. Toss the apples with the coconut oil, sugar, vanilla, and cinnamon.
2. Pour ¼ cup of water into an Air Fryer safe dish. Place the apples in the dish.
3. Select Bake. Set temperature to 340ºF (170ºC), and set time to 17 minutes. Serve at room temperature. Bon appétit!

## Honey Pumpkin Cake

**Prep time: 10 minutes | Cook time: 13 minutes | Serves 3**

4 tablespoons all-purpose flour
4 tablespoons almond flour
1 teaspoon baking powder
4 tablespoons honey

1 teaspoon pumpkin pie spice blend
A pinch of Himalayan salt
¼ cup milk
¼ cup canned pumpkin
1 egg, beaten

1. Mix all the ingredients to make the batter. Pour the batter into a lightly oiled baking pan.
2. Place the pan in the Air Fryer cooking tray.
3. Select Bake. Set temperature to 350ºF (180ºC), and set time to about 13 minutes or until it is golden brown around the edges.
4. Bon appétit!

## Simple Chocolate Cupcakes

**Prep time: 10 minutes | Cook time: 15 minutes | Serves 6**

¾ cup all-purpose flour
1 teaspoon baking powder
¼ teaspoon ground cinnamon
¾ cup granulated sugar
¼ cups unsweetened

cocoa powder
A pinch of sea salt
1 stick butter, at room temperature
¾ cup milk
2 eggs, beaten

1. Preheat your Air Fryer oven to 330ºF (165ºC).

2. Mix all the ingredients in a bowl. Scrape the batter into silicone baking molds; place them in the Air Fryer cooking tray.
3. Select Bake. Set temperature to 330ºF (165ºC), and set time to 15 minutes or until a tester comes out dry and clean.
4. Allow the cupcakes to cool before unmolding and serving. Bon appétit!

## Thai-Style Goreng Pisang

**Prep time: 10 minutes | Cook time: 13 minutes | Serves 2**

4 tablespoons rice flour
4 tablespoons all-purpose flour
¼ teaspoon ground cinnamon
A pinch of sea salt
A pinch of grated nutmeg

4 tablespoons coconut flakes
2 teaspoons coconut oil
2 eggs, whisked
2 bananas, peeled and sliced

1. Preheat your Air Fryer to 390ºF (200ºC).
2. In a mixing dish, thoroughly combine the flours, cinnamon, salt, nutmeg, and coconut flakes.
3. Now, add in the coconut oil and eggs. Roll each slice of banana over the egg/flour mixture.
4. Select Bake. Set temperature to 390ºF (200ºC), and set time to 13 minutes, turning them over halfway through the cooking time. Bon appétit!

## German Giant Pancake

**Prep time: 10 minutes | Cook time: 12 minutes | Serves 3**

1 small apple, peeled, cored, and sliced
1 tablespoon coconut oil, melted
1 egg, whisked
¼ cup plain flour
¼ teaspoon baking

powder
¼ cup full-fat coconut milk
A pinch of granulated sugar
A pinch of kosher salt
½ teaspoon vanilla paste

1. Drizzle the apple slices with the melted coconut oil; arrange the apple slices in a baking pan.
2. Mix the remaining ingredients to make the batter. Pour the batter over the apples. Transfer the baking pan to the Air Fryer cooking tray.
3. Select Bake. Set temperature to 350ºF (180ºC), and set time to about 12 minutes or until it is golden brown around the edges.
4. Bon appétit!

# Cinnamon Donuts

**Prep time: 5 minutes | Cook time: 10 minutes | Serves 4**

12 ounces (340 g) flaky large biscuits
¼ cup granulated sugar
1 teaspoon ground cinnamon

¼ teaspoon grated nutmeg
2 tablespoons coconut oil

1.  Separate the dough into biscuits and place them in a lightly oiled Air Fryer cooking tray.
2.  Mix the sugar, cinnamon, nutmeg, and coconut oil until well combined.
3.  Drizzle your donuts with the cinnamon mixture.
4.  Select Bake. Set temperature to 340ºF (170ºC), and set time to 10 minutes or until golden. Repeat with the remaining donuts.
5.  Bon appétit!

# Frosted Peanut Butter Chocolate Cookie

**Prep time: 10 minutes | Cook time: 8 minutes | Serves 4**

3 tablespoons butter, at room temperature
⅓ cup plus 1 tablespoon brown sugar
1 egg yolk
⅔ cup flour

5 tablespoons peanut butter, divided
¼ teaspoon baking soda
1 teaspoon vanilla
½ cup semisweet chocolate chips

1.  In a medium bowl, beat the butter and brown sugar together until fluffy. Stir in the egg yolk.
2.  Add the flour, 3 tablespoons of the peanut butter, the baking soda, and vanilla, and mix well.
3.  Line a 6-by-6-by-2-inch baking pan with parchment paper.
4.  Spread the batter into the prepared pan, leaving a ½-inch border on all sides.
5.  Select COOKIES, cook for 7 to 10 minutes at 350 ºF (180ºC) or until the cookie is light brown and just barely set.
6.  Remove the pan from the air fryer and let it cool for 10 minutes. Remove the cookie from the pan, remove the parchment paper, and let cool on a wire rack.
7.  In a small heatproof cup, combine the chocolate chips with the remaining 2 tablespoons of peanut butter. Bake for 1 to 2 minutes or until the chips are melted. Stir to combine and spread on the cookie.

# Chapter 12 Sauces, Dipping, and Spice Mixes

## Thai Spicy Peanut Sauce

**Prep time: 10 minutes | Cook time: 0 minutes | Makes ⅔ cup**

½ cup natural peanut butter
4 teaspoons sesame oil
2 tablespoons rice vinegar
2 to 4 teaspoons freshly squeezed lime juice
2 to 2½ teaspoons hot

sauce (optional)
1 teaspoon low-sodium soy sauce
1 teaspoon honey
1 teaspoon chopped peeled fresh ginger or pinch ground ginger

1. Place the sesame oil, rice vinegar, and peanut butter in a small bowl and stir until thoroughly mixed.
2. Whisk in the lime juice, hot sauce (if desired), soy sauce, honey, and ginger.
3. Store in an airtight container for up to 2 weeks and stir well before using.

## Ghee

**Prep time: 5 minutes | Cook time: 20 minutes | Makes: 2 cups**

1 pound (454 g) unsalted butter

1. Place the butter in a heavy-bottomed saucepan over medium-low heat. Set a timer for 20 minutes and leave it alone! Don't stir the butter or mess with it in any way. Just let it be. (During this time, the water from the butter will evaporate. You'll see a light foam forming on top of the bubbling butter. It will sound like popcorn popping, but much softer.)
2. At the 20-minute mark, stir the butter and raise the heat to medium-high. Cook, stirring occasionally, until you see the milk solids start to turn brown and settle on the bottom of the pan. If you give up before this stage you are either: a) a quitter, or b) trying to make clarified butter, not ghee.
3. Let the butter cool a little, then strain the clear yellow liquid through a fine-mesh strainer into a jar with a lid. (Discard the brown milk solids.) Seal the jar tightly, and you're done.
4. You can store the ghee on your countertop. As long as you keep the jar sealed and use a clean spoon each time you dig into the ghee, it lasts almost indefinitely.

## Kebab Spice Mix

**Prep time: 5 minutes | Cook time: 0 minutes | Makes: 4 tablespoons**

1 tablespoon coriander seeds
1 tablespoon cumin seeds
1 teaspoon whole black peppercorns
1 teaspoon whole

allspice berries
½ teaspoon cardamom seeds (from green/white pods)
½ teaspoon ground turmeric

1. Combine the coriander, cumin, peppercorns, allspice, cardamom, and turmeric in a clean coffee or spice grinder. Grind, shaking the grinder lightly so all the seeds and bits get into the blades, until the mixture is broken down to the consistency of a fine powder.
2. Unplug the grinder and turn it upside down. (You want all the ground spices to collect in the lid so you can easily scoop them out without cutting yourself on the blades.)
3. Transfer the spice mix to an airtight container and store in a cool, dark place for up to 3 months.

## Tomatillo Salsa Verde

**Prep time: 5 minutes | Cook time: 15 minutes | Serves: 4**

12 tomatillos
2 fresh serrano chiles
1 tablespoon minced garlic
1 cup chopped fresh

cilantro leaves
1 tablespoon vegetable oil
1 teaspoon kosher salt

1. Remove and discard the papery husks from the tomatillos and rinse them under warm running water to remove the sticky coating.
2. Place the tomatillos and peppers in a 7-inch round baking pan with 4-inch sides. Place the pan in the air-fryer cooking tray. Select Bake, set the temperature to 350ºF (180ºC), and set the time to 15 minutes.
3. Transfer the tomatillos and peppers to a blender, add the garlic, cilantro, vegetable oil, and salt, and blend until almost smooth. (If not using immediately, omit the salt and add it just before serving.)
4. Serve or store in an airtight container in the refrigerator for up to 10 days.

## Cilantro Pesto

**Prep time: 10 minutes | Cook time: 0 minutes | Serves: 4**

1 cup fresh cilantro leaves
1 jalapeño
2 tablespoons vegetable oil
2 tablespoons fresh

lemon juice
2 tablespoons minced fresh ginger
2 tablespoons minced garlic
1 teaspoon kosher salt

1. In a blender, combine the cilantro, jalapeño, vegetable oil, lemon juice, ginger, garlic, and salt. Blend until smooth.

## Simple Ginger Teriyaki Sauce

**Prep time: 5 minutes | Cook time: 0 minutes | Serves 4**

¼ cup pineapple juice
¼ cup low-sodium soy sauce
2 tablespoons packed brown sugar

1 tablespoon arrowroot powder or cornstarch
1 tablespoon grated fresh ginger
1 teaspoon garlic powder

1. Mix together all the ingredients in a small bowl and whisk to incorporate.
2. Serve immediately, or transfer to an airtight container and refrigerate until ready to use.

## Gochujang Sauce

**Prep time: 5 minutes | Cook time: 0 minutes | Makes: a scant ½ cup**

2 tablespoons gochujang (Korean red pepper paste)
1 tablespoon mayonnaise
1 tablespoon toasted

sesame oil
1 tablespoon minced fresh ginger
1 tablespoon minced garlic
1 teaspoon agave nectar

1. In a small bowl, combine the gochujang, mayonnaise, sesame oil, ginger, garlic, and agave. Stir until well combined.
2. Use immediately or store in the refrigerator, covered, for up to 3 days.

## Easy Remoulade Sauce

**Prep time: 5 minutes | Cook time: 0 minutes | Serves 4**

¾ cup mayonnaise
1 garlic clove, minced
2 tablespoons mustard
1 teaspoon horseradish
1 teaspoon Cajun seasoning

1 teaspoon dill pickle juice
½ teaspoon paprika
¼ teaspoon hot pepper sauce

1. Whisk together all the ingredients in a small bowl until completely mixed.
2. It can be used as a delicious dip for a sandwich, burger spread or veggies, or you can serve it with chicken fingers for a dipping sauce.

## Lemony Cashew Dip

**Prep time: 10 minutes | Cook time: 0 minutes | Makes 1 cup**

¾ cup cashews, soaked in water for at least 4 hours and drained
Juice and zest of 1 lemon
¼ cup water

2 tablespoons chopped fresh dill
¼ teaspoon salt, plus additional as needed

1. Blend the lemon juice, cashew, and lemon zest, and water in a blender until smooth and creamy.
2. Fold in the dill and salt and blend again.
3. Taste and add additional salt as needed.
4. Transfer to the refrigerator to chill for at least 1 hour to blend the flavors.
5. This dip perfectly goes with the crackers or tacos. It also can be used as a sauce for roasted vegetables or a sandwich spread.

## Cajun Spice Mix

**Prep time: 10 minutes | Cook time: 0 minutes | Makes: ½ cup**

1 tablespoon dried parsley
1 tablespoon dehydrated onion flakes
1 tablespoon smoked paprika
1 teaspoon dried oregano

1 teaspoon dried thyme
1 teaspoon cayenne pepper
1 teaspoon garlic powder
1 teaspoon kosher salt
1 teaspoon black pepper

1. In a clean coffee grinder or spice mill, combine all the spices and process to a moderately fine powder.
2. Unplug the grinder and turn it upside down. (You want all the ground spices to collect in the lid so you can easily scoop them out without cutting yourself on the blades.) Store in an airtight container in a cool, dark place for up to 2 months.

## Lebanese Shawarma Spice

**Prep time: 10 minutes | Cook time: 0 minutes | Makes: 4 tablespoons**

2 teaspoons dried oregano
1 teaspoon ground cinnamon
1 teaspoon ground cumin
1 teaspoon ground coriander
1 teaspoon kosher salt
½ teaspoon ground allspice
½ teaspoon cayenne pepper

1. In a small bowl, stir together the oregano, cinnamon, cumin, coriander, salt, allspice, and cayenne. Store in an airtight container in a cool, dark place for up to 3 months.

## Mushroom Apple Gravy

**Prep time: 5 minutes | Cook time: 10 minutes | Serves 4**

2 cups vegetable broth
½ cup finely chopped mushrooms
2 tablespoons whole-wheat flour
1 tablespoon unsweetened applesauce
1 teaspoon onion powder
½ teaspoon dried thyme
¼ teaspoon dried rosemary
⅛ teaspoon pink Himalayan salt
Freshly ground black pepper, to taste

1. In a nonstick saucepan over medium-high heat, combine all the ingredients and mix well. Bring to a boil, stirring frequently, reduce the heat to low, and simmer, stirring constantly, until it thickens.

## Greek Tzatziki

**Prep time: 10 minutes | Cook time: 0 minutes | Makes: 2 cups**

1 large cucumber, peeled and grated
1 cup plain Greek yogurt
2 to 3 garlic cloves, minced
1 tablespoon tahini (sesame paste)
1 tablespoon fresh lemon juice
½ teaspoon kosher salt, or to taste
Chopped fresh parsley or dill, for garnish (optional)

1. In a medium bowl, combine the cucumber, yogurt, garlic, tahini, lemon juice, and salt. Stir until well combined. Cover and chill until ready to serve.
2. Right before serving, sprinkle with chopped fresh parsley, if desired.

## Honey Dijon Sauce

**Prep time: 10 minutes | Cook time: 0 minutes | Makes about 1 cup**

½ cup raw honey or maple syrup
½ cup Dijon mustard
1 teaspoon toasted sesame oil
1 garlic clove, minced

1. Whisk together all the ingredients in a small bowl until smooth.
2. Refrigerate to chill for at least 2 hours for best flavor.
3. This sauce can be served as a dip for fresh vegetables or a spread for wraps and sandwiches. It's perfect for salads, grilled or roasted meats.

## Peanut Sauce

**Prep time: 10 minutes | Cook time: 0 minutes | Serves: 4**

⅓ cup peanut butter
¼ cup hot water
2 tablespoons soy sauce
2 tablespoons rice vinegar
Juice of 1 lime
1 teaspoon minced fresh ginger
1 teaspoon minced garlic
1 teaspoon black pepper

1. In a blender container, combine the peanut butter, hot water, soy sauce, vinegar, lime juice, ginger, garlic, and pepper. Blend until smooth.
2. Use immediately or store in an airtight container in the refrigerator for a week or more.

## Nigerian Suya Spice

**Prep time: 10 minutes | Cook time: 0 minutes | Makes: ½ cup**

¼ cup dry-roasted peanuts
1 teaspoon cumin seeds
1 teaspoon garlic powder
1 teaspoon smoked paprika
½ teaspoon ground ginger
1 teaspoon kosher salt
½ teaspoon cayenne pepper

1. In a clean coffee grinder or spice mill, combine the peanuts and cumin seeds. Process until you get a coarse powder. (Do not over-process or you will wind up with peanut butter!)
2. Pour the peanut mixture into a small bowl, add the garlic powder, paprika, ginger, salt, and cayenne, and stir to combine.
3. Store in an airtight container in a cool, dark place for up to 2 months.

## Asian Hot Sauce

**Prep time: 5 minutes | Cook time: 0 minutes | Makes ½ cup**

⅓ cup low-fat mayonnaise

2 teaspoons rice vinegar

1 to 2 teaspoons hot sauce

1 teaspoon sesame oil

1. Stir together all the ingredients in a small bowl until well combined.
2. Serve it with chicken or veggie stir-fry over rice. It can be refrigerated in an airtight container for up to 2 weeks.

## South Indian Spice Mix

**Prep time: 10 minutes | Cook time: 0 minutes | Makes: 3 tablespoons**

1½ teaspoons coriander seeds

1 teaspoon fennel seeds

1 teaspoon cumin seeds

1 teaspoon black peppercorns

½ teaspoon cardamom seeds

1 dried red chile, or ½ teaspoon dried red pepper flakes

1 (1-inch) piece cinnamon stick

¼ teaspoon ground turmeric

1 teaspoon kosher salt

1. In a clean coffee grinder or spice mill, combine the coriander, fennel, cumin, peppercorns, cardamom, dried chile, and cinnamon stick. Grind, shaking the grinder lightly so all the seeds and bits get into the blades, until the mixture is broken down to moderately fine powder. Stir in the turmeric and salt.
2. Store in an airtight container in a cool, dark place for up to 2 months.

## Vegan Tahini Lentil Dip

**Prep time: 10 minutes | Cook time: 15 minutes | Makes 3 cups**

2½ cups water, divided

1 cup dried green or brown lentils, rinsed

⅓ cup tahini

1 garlic clove

½ teaspoon salt, plus additional as needed

1. Mix 2 cups of water and lentils in a medium pot and bring to a boil over high heat.
2. Once it starts to boil, reduce the heat to low, and bring to a simmer for 15 minutes, or until the lentils are tender. If there is any water remaining in the pot, simply drain it off.

3. Transfer the cooked lentils to a food processor, along with the remaining ingredients. Pulse until a hummus-like consistency is achieved.
4. Taste and add additional salt as needed.
5. It's tasty used as a sandwich spread, and you can also serve it over crackers or whole-wheat pita bread.

## Harissa Paste

**Prep time: 10 minutes | Cook time: 5 minutes | Makes: 1 cup**

½ cup olive oil

6 cloves garlic, minced

2 tablespoons smoked paprika

1 tablespoon ground coriander

1 tablespoon ground

cumin

1 teaspoon ground caraway

1 teaspoon kosher salt

½ to 1 teaspoon cayenne pepper

1. In a medium microwave-safe bowl, combine all the ingredients. Microwave on high for 1 minute, stirring halfway through the cooking time.
2. You can also heat this on the stovetop until the oil is hot and bubbling. Or, if you must use your air fryer for everything, cook in the air fryer oven at 350ºF (180ºC), and set time to 5 to 6 minutes, or until the pasta is heated through.
3. Cool completely. Store in an airtight container in the refrigerator for up to 1 month.

## Homemade Garam Masala

**Prep time: 10 minutes | Cook time: 0 minutes | Makes: ¼ cup**

2 tablespoons coriander seeds

1 teaspoon cumin seeds

½ teaspoon whole black cloves

½ teaspoon cardamom seeds

2 dried bay leaves

3 dried red chiles; or ½ teaspoon cayenne pepper or red pepper flakes

1 (2-inch) piece cinnamon stick

1. In a clean coffee grinder or spice mill, combine all the spices and grind, shaking so all the seeds and bits get into the blades, until the mixture has the consistency of a moderately fine powder.
2. Unplug the grinder and turn it upside down. (You want all the ground spices to collect in the lid so you can easily scoop them out without cutting yourself on the blades.) Store in an airtight container in a cool, dark place for up to 2 months.

## Lebanese Spice Mix

**Prep time: 10 minutes | Cook time: 0 minutes | Makes: 1/3 cup**

1 tablespoon ground allspice
1 tablespoon ground cloves
1 tablespoon grated nutmeg
1 tablespoon ground fenugreek

1 tablespoon ground ginger
2 teaspoons ground cinnamon
2 teaspoons black pepper

1. In a small bowl, stir together all the ingredients. Store in an airtight container in a cool, dark place for up to 2 months.

## Ras Al Hanout

**Prep time: 10 minutes | Cook time: 0 minutes | Makes: 1/3 cup**

2 teaspoons ground cumin
2 teaspoons ground ginger
2 teaspoons ground turmeric
1 teaspoon ground cardamom
1 teaspoon ground cinnamon

1 teaspoon ground coriander
1 teaspoon cayenne pepper
1 teaspoon ground allspice
2 teaspoons kosher salt
2 teaspoons black pepper

1. In a small bowl, stir together all the ingredients. Store in an airtight container in a cool, dark place for up to 2 months.

South Indian Spice Mix, page 155

Honey Dijon Sauce, page 154

# Appendix 1: Measurement Conversion Chart

## Volume Equivalents (Dry)

| US STANDARD | METRIC (APPROXIMATE) |
|---|---|
| 1/8 teaspoon | 0.5 mL |
| 1/4 teaspoon | 1 mL |
| 1/2 teaspoon | 2 mL |
| 3/4 teaspoon | 4 mL |
| 1 teaspoon | 5 mL |
| 1 tablespoon | 15 mL |
| 1/4 cup | 59 mL |
| 1/2 cup | 118 mL |
| 3/4 cup | 177 mL |
| 1 cup | 235 mL |
| 2 cups | 475 mL |
| 3 cups | 700 mL |
| 4 cups | 1 L |

## Temperatures Equivalents

| FAHRENHEIT (F) | CELSIUS(C) (APPROXIMATE) |
|---|---|
| 225 °F | 107 °C |
| 250 °F | 120 °C |
| 275 °F | 135 °C |
| 300 °F | 150 °C |
| 325 °F | 160 °C |
| 350 °F | 180 °C |
| 375 °F | 190 °C |
| 400 °F | 205 °C |
| 425 °F | 220 °C |
| 450 °F | 235 °C |
| 475 °F | 245 °C |
| 500 °F | 260 °C |

## Volume Equivalents (Liquid)

| US STANDARD | US STANDARD (OUNCES) | METRIC (APPROXIMATE) |
|---|---|---|
| 2 tablespoons | 1 fl.oz. | 30 mL |
| 1/4 cup | 2 fl.oz. | 60 mL |
| 1/2 cup | 4 fl.oz. | 120 mL |
| 1 cup | 8 fl.oz. | 240 mL |
| 1 1/2 cup | 12 fl.oz. | 355 mL |
| 2 cups or 1 pint | 16 fl.oz. | 475 mL |
| 4 cups or 1 quart | 32 fl.oz. | 1 L |
| 1 gallon | 128 fl.oz. | 4 L |

## Weight Equivalents

| US STANDARD | METRIC (APPROXIMATE) |
|---|---|
| 1 ounce | 28 g |
| 2 ounces | 57 g |
| 5 ounces | 142 g |
| 10 ounces | 284 g |
| 15 ounces | 425 g |
| 16 ounces (1 pound) | 455 g |
| 1.5 pounds | 680 g |
| 2 pounds | 907 g |

# Appendix 2: Dirty Dozen and Clean Fifteen

The Environmental Working Group (EWG) is a widely known organization that has an eminent guide to pesticides and produce. More specifically, the group takes in data from tests conducted by the US Department of Agriculture (USDA) and then categorizes produce into a list titled "Dirty Dozen," which ranks the twelve top produce items that contain the most pesticide residues, or alternatively the "Clean Fifteen," which ranks fifteen produce items that are contaminated with the least amount of pesticide residues.

The EWG has recently released their 2021 Dirty Dozen list, and this year strawberries, spinach and kale – with a few other produces which will be revealed shortly – are listed at the top of the list. This year's ranking is similar to the 2020 Dirty Dozen list, with the few differences being that collards and mustard greens have joined kale at number three on the list. Other changes include peaches and cherries, which having been listed subsequently as seventh and eighth on the 2020 list, have now been flipped; the introduction – which the EWG has said is the first time ever – of bell and hot peppers into the 2021 list; and the departure of potatoes from the twelfth spot.

| DIRTY DOZEN LIST | | CLEAN FIFTEEN LIST | |
|---|---|---|---|
| Strawberries | Cherries | Avocados | Broccoli |
| Spinach | Peaches | Sweet corn | Cabbage |
| Kale, collards and mustard greens | Pears | Pineapple | Kiwi |
| | Bell and hot peppers | Onions | Cauliflower |
| Nectarines | Celery | Papaya | Mushrooms |
| Apples | Tomatoes | Sweet peas (frozen) | Honeydew melon |
| Grapes | | Eggplant | Cantaloupe |
| | | Asparagus | |

These lists are created to help keep the public informed on their potential exposures to pesticides, which then allows for better and healthier food choices to be made.

This is the advice that ASEQ-EHAQ also recommends. Stay clear of the dirty dozen by opting for their organic versions, and always be mindful of what you are eating and how it was grown. Try to eat organic as much as possible – whether it is on the list, or not.

# Appendix 3: Breville Air Fryer Oven Time Table

## Chicken

| INGREDIENT | AMOUNT | PREPARATION | AVG.TIME | TEMP.($^{o}F$) |
|---|---|---|---|---|
| Tender | 1-inch | strips | 8 min | 360 |
| Breast | 4 ounces | Boneless | 11 min | 380 |
| Wings | 2 pounds | / | 13 min | 380 |
| Thighs | 1.5 pounds | Boneless | 17 min | 380 |
| Drumsticks | 2.5 pounds | / | 19 min | 370 |
| Thighs | 2 pounds | Bone-in | 21 min | 380 |
| Breast | 1.25 pounds | Bone-in | 24 min | 370 |
| Legs | 1.75 pounds | Bone-in | 30 min | 380 |
| Cornish Hen | 2 pounds | Whole | 32 min | 370 |
| Roast Chicken | 4 pounds | Whole | 55 min | 350 |

## Seafood

| INGREDIENT | AMOUNT | PREPARATION | AVG.TIME | TEMP.($^{o}F$) |
|---|---|---|---|---|
| Calamari | 8 ounces | / | 4 min | 400 |
| Shrimp | 1 pound | Whole | 4 min | 400 |
| Lobster Tails | 1 | Whole | 5 min | 370 |
| Scallops | 1 pound | Whole | 6 min | 400 |
| Tuna Steak | 2 inches | thick | 6 min | 400 |
| Fish Fillet | 8 ounces | / | 9 min | 400 |
| Swordfish Steak | 2 inches | thick | 9 min | 400 |
| Crab Cakes | 1-2 inches | thick | 9 min | 400 |
| Salmon Fillet | 12 ounces | / | 10 min | 380 |

## Beef

| INGREDIENT | AMOUNT | PREPARATION | AVG.TIME | TEMP.($^{o}F$) |
|---|---|---|---|---|
| Meatballs | 2-inch | / | 8 min | 380 |
| Flank Steak | 1.5 pounds | / | 11 min | 400 |
| Ribeye | 8 ounces | Bone-in | 11 min | 400 |
| Sirloin Steak | 12 ounces | / | 11 min | 400 |
| Burger | 4 ounces | / | 14 min | 370 |
| Filet Mignon | 8 ounces | / | 16 min | 400 |
| London Broil | 2 pounds | / | 18 min | 400 |
| Beef Eye Round | 4 pounds | / | 45 min | 380 |

## Vegetable

| INGREDIENT | AMOUNT | PREPARATION | AVG.TIME | TEMP.(°F ) |
|---|---|---|---|---|
| Brussels Sprouts | / | Halved | 15 min | 380 |
| Eggplant | 1-inch | Chopped | 15 min | 400 |
| Fennel | / | Quartered | 15 min | 370 |
| Parsnips | 1/2-inch | Chopped | 15 min | 380 |
| Peppers | 1/2-inch | Chopped | 15 min | 400 |
| Baby Potatoes | 1.5 pounds | Small | 16 min | 400 |
| Cherry Tomatoes | / | Whole | 20 min | 340 |
| Carrots | / | Whole | 20 min | 380 |
| Sweet Potato | / | Whole | 35 min | 380 |
| Beets | / | Whole | 40 min | 400 |
| Potatoes | / | Whole | 40 min | 400 |

## Frozen

| INGREDIENT | AMOUNT | PREPARATION | AVG.TIME | TEMP.(°F ) |
|---|---|---|---|---|
| Onion Rings | 12 ounces | / | 7 min | 370 to 400 |
| Mozzarella Sticks | 12 ounces | / | 7 min | 370 to 400 |
| Pot Stickers | 10 ounces | / | 7 min | 370 to 400 |
| Breaded Shrimp | 12 ounces | / | 9 min | 370 to 400 |
| Fish Sticks | 10 ounces | / | 9 min | 370 to 400 |
| Chicken Nuggets | 12 ounces | / | 10 min | 370 to 400 |
| Thin Fries | 20 ounces | / | 14 min | 370 to 400 |
| Fish Fillet | 10 ounces | / | 14 min | 370 to 400 |
| Chicken Wings | 6 ounces | Precooked | 17 min | 370 to 400 |
| Thick Fries | 20 ounces | / | 17 min | 370 to 400 |

# Appendix 4: Recipes Index